Of Course, God is Blatantly Against Abortion

Second Edition

Christina L. Barr

For my beloved family,

thank you for your unwavering support.

Contents

Need to Know Definitions

fe·tus

/ˈfētəs /

noun

An unborn offspring of a mammal, in particular an unborn human baby more than eight weeks after conception.

child

/CHīld/

noun

a young human being below the age of puberty or below the legal age of majority.

a son or daughter of any age.

per·son

/ˈpərs(ə)n/

noun

    a human being regarded as an individual.

in·di·vid·u·al

/ˌində'vij(oō)əl/

noun

    a single human being as distinct from a group, class, or family.

hu·man be·ing

noun

    a man, woman, or child of the species *Homo sapiens*, distinguished from other animals by superior mental development, power of articulate speech, and upright stance.

Definitions from the Oxford English Dictionary

For I wrote to you out of much affliction and anguish of heart and with many tears, not to cause you pain but to let you know the abundant love that I have for you. (2 Corinthians 2:4, ESV)

Introduction

The abortion debate has dramatically intensified in the United States after the overturning of *Roe v. Wade* and *Planned Parenthood v. Casey*, bringing the issue of abortion back to the state level. It's a passion issue for both sides of the political spectrum, even a singular voting issue for many Americans. The pro-life argument is simple: human beings in the womb are alive and deserve to have their right to life honored and protected. But even if you keep your explanation concise and without one utterance of religious dogma, you'll still be told to keep your religion out of women's uteruses. Even secular pro-life advocates have suffered with accusations of being religious control freaks who want to punish women. No one is safe from this disingenuous argument.

The question is why?

Abortion has a long history of being looked upon as a necessary evil. In a 2006 interview, then-Senator Joe Biden (D-DE) said he did not view abortion as "a choice and a right."[1] Biden said, "It's always a tragedy." Like many democrats, he believed abortion should be safe, legal, and rare. That was the mantra I heard repeated in my childhood from strong pro-choice advocates like Hillary Clinton (D), former First Lady, U.S. Senator from New York, and U.S. Secretary of State.

Abortion is never safe for the sons and daughters killed during the procedure or permanently scarred—if they miraculously survive. They mean "safe" for the mother, though there are risks to women. Women can die in botched abortions, some are never able to bring another child to term, and many carry the mental scars and guilt from taking the lives of their children.

Abortion is obviously not good. That is why politicians who wanted it to be legal, still professed it needed to be rare. It wasn't simply because of the physical and mental harm that can occur to a woman. It was a tragedy for professing Catholics—like Biden—because they knew a life was taken. And even if they viewed it as a "potential life," they acknowledged even that potential required some sort of moral consideration.

But an unborn child in the womb isn't a "potential life." It's a life *with* potential. "Safe, legal, and rare" implied abortion was a *necessary* evil. And let's, for a moment, agree with that sentiment. Let's say abortion is a tragedy, but something that should be allowed for rare circumstances and sparsely. That's not happening when you look at the numbers. Nearly all abortions are elective. Even abortions in cases of rape are less than one percent.[2] In 2020, there were 930,160 abortions in the United States.[3] That's an 8% increase from the 2017 numbers. If abortion is necessary, it should not be Option A, B, C, and so on. It should be Option Z, all the way to the end.

The abortion industry cannot survive Option Z.

The abortion industry pulls in too much money. In 2020, Planned Parenthood reported $1.6 billion in revenue[4] and over $2 billion in net assets. Abortion chains like Planned Parenthood are allocated government funds, and their PACs return the favor by pouring money into candidates who will keep their business going. *The Associated Press* reported Planned Parenthood prepared to spend $50 million in the 2022 U.S. midterm elections.[5] By October 23, Reproductive Freedom for All raised $40.2 million for the 2022 Michigan midterm election to create a right for abortion, even late into the pregnancy.[6]

That's why a radical shift in the ideology of pro-choice activists had to take place. They know abortion isn't used as a "necessary" evil. Therefore, they have to remove the idea that abortion is "evil" at all.

If you utter the word "baby" or "child," you'll be met with scorn and mockery, even though a fetus is an "unborn human baby," and a child is a son or daughter of any age. "It's a fetus," they *hiss* as if they weren't merely acknowledging a stage in human development. It's not new. It's not unique. We've all been there and done that, yet they'll point to pictures of embryos and ask with a straight face, "Do you honestly believe this is a human?" Some will swap out a picture of a human fetus with a dolphin or elephant to pull one over on anti-abortion activists who don't know any better. Arguing humans can be killed based on how ugly they are, is profoundly immoral, but that's where we are as a society.

They will do anything to claim abortion isn't homicide. It takes a serious leap of logic to convince yourself a fetus at 15 weeks—who has started to form all of their major organs, has fingernails, and can suck their thumb—isn't alive. According to a Harvard-Harris poll, a majority of Americans don't want abortion past 15 weeks.[7] If that's the case, Americans should be happy *Dobbs v. Jackson Women's Health Organization* struck down *Roe* and *Casey*, which was preventing *Dobbs* from saving the unborn past 15 weeks. Yet, abortion advocates will claim those children are not alive because they cannot survive outside of the womb, and they are not yet sentient. Newborns don't have a sense of the world, nor can they survive without the care and resources from another, yet pro-choice activists hold onto their beliefs like zealots grasping onto a religion to justify discrimination against a class of people.

Since they are clasping onto a belief, they need to distract from their dogma by accusing their opposition of doing the same.

When I state, "Life starts at conception," I'm not making a declaration of faith. I'm stating a scientific fact. Whether you *choose* to value that life, is a subjective opinion. Whether you want to grant them "personhood," is centered around a philosophical concept. Whether someone considers humanity to possess intrinsic value is irrelevant. Protecting life at conception is about being the most consistent with human rights as possible. A rigid principle like that flies in the face of a "woman's choice."

During the 2016 presidential campaign, Democratic candidate Hillary Clinton repeatedly said the unborn had no constitutional rights (technically, our unalienable rights are not granted by the Constitution; they're acknowledged, and the Constitution limits the power of the federal government). Even while being interviewed on *The View*, Hillary Clinton maintained this opinion, even hours before the baby's due date. On the final debate stage with Donald Trump (R), Clinton defended—perhaps begrudgingly—partial-birth abortion. Businessman Donald Trump promised to appoint conservative justices, then went on to win the presidency. All three of his appointments, Justices Neil Gorsuch, Brett Kavanaugh, and Amy Coney Barrett, joined Justices Samuel Alito and Clarence Thomas in the major opinion of *Dobbs v. Jackson*.

Clinton, who has been awarded the Margaret Sanger Award in the past, was a bit too radical back then. However, her Democratic counterparts have not corrected the course. Stacey Abrams, who ran unsuccessfully for Georgia governor in 2018 and 2022, also refused to condemn nine-month abortions on *Fox News*.[8] In 2019, Francis "Beto" O'Rourke—who unsuccessfully ran for U.S. Senate, president, and Texas governor—was asked by a woman in Cleveland if he supported third-trimester abortions. The woman even explained they can take days and doctors are better off inducing if it's to save the life of the mother. He said, "That should be a decision that the woman makes."[9] During an event at Plymouth State University in the same year, O'Rourke refused to support the Born-Alive Abortion Survivors Protection Act. Even though this bill would have given care to infants who survive abortion, O'Rourke said, "The way that I would approach your question, and this issue generally, is to trust women to make their own decisions about their own bodies."[10] If O'Rourke had defeated Senator Ted Cruz in 2018, he would have had the opportunity to vote down the bill.

Abortion advocates don't find it absurd that Christians defer to a higher moral authority. They simply resent the fact Christians won't bow down to *their* moral authority. Support for abortion is *extraordinarily* religious. "My body, my choice" is their chant, regardless of the fact, that there's another body inside of their body, due to the choice of engaging in procreation (consensual more than 99 percent of the time). Abortion is literally child sacrifice. It's the highest possible form of self-idolatry. Starlets like Michelle Williams have even accepted golden idols and praised abortion, claiming her hunk of metal wouldn't have been possible without the freedom of choice, and that choice is to trade the lives of children for money and fame.[11] They will smile and state—without godlike omniscience to possibly know—that they made the best decision.

To make their religious sacrament seem less heinous, they have to make Christianity selfish and frivolous. Democratic New York Congresswoman Alexandria Ocasio Cortez berated Christians who believe abortion harms a life.[12] "Well, some religions don't. So, how 'bout that?" It's not a religious opinion that abortion ends a life. Many non-religious people acknowledge that scientific fact. Even many people who consider themselves to be pro-choice can acknowledge the unborn are alive.

She went on to say, "Our Jewish brothers and sisters are able to have abortions according to their faith. You know, there are so many faiths that do not have the same definition of life as fundamentalist Christians."

Ben Shapiro, a Jewish major conservative commentator, mocked AOC on his podcast. "Explain to me where in Jewish law abortion is widely permissible. I'm waiting to hear, rabbi." [13]

President Joe Biden believes *Roe* says what "all basic mainstream religions have historically concluded." He says, "The existence of the human life and being is a question. Is it at the moment of conception? Is it six months? Is it six weeks? Is it…is it the quickening like the Aquinas argued?" [14] Not only do you have abortion advocates telling the pro-life community they cannot interject their religious arguments; you have politicians making religious arguments in favor of abortion! Before Barrack Obama became president, Americans seem to remember Obama infamously stating when life begins is "above my paygrade." [15] If that's the case, why not err on the side of caution? If you thought there was a possibility a baby was laying directly in front of your right tire, would you put the car in drive and hit the gas, or would you get out and bring the infant to safety?

A majority of Americans do not believe in hitting the gas. 37 percent of Americans only want legal abortions for rape and incest. That is the plurality. If we add in the 12 percent who believe abortion shouldn't be allowed past 6 weeks and the 23 percent who don't believe abortion should be allowed past 15 weeks, that means a majority of Americans don't believe in the restrictions imposed by *Roe v. Wade*. 18 percent don't believe abortion should be allowed past 23 weeks, which is around the time of "fetal viability." Only 10 percent believe abortion should be allowed for up to nine months.[16] Why is this the directional push of the abortion lobby and its political sycophants?

It's the only logical conclusion.

The truth is Obama's past abortion comments are much more egregious once you realize he was not asked when life begins. Pastor Rick Warren of Saddleback Church asked, "At what point does a baby get human rights?" That's not a theological or scientific question. As a politician who signed his name to abortion-related legislation and executive orders, Obama obviously had an answer. But Obama realized his honest opinion was far too radical.

Personhood based on size, level of development, environment, or degree of dependency (S.L.E.D.) has inconsistent standards that wouldn't be applied outside of the womb. They're used as discrimination tactics with the foreknowledge of what a fetus lacks. For example, you wouldn't kill a person just because they temporarily don't possess consciousness or sentience, yet pro-choice activists rationalize abortion because the fetus temporarily doesn't possess those either. Viability is also a ridiculous standard. A newborn can't survive outside the womb on their own. Some adults cannot survive without physical or medical assistance; that doesn't mean they should be stripped of their rights. Bodily autonomy isn't absolute; it doesn't grant you the freedom to infringe on someone else's rights. It also ignores how the baby got into a woman's uterus in the first place. And as far as "choice," women make terrible choices every day. Not all of them are—or should be—legal.

If a woman has the "right to abortion," and the unborn has no right to life, nine-month abortions are justified. It's the opposite end of the pro-life position, that all humans deserve equal rights from the moment their human life begins. The abortion lobby cannot take the risk of the world waking up to its immoral atrocities.

One of their best tactics is to misrepresent religion and use it to shame Christians into backing away from their objective worldview. I've seen TikTok accounts with millions of followers, shame Christians for having a belief system, then turn around and claim the Bible is okay with abortions. They claim God sanctions abortions, life starts at first breath, God killed kids in the Bible so they can too, and abortion should be a woman's choice because God grants free will.

Christian influencers have been very silent or even grieved about the overturning of Roe v. Wade. Emmanuel Acho premiered an episode of The Uncomfortable Conversation about the subject. [17] No one on the panel represented the pro-life position. He had women who identified as Christians and had abortions, but there was never a call for repentance or discouragement of the act. They acknowledged grief and guilt, but they never expressed regret, even though two women had their abortions out of financial gain and to advance their careers. The other woman had an ectopic pregnancy, which is not considered an abortion. No one acknowledged abortion takes a life, and no one urged Christians to grant moral consideration for the child. The conversation surrounded *their* feelings and not God's truth.

The pro-life movement is not solely made up of believers, but they are the force behind it. Critics now claim overturning *Roe v. Wade* was about white people trying to maintain their population, and not about saving innocent babies. This ignores the nefarious history of eugenics in America, especially within the leadership of Planned Parenthood like Margaret Sanger and Alan Guttmacher. Besides, the pro-life organization Right to Life—which began with the National Conference of Catholic Bishops—predated the ruling. First-century Jewish historian Flavius Josephus said, "The law moreover enjoins us to bring up all our offspring: and forbids women to cause abortion of what is begotten; or to destroy it afterward. And if any woman appears to have so done, she will be a murderer of her child; by destroying a living creature, and diminishing human kind."[18] Early Christian literature such as the *Didache*, *The Letter of Barnabas*, and *The Apocalypse of Peter* also condemns abortions and infanticide, and these date to the late-first and second century.

"The second commandment of the teaching: You shall not murder. You shall not commit adultery. You shall not seduce boys. You shall not commit fornication. You shall not steal. You shall not practice magic. You shall not use potions. You shall not procure [an] abortion, nor destroy a newborn child" (*Didache* 2:1–2 [A.D. 70]).

"Thou shalt not slay the child by procuring abortion; nor, again, shalt thou destroy it after it is born" (*Letter of Barnabas* 19 [A.D. 74]).

"And near that place I saw another strait place...and there sat women...And over against them many children who were born to them out of due time sat crying. And there came forth from them rays of fire and smote the women in the eyes. And these were the accursed who conceived and caused abortion" (*The Apocalypse of Peter* 25 [A.D. 137]).

Early Christian authors and philosophers also acknowledged that abortion was murder. When Athenagoras defended Christianity to the Roman Emperor, he said that women who take drugs for an abortion are murderers and will have to give an account to God (*A Plea for the Christians* 35 [A.D. 177]). Tertullian said, "In our case, a murder being once for all forbidden, we may not destroy even the fetus in the womb, while as yet the human being derives blood from other parts of the body for its sustenance. To hinder a birth is merely a speedier man-killing; nor does it matter whether you take away a life that is born, or destroy one that is coming to birth. That *is* a man which is *going to be* one; you have the fruit already in its seed," (*Apology* 9:8 [A.D. 197]). Marcus Minucius Felix and Hippolytus condemned abortion in the third century. Basil the Great said women who procure an abortion should undergo "ten years' penance, whether the embryo were perfectly formed, or not," (*First Canonical Letter*, canon 2 [A.D. 374]). John Chrysostom condemned fornication and abortion. "For even the harlot you do not let continue a mere harlot, but make her a murderess also." He referred to abortion as "murder before the birth," (*Homilies on Romans* 24 [A.D. 391]). St. Jorome also condemned abortion as "child murder" in the fourth century (*Letters* 22:13 [A.D. 396]).

That doesn't mean Christian leaders haven't been on the wrong side of history. Margaret Sanger once urged in a letter to Dr. C. J. Gamble to enlist colored physicians and ministers to put the minds of the negros at ease, while they pushed their agenda. "We do not want word to go out that we want to exterminate the Negro population, and the minister is the man who can straighten out that idea if it ever occurs to any of their more rebellious members."[19] In Sanger's article, "A Better Race Through Birth Control," she wrote, "Given birth control, the unfit will voluntarily eliminate their kind."[20] Sanger's apologists argue her quotes have been widely mischaracterized and her goal was to grant women options to make their lives better. To be fair, Sanger was not as nearly extreme on abortion as modern pro-choice advocates. But she did make several comments that leaned heavily into eugenics, which was more accepted in her day. Sanger even supported the ruling of *Buck v. Bell* that opened the door for forced sterilization of the "feeble-minded." Even Planned Parenthood has begun to throw Sanger under the bus, writing in *The New York Times*: "We're done making excuses for our founder."[21]

Sadly, on Acho's panel, a black woman and TV analyst MJ Acosta-Ruiz, said *Roe v. Wade*'s overturning would hurt women of color and low-income women. Eugenics seeks to limit the population of those types of "undesirables." This is antithetical to the gospel. You are no less or more valuable to God whether you are rich or poor, black or white, born or unborn. God is no respecter of persons (Acts 10:34).

There is a goal to dull Christianity, to make it spiritually ineffective and socially compliant with sin. If we lose the moral values that have helped to build and liberate America, our country will fall. Communists know this. They come into countries, offering to be friendly toward Christianity, expecting compliant Christians to water down their messages. Then they take a dramatic turn and brutally oppress the faithful. Romanian pastor Richard Wurmbrand wrote about this in *Tortured for Christ*, detailing his experiences in communist prisons.

More than 60 million lives have been stolen since the passage of *Roe v. Wade*. Every single one was God's creation, and they held value to him. *Roe* is gone, but the fight for abolition continues. Will Christians stand for life and life more abundantly? Or will they stand with Moloch?

The goal of this book is not to condemn women who have had abortions and the men who have supported them along the way. As Apostle Paul wrote to the Christians in Corinth, his corrections and teachings could come off as harsh at times, but Paul never meant to cause pain. He spoke from a place of abundant love. I believe in God's power of redemption, and I pray for that over condemnation. God can deliver us from our sins, and abortion is, undoubtedly, a terrible sin. If Christians truly claim to love these women, we cannot rejoice in wrongdoing; we must rejoice in truth (1 Corinthians 13:6). No, we don't have to condemn these men and women to hell, but we should want them to be convicted and to turn toward a righteous path.

An induced abortion is designed to take the life of an innocent child, an image bearer of God. We must never allow these conversations to occur without acknowledging the humanity of the preborn, and we must seek mercy, protection, and justice for the littlest among us.

It is vitally important to state that abortion is a great evil, and we must turn away from this horrific sin. Abortion should not only be illegal; it should be antithetical to everything we believe and stand for in a civilized society filled with spirit-led, Holy Ghost-filled Christians preaching the gospel. But we're not there. Some days, it feels like we're Abraham bargaining to spare

Sodom and Gomorrah. I believe enough righteous people are willing to fight for life, and by the end of this book, your faith will be affirmed, and your iron will be sharpened.

Chapter One

When Does Life Begin?

What Biology Says

The origin of a human being's life is settled science. The answer is at conception. If you read biology and embryological textbooks, you'll find this to be the point when a new and unique human individual comes into existence and develops. "Human development begins at fertilization, when a sperm fuses with an oocyte to form a single cell, the zygote."[1] Half of your chromosomes come from your mother, and the other half comes from your father. "Hence, the zygote contains a new combination of chromosomes different from both parents. Determination of the sex of the new individual."[2] Even the child's sex is determined at birth by either the X-carrying sperm (XX) or the Y-carrying sperm (XY).

Humans in the womb meet the characteristics of life: cellular organization, ability to reproduce, metabolism, heredity, response to stimuli, growth and development, and homeostasis. Plants and animals also meet these criteria, so it's important to note these are not traits of "personhood." Nevertheless, the child in the womb is human, alive, and growing.

In a survey of 5,577 biologists, 96 percent agreed life begins at fertilization. Dr. Steve Jacobs collected this data while working on his dissertation, "Balancing Abortion Rights and Fetal Rights: A Mixed Methods Mediation of the U.S. Abortion Debate."[3] He received a firestorm of media after his results since it's a very inconvenient truth that can be used in the abortion debate.

Now, a consensus isn't science, but the science is clear.

As a matter of fact, the biologists held this opinion, even though 89 percent identified as liberal, 85 percent identified as pro-choice, 63 percent were non-religious, and 92 percent were Democrats. In his study, Jacobs also found that 82 percent of surveyed Americans believe "when life begins" is an important aspect of the abortion debate, and 76 percent of Americans deserve to know in order to grant true informed consent during an abortion. 93 percent of Americans also believe legal protections should start when that life begins. When the respondents were asked who was the most qualified to make that determination, 80 percent selected biologists, viewing them as objective experts.

Even famous atheist Christopher Hitchens acknowledged that life begins at conception and mocked feminists for pretending otherwise. He said they have a "contempt for science and the theory of evolution—which establishes beyond reasonable doubt that life is a continuum that begins at conception because it can't begin anywhere else." Hitchens also said, "Once you allow that the occupant of the womb is even potentially a life, it cuts athwart any glib invocation of 'the woman's right to choose.'"[4]

But even if pro-choice activists acknowledge the science, they believe there's more nuance involved. Many biologists think the question of life is one of morality and politics.

Scott Gilbert, who is a development biologist, said, "I couldn't say when personhood begins, but I can say with absolute certainty scientists don't have a consensus."[5] Signs of life have evolved from the "quickening," when a mother could feel her baby kick, to fertilization. But just because two people have sex, doesn't mean an egg will be fertilized or that it will happen immediately. Sperm can live five days inside a woman, according to Mayo Clinic.[6] And just because an egg is fertilized doesn't mean it will implant, and some implanted embryos spontaneously abort. Even the threshold of fetal viability has greatly changed and will continue as we make more technological advancements. Whether a fetus at 22 weeks can survive outside of the womb can greatly depend on whether they're born in a well-equipped hospital and staffed with talent.

Many medical professionals believe the pregnant woman should have sole authority to decide when her child is a person. But that is a dangerously extreme position. If a woman doesn't know the science and hasn't pondered the philosophical concepts, how can she make a truly informed decision for herself and her child? And if she solely gets to decide, there's no stopping her from deciding that the moment is when her child passes through the birth canal. Many abortion activists have even made this argument.

Sahotra Sarkar, a Professor of Philosophy and Integrative Biology, doesn't believe biology can answer when life begins. He says, "It's a question of politics and ethical values."[7] He even goes on to critique Dr. Steve Jacobs' survey, noting that only 70 of the respondents "supported Jacob's legal argument enough to sign the amicus brief, which makes a companion argument to the main case."

He then cites Scott Gilbert, the Howard A. Schneiderman Professor of Biology emeritus at Swarthmore College. Gilbert has identified at least five possible stages of life in human development.

"The first of these stages is fertilization in the egg duct, when a zygote is formed with the full human genetic material." Then Sarkar criticizes this point, "If genetic material alone makes a potential human being, then when we shed skin cells—as we do all the time—we are severing potential human beings."

This critique is ridiculous. My skin cells are not the same as my mother's. Does Sarkar truly believe a dead skin cell is a "potential human being?" What are the odds of scratching dandruff off my head and rapidly developing into a separate human being with their own thoughts, feelings, and social security number?

"The second plausible stage is called gastrulation, which happens about two weeks after fertilization. At that point, the embryo loses the ability to form identical twins—or triplets or more. The embryo, therefore, becomes a biological individual but not necessarily a human individual."

The critique here is that human life may actually be two or three lives. I don't find it particularly compelling that we must not protect life at gastrulation because there could be multiple victims instead.

Regarding the first two instances, they would play little to no role in the major abortion debate. A woman won't likely know she is pregnant this early. It's only relevant concerning birth control that can prevent a fertilized egg from implantation.

"The third possible stage is at 24 to 27 weeks of pregnancy, when the characteristic human-specific brain-wave pattern emerges in the fetus's brain. Disappearance of this pattern is part of the legal standard for human death; by symmetry, perhaps its appearance could be taken to mark the beginning of human life."

But doctors would not consider this a legal standard for human death if there was a guarantee a human being was going to be as good as brand-new in nine months. If the brain has shut down, everything is going to shut down. A brain-dead individual needs machinery to keep their body working. By week 24, a fetus has all of their major organs formed. Their heart has been beating, they can feel pain, suck their thumbs, and touch their face; they've even been working on strengthening their muscles, so they can get ready for that first big gasp of air! If you are having a daughter, one million eggs would already be in her uterus. Their body is booting up. You just have to give them some time to log on. A brain-dead human at the end of their life is not the same as a human child at the beginning of theirs. If your baby has a rare defect such as Anencephaly, when parts of the brain and skull are missing, the baby would not be viable and would most likely die within minutes, hours, or days after birth.

The fourth possible stage is viability. Fetal viability is when a fetus is considered "viable" outside of the womb, even with medical intervention. Most people consider this to be about 24 weeks.

But babies have been born and survived earlier than 24 weeks. Babies have survived at 21. Would it be just to cut off legal protections for a child at 20 weeks? And viability doesn't make much sense. Viability means the "ability to survive or live successfully." A fetus is viable within the environment they're meant to be in—the mother's womb. If I launched you into outer space, sunk you to the ocean's depths, or placed you in a burning building, you wouldn't be viable in those spaces either. People with severe autoimmune deficiencies require protected environments or else they will die. Viability is extremely relative. "Fetal viability" relates to when a fetus can survive outside of the womb, but there is no such answer without the resources and labor of another human being. Newborns are not independently viable either.

The final possibility is birth.

It would be heinous if our society justified abortions at nine months. There is nothing so magical about the vagina that it should instill personhood in a baby, who could very well be ten pounds, like my youngest sister. How can a few inches of skin possibly be enough to convince a rational mind that it makes a justifiable difference between life and death?

But even "rational" people can reason themselves out of a rational position. Everyone has a bias, and if those biases are not challenged, they cannot be battle-tested. Even an entry-level pro-life debater could debunk the biologist's claim that shed skin could be "potential human beings."

Americans want to look at biologists for objectivity. The most consistent standard is conception. But what do we do when biologists want to pass the ball? Sakar says, "When human life begins during fetal developments is a question for philosophers and theologians."

What Philosophers Say

Personhood

When it comes to the abortion debate, there are people who don't see the unborn as persons, may see them as a person but not enough to supersede the bodily autonomy of the mother, and then there are activists who do not care if the child is alive because it's still immoral to deny a woman an abortion.

The argument of bodily autonomy is made more palatable by downplaying the sanctity of human life. To do that, you must argue that even though a human mother is carrying a cellular life in her womb, the child is still not a person.

Technically, a person is a human being individual. A zygote/embryo/fetus has distinct DNA. The child may be attached to the mother, but the child isn't the mother. The fetus qualifies. Sons and daughters in the womb are undoubtedly alive. But "personhood" is a philosophical concept.

Philosopher Mary Anne Warren believes there are five traits of personhood we should consider: consciousness (and in particular, the capacity to feel pain), reasoning, self-motivated activity, capability to communicate, and self-awareness.[8]

There are born human beings who don't possess all of these traits—whether through a temporary state like a coma or an illness—and some animals like squirrels, chimps, and dolphins would qualify. Not all humans can feel pain. And in the past, scientists and doctors have certainly made egregious mistakes regarding babies and pain. Back in 1848, Henry J. Bigelow, M.D. wrote in the Journal of the *American Medical Association:* "Indeed, the facility of controlling a child of this age, together with the fact that it has neither the anticipation nor remembrance of suffering, however severe, seems to render this stage of narcoticism [anesthesia] unnecessary."[9] In the 1940s, it was believed infants lacked the neurological capacity for pain because of their limited reactions during pinprick tests. Doctors didn't begin giving anesthesia to newborns during surgery until the mid-1980s. Newborns were given muscle relaxers to keep them from intensely moving on an operation table, but doctors didn't think they experienced pain based on their body language. In 1987, the American Academy of Pediatrics declared operating on newborns without anesthetics unethical.[10] Even fetuses in the womb receive anesthesia for surgery now. Historically, there is much we have been certain of that has turned out to be barbarism.

Philosophers don't necessarily believe you need to possess all of Warren's stated personhood traits at once, but they do normally argue for some form of consciousness or sentience. But if a newborn came out of the womb with complications and was in a coma, would they not be a person? Would they not qualify to be protected from violence?

Warren believes it is crucial to disqualify the unborn from personhood, because "once we allow the assumption that a fetus has full moral rights it becomes an extremely complex and difficult question whether and when abortion is justifiable."

Imagine if you sent a child to school in a purple shirt and at recess, all of the other kids in the class decide to create a new kickball game. But according to the rules they just made up, no one in purple shirts can participate. If your child came home in tears for being purposely singled out, I imagine you'd be very angry they were so obviously discriminated against. That's how we treat "personhood." We already know (or we think we do) the characteristics of a fetus. So, we use that information to discriminate against the unborn, even though the qualifying traits of "personhood" are within their nature, and you wouldn't unperson someone outside of the womb for temporarily not possessing those inherent traits.

It's fascinating how human beings can rationalize themselves into immoral positions. If one day made all the difference between whether a human being in the womb felt pain or possessed consciousness, do you truly believe that a single day is enough to end their life? And if not a day, why a week? How about one month or five? They're trying to take the life of a child before they're too great of a moral conundrum. They're like Skynet from *Terminator*, fighting in the present to protect their future. Skynet knows John Connor will be their end, and a woman knows the same fetus at six weeks will be a person with a social security number and a qualifying dependent on her tax return after they exit her vagina. From the moment of conception, her child is on a self-determined path to maturity.

The mother doesn't need to learn to code or use complicated directions from IKEA. The child is not going through a dramatic metamorphosis like a tadpole or caterpillar. They are simply growing up and experiencing normal stages of human development. The capacity to feel pain and rationalize is inherent to human nature. Regardless of whether that is actualized in the first few weeks of existence doesn't erase that reality. That's why human rights should begin when one's human existence begins.

It is also important to note Congressman John A. Bingham, the author of the 14th Amendment, used "person" and "human being" interchangeably. "If a State has not the right to deny equal protection to any human being under the Constitution of this country in the rights of life, liberty, and property, how can State rights be impaired by penal prohibitions of such denial as proposed?"[11] His purpose in writing the 14th Amendment was to guarantee equal protection to human beings, and there is no distinction made to separate a legal person from a biological human being.

Using the concept of "personhood" to disqualify human beings from human rights is using a belief to justify discrimination. It's bigotry used to excuse and endorse violence.

Bodily Autonomy

Many philosophical arguments today talk past the point of when life begins, claiming it doesn't matter. Bodily autonomy is the prevalent pro-choice argument, with variations of the "violinist" scenario, made famous in Judith Jarvis Thomson's "A Defense of Abortion" essay. In short, you wake up one day, attached to the world's greatest violinist with a fatal kidney ailment. You've been kidnapped by the Society of Music Lovers, and you're the only person who can save this violinist. Do you have the right to deny your bodily resources, even at the expense of their life?

In this contrived scenario, you have been violently aggressed upon without your consent, vocal or implied. It's tragic the violinist is dying, but he does not have a God-given right to never die. He has a right to life, which equates to a right to not be killed. Being involuntarily hooked to a stranger isn't the same as creating a life inside of you, almost always through deliberate actions of procreation. The child isn't an intruder; they were invited into existence by the mother and father, and their genetic material was inherited from their parents. With abortion, the point of the procedure is to end the pregnancy by terminating the life of the embryo or fetus. And whether you take the pill early on or have the baby sucked out of you, it will be killed before passing through.

I recently explained to a pro-choice advocate that I didn't find the "violinist" scenario analogous to abortion, because the violinist isn't ripped apart, limb from limb, as the cause of death. They pushed back, believing since less than one percent of abortions are done after 21 weeks according to the CDC (which does not always include all states), few involve dismemberment.

Well, if there are nearly one million abortions yearly in the US, less than one percent is still thousands of babies. And just because an abortion is done early, doesn't mean they aren't being dismembered. According to Michigan's 2021 abortion data, 381 induced abortions took place after 21 weeks. But if you look at the procedures, there were 1,783 dilation & evacuations and 12,732 suction curettages.[12] Those are nearly half the abortions in my home state. Don't you think the analogy is vastly different if instead of merely unplugging the violinist, who doesn't belong attached to my body, I take out an axe and start hacking him to bits?

While pro-life debaters are correct to point out that Thomson's scenario isn't analogous to pregnancy, it's important to note that wasn't Thomson's point. She even adjusts the parameters of her scenario to prove her theory. "Having a right to life does not guarantee having either a right to be given the use of or a right to be allowed continued use of another person's body—even if one needs it for life itself." The true issue with Thomson's essay is that it's nonsensical in the real world. Mothers who refuse care for their infants are punished for their neglect and seen as murderers, even though their refusal of care is far more like the unplugging scenario compared to the intentionally aggressive forms of violence in abortion, yet abortion advocates believe parents are obligated to use their body and provide care for their born children. During the 2020 COVID-19 pandemic, humans were also coerced into taking a vaccine to possibly save their neighbor. If your neighbor isn't viable in a post-COVID world, why is it the moral obligation of others to alter their body for their neighbor's benefit? You could argue the scenarios I've offered deal with born people who have obtained consciousness and can experience suffering, but the same is true for the violinist. The thesis for the entire essay simply isn't true.

Pro-life Stanford University refutes the "violinist" argument by pointing out the difference between extraordinary life-saving measures vs ordinary ones.[13] For example, diving on train tracks to save you after fainting, with a train on the way, would be an extraordinary measure. It would be heroic, but it would be understandable if someone didn't risk their life. However, if you fainted on the tracks next to me, and I allowed you to lay there for hours, that would be immoral. Despite how much pro-choice women make it seem like getting pregnant is the end of the world, it's actually very ordinary. Granted, it can be difficult—even miserable—but it's ordinary. After all, over one hundred million children are born every year. Extraordinary circumstances—such as life-threatening pregnancies—can arise, but they are rare and hardly the reasons for abortions.

Another famous bodily autonomy argument goes even further. Philosopher David Boonin argues even if a fetus is a living person, you should still be able to legally kill that person while appealing to *McFall v. Shimp*.[14] A court in Pennsylvania ruled the state cannot force another person to donate body parts after McFall sued his cousin for backing out of donating bone marrow. The logic is if Shimp can refuse to donate his organs, the state shouldn't force a mother to donate her uterus, even at the expense of her child's life. Abortion is the only way to be free from the donation, therefore, she must be entitled to an abortion, or it would be "force."

A big difference between the cousins and the child-mother dynamic is that the donation has already occurred in pregnancy. If Shimp had already donated the bone marrow to McFall, the courts wouldn't likely rule that Shimp had a right to repossess it, especially if it would kill McFall. Shimp's bone marrow is also for Shimp. The purpose of the uterus is to be a safe space for a woman's child—a child who only exists because actions were taken to create them. The use of a mother's body is inherent to the mother-child relationship.

The accusation of "force" is also problematic. Let's imagine for a moment that divorce becomes illegal. If the woman wants out of her marriage and kills her husband, would she be able to avoid judgment by claiming the state "forced" her to stay in her marriage? If you are already in a state—especially one through voluntary means—is it "force" if the government penalizes the exit? Perhaps it is. After all, when the government gets involved, they are threatening with a gun. Many Americans don't believe the government should involve itself in everything, including marriage. But is government interference *always* wrong? The state "forces" men to pay child support, yet I've never seen pro-choice women start a campaign to end their parental obligations of 18-25 years. If a man killed their child to avoid paying child support, could he get off by reminding the court it was his only way of getting out of providing for his child? No. We wouldn't tolerate a father ending his parental obligations through violence.

If I were in a dire financial situation and the only immediate method to alleviate the burden was to beat up my neighbor and rob them, would the government be "forcing" me to stay poor because they have laws in place disincentivizing me from committing the robbery? There are other legal means of acquiring money that would require patience, and this is true of women who are pregnant. Birth can't be avoided; their offspring is coming out dead or alive. The "donation" in pregnancy will cease. The child will not be in their body forever. Abortion is not the only way to end the "donation." It's a means to immediately end it, and facilitating that desire requires more justification than, "I want, I want, I want," since it's at the expense of a child's life.

If I invited you to fly in my private airplane and decided you were unbearably annoying, would it be moral to push you out of my property from 30,000 feet, or should I hold my peace until we're safely on the ground? What if a couple went on a sailing adventure with their toddler and got tired of their parental obligations while surrounded by sparkling blue waters? Is it fine to submit the child over to the ocean's mercy, or should they endure their responsibilities? What if the couple discovered a toddler on their boat who wasn't their child? Could they still chuck the child into the water? What if the old man from Pixar's *UP* never let Russell into his house after he launched it into the air? If Carl shoved Russell with his cane until the boy fell to his death, would we say that wasn't murder and Carl deserves no penalties?

Abortion activists claim they want the government to stay out of a woman's abortion, yet they want the government to sign onto state-sanctioned murder and provide immunity to the woman and her hitman. Nowadays, they even want federal and financial backing. The abortion industry has even lobbied the government to force Christians to cover abortion in their insurance plans in California.[15] In 2019 and 2021, the majority of Michigan Democrats in the state legislature introduced the Reproductive Health Act to repeal barriers from tax dollars funding abortion.[16] These politicians went on to support Proposal 3 in 2022, which its opponents warned could provide taxpayer-funded abortions. Abortion is very much an issue beyond a woman and her doctor.

Bodily autonomy is also not absolute. For example, the Affordable Care Act aka Obamacare charged Americans for not purchasing health insurance. This wasn't like paying a tax because you use a service. This is a fee for simply being alive. The Obama Administration was sued, but the Supreme Court ruled (controversially) that Congress had the power to impose the fee as a tax.

In *Jacobson v. Massachusetts*, the Supreme Court ruled states can enforce compulsory vaccination laws, and individual liberty is not absolute, especially when the lives of others are on the line. If the state can make someone take a vaccination to potentially save someone's life, how is it not reasonable for the state to enact an abortion ban to prevent a woman from deliberately killing her baby?

The state also forces men to sign up for the draft when they reach maturity. Granted, they don't have uteruses, but all of their organs are still inside their body that could potentially be blown up while serving the country. The Selective Service's Twitter account even wrote, "Parents, if your son is an only son and the last male in your family to carry the family name, he is still required to register with SSS."[17] The United States military operates off of volunteers today, but we had drafts in the Civil War (which led to terrible riots), Vietnam, and more. Some countries like South Korea require men to serve. In Israel, service is mandatory for both sexes.

Some activists argue if women cannot have abortions, we are granting a fetus a special right that no one else has: a right to use someone else's body. To that I say, there is nothing special about being a fetus. Everyone alive today has had the privilege of using someone else's uterus. Women are the ones demanding a special right that men certainly don't possess: free reign to end the lives of their children.

Besides, pregnancy doesn't erase your bodily autonomy. A government lab can't just confiscate pregnant women for experiments because they have no rights. She's still a human being who should be treated with dignity; she just shouldn't be able to kill the child.

The United Nations Population Fund debunked the "myth" that "one person's bodily autonomy could end up undermining the autonomy of others." They said:

> Having bodily autonomy does not mean any person gets to undermine the health, rights or autonomy of others. Individuals have the right to choose whether to have sex or get pregnant, for example, but they are not entitled to impose these choices on others.
>
> No one has the right to violate the rights, autonomy, or bodily integrity of anyone else. [18]

Bodily autonomy doesn't grant you the freedom to use that bodily autonomy to actively kill another human being, especially if the victim only exists because of actions taken with *your* bodily autonomy. Bodily autonomy is not a free pass for lawlessness. You can't infringe on another person's rights, especially their right to life, simply because you wish to do so. Besides, bodily autonomy is about making decisions about *your* body, *your* life, and *your* future. Abortion involves *two* bodies, *two* lives, and *two* futures.

Positive and Negative Rights

Negative rights are rights we come into the world with. They are natural, God-given rights and do not require the duty or the action of another person. For example, I don't need another person to have free speech. Negative rights can be considered liberties.

Positive rights impose a positive duty on another person. An example would be if a government creates a right to education or health care. Positive rights are entitlements.

In an ideal world, we would all live out our liberties and agree to respect them, but there are times when our rights conflict. When a landlord wants to evict someone from their property, there is a legal process. Even a squatter has rights. But what the landlord can't do is murder their former tenant because it's faster than eviction or makes the process smoother.

The right to life would be a negative right. Another way to look at the right to life is the right to not be killed (after all, we mortals don't live forever). The right to an abortion, especially in the United States, is not a right recognized by the Constitution at all. That is why, under the 10th Amendment, it falls back to the states to legislate. However, it can be argued abortion shouldn't be legislated from state to state—or permitted at all—because equal protection from the 14th Amendment should apply to the unborn.

When a woman is pregnant, there are conflicting rights at play. The mother has a right to autonomy, but the baby has a right to not be killed. Wouldn't the best compromise be the least violent that maximizes the most liberty? Unless there's a reasonable statistical likelihood the pregnancy would result in the mother's death (after all, she has a right to life), wouldn't it be the most moral to carry that child to term?

Pro-choice activists would disagree. They'd say it's immoral to make her carry the pregnancy. Of course, no one is "making" her do that. But can we prevent her from terminating?

An induced abortion is also not a natural or negative right. Pro-choice activists argue an abortion procedure through the pill is simply denying the baby of the mother's resources and not killing them. They say it's no different than deciding to unplug yourself in the "violinist" scenario. However, you're naturally connected to your human baby, and you cannot will yourself to stop providing resources to your child.

Let's for a moment imagine a small child has been placed in my care, but I have decided to not go out of my way to help them. They're big enough to maneuver to different cabinets and open the refrigerator if they're hungry, but I don't have to purposely feed them. Well, what if I decide they aren't entitled to any of my resources, and instead of allowing the process to continue until I can transfer care, I acquire locks from my neighbor and place them on all the cabinets and the refrigerator until the child starves to death? If I told my neighbor what the locks were for, do you think they would have provided them? Most people would find this to be irreprehensible, yet this is what happens in two-thirds of abortions.

A woman has to take a mifepristone pill to stop a natural hormone called progesterone, which stabilizes the lining of the uterus. When the lining breaks down, blood and nourishment are cut off from the baby, and it suffocates/starves to death in the womb (it is possible to reverse the procedure if done quickly enough). A woman then takes misoprostol to force contractions and heavy bleeding to expel the dead baby.

Whether the mother is taking the pill or having a surgical abortion, she requires the products and labor of individuals. She needs quite a bit of participation to override the baby's natural right to life.

She also expects the government not to intervene on the child's behalf, but is this a reasonable desire? If a company was specifically making poison pills for women to give to their toddlers when they want out of motherhood, the government wouldn't allow that. U.S. Citizens have a right to bear arms, but if you tried to buy a gun and wrote on the ATF form that you were specifically purchasing a firearm to kill your neighbor, there's a good chance you'll be denied, investigated, and arrested for conspiracy to commit murder.

Even if a woman has the right to decide what to do with her bodily resources, society isn't obligated to keep abortion accessible or legal. The government is obligated to "secure" our unalienable rights. According to the Declaration of Independence, that's why men form governments. Life is one of those unalienable rights our government is meant to secure. Not only should the government intervene and end abortion on demand; the government is violating its purpose by not protecting children in the womb.

Deep down, I believe our elected officials understand this. Vice President Kamala Harris (D) gave a speech during the anniversary of *Roe v. Wade*, lamenting its overturning.[19] "America is a promise. It is a promise of freedom and liberty— not for some, but for all," Harris said, ignoring the irony of her statement. "A promise we made in the Declaration of Independence that we are each endowed with the right to liberty and the pursuit of happiness." It was not a mistake Harris omitted "Life" from the conversation. She couldn't bring herself to admit that "Life" is also a promise, and America is failing to protect that liberty. Harris actively objects to that obligation.

Harris then went on to say, "Be clear. These rights were not bestowed upon us. They belong to us as Americans." But unalienable rights don't simply belong to Americans. There are certain privileges we're entitled to as U.S. citizens, but if someone illegally enters the country and is murdered, we will still seek justice for that human being. No one has the right to unjustly take their life. And you cannot believe our rights are *not* "bestowed upon us" if they are only allowed if we are wanted.

Abortion is treated with remarkable inconsistency, and one can argue pregnancy is such a unique situation of conflicting rights. But parental obligation presents conflicting rights anyway. A parent can't refuse to feed their child simply because the food is their property. This would be neglect; the child could be removed, and the parents could be prosecuted. A woman doesn't have a God-given right to have an induced abortion, but the baby does have a God-given right to life. The baby deserves more moral consideration than a squatter, especially since they were invited into existence by deliberate actions (despite intentions), in a consensual manner more than 99 percent of the time.

"Do No Harm"

Back in 400 BC, a famous Greek physician by the name of Hippocrates created *the Hippocratic Oath*. The famous phrase "Do no harm," associated with the medical field, is attributed to Hippocrates. In the original text of the oath, there is the following:

> I will not give a lethal drug to anyone if I am asked, nor will I advise such a plan; and similarly I will not give a woman a pessary to cause an abortion.

After the medical horrors committed by Nazis in WWII, the World Medical Association created the Declaration of Geneva, in 1948. The original text reads:

> I WILL MAINTAIN the utmost respect for human life, from the time of conception; even under threat, I will not use my medical knowledge contrary to the laws of humanity. [20]

Germans heavily discouraged abortions for their women while building their master race (unless the children were "undesirables"). However, Jewish and Roma women were subjected to forced sterilizations and abortions. The women were beaten and raped, and if a pregnancy occurred, "race experts" would determine if the children were capable of "Germanization." If not, the women were either forced to have an abortion or kept in conditions so abhorrent, the child would not survive.[21]

It's no wonder why the medical world rallied around the preservation of life at conception. Picking and choosing who does and doesn't produce is barbaric. It wasn't until 1983 that the declaration was amended to remove the phrasing about conception. Medical professionals have valued and dedicated their lives to healing for a very long time, and their oaths have recognized the sanctity of life for the unborn as well.

Today, doctors vary in their beliefs regarding life. There are abortion doctors very candid about what abortion is and that it takes a human life, but the pro-choice movement is hidden in euphemisms. When abortion is called "health care," I always ask, "How healthy is the baby after the abortion?"

In a viral abortion debate on conservative commentator Michael Knowles' YouTube channel, Bronte Remsik—a third-year medical student and social media influencer—admitted she is being taught to change her language based on the patient's desires toward the child, even though Bronte knows the feelings of the mother doesn't change the ontology of her child. "Calling it a fetus when it is a wanted pregnancy can make them feel detached from that pregnancy but also calling it a baby when it is an unwanted pregnancy can put—you know—unnecessary pressure and fear onto that pregnant person."[22] Remsik understands that language is "emotional" and even though she knows a fetus is human and alive, medical professionals are willing to downplay the baby's humanity to perform an abortion. Instead of "do no harm," harm is now a matter of controlled perspective.

Health care is about maintaining and restoring health. Pregnancy is not a disease and children should not be treated like cancer. It may not be what every woman desires, and it certainly isn't easy, but the amount of vitriol associated with pregnancy, as if motherhood—something women are biologically designed to achieve—is somehow debilitating, is extraordinarily sexist.

What the Bible Says

Origin of Mankind

One of the most common rebuttals, whether I'm having a conversation with Christians or not, is that "life starts at first breath." This is a reference to Genesis chapter two, the creation of Adam. Normally, this is thrown out by atheists or disgruntled ex-Christians, but I have met a Jewish person or two who believed the same thing.

First and foremost, the objective scientific reality is that a unique individual comes into existence at the moment of conception. It is cellular life. It is a whole human organism. Whether you value their life, is a subjective opinion. Whether God values that life, is obvious, but we'll address this later.

If we are to believe a baby is not literally alive until it's birthed out of their mother's womb and takes their first breath—even if they're mostly or perfectly healthy—that would be a complete contradiction with reality.

When science and the word of God don't line up properly, a Christian should come to one of two conclusions. The first is that science simply hasn't caught up with the inspired word written in the text. God is all-knowing. He doesn't make mistakes, and if the authors of the Bible were truly hearing from God as they wrote the compiled books, it should all make sense.

If there is a contradiction with absolute settled science, the believer should question whether they are understanding the scripture correctly. In the case of "first breath," it's clear.

First and foremost, fetuses do breathe in the womb. They just don't breathe like us. When the mother breathes air into her lungs, oxygen filters into her blood, and the oxygen and nutrients in her blood transfer to her child via the umbilical cord and placenta. Carbon dioxide is also removed through the umbilical cord until the baby is ready to exit the birth canal.

Babies even prepare their lungs for air before birth. Between 10-12 weeks, the baby will begin to practice breathing. As time goes on, they'll strengthen their muscles by swallowing the amniotic fluid that surrounds them. MRIs of this sight do not paint the picture of a lifeless hunk of flesh waiting for validation. It's a human baby, discovering the pathway to strength and survival like they will continue to do outside of the womb. It's not very different than watching my helpless nephew as a newborn grow and strengthen his muscles, gradually testing his body, until he was able to take his first step.

Now, let's go to the scripture. The Bible says, "Then the LORD God formed the man of dust from the ground and breathed into his nostrils the breath of life, and the man became a living creature," (Genesis 2:7, ESV). The King James Version says man became a "living soul."

Adam is the origin of mankind. So, we see Adam was assembled from the dust of the ground. God took the necessary particles and minerals from within the earth and built him molecule by molecule. He was only a hunk of flesh until God breathed into his nostrils, and then Adam came alive. Adam was not birthed out of a womb. He probably wouldn't have a belly button from a missing umbilical cord like you and me. He's distinctly different, and God only explained this process once.

²¹ So the LORD God caused a deep sleep to fall upon the man, and while he slept took one of his ribs and closed up its place with flesh. ²² And the rib that the LORD God

had taken from the man he made into a woman and brought her to the man. (Genesis 2:21-22, ESV)

God placed Adam into a deep sleep for surgery, removed his rib, closed him up, and then altered that genetic material to create another human being. God made her chromosomes XX instead of XY and created distinct sex organs, so the two could come together and become one flesh.

> Now Adam knew Eve his wife, and she conceived and bore Cain, saying, "I have gotten a man with the help of the LORD." [2] And again, she bore his brother Abel. Now Abel was a keeper of sheep, and Cain a worker of the ground. (Genesis 4:1-2, ESV)

Now, there is a natural process of procreation established. God doesn't build anyone else from "dust." He doesn't need to clone anyone else. Humans can be fruitful and multiply on autopilot. The text doesn't note that God needs to breathe "the breath of life" in anyone else to make humanity continue. God's breath was necessary to create man, and humanity was built capable of reproducing without God supernaturally intervening repeatedly.

But let's, for a moment, assume God does need to supernaturally intervene for every human being to become alive. There is no reason to assume this doesn't happen within the womb since the Holy Spirit interacts with John the Baptist while he is an unborn baby.

And referencing Genesis 2:7 also presents another glaring problem for the abortion debate. Human beings are not merely hunks of flesh, blood, and electrical signals. We contain a soul. Not only is abortion taking a life, but it's robbing a soul of its vessel. Pro-Choice advocates will deny the humanity of the unborn because they lack consciousness or sentience, but how can they judge a person's soul?

Early debates about when life began or ensoulment lacked the knowledge that we possess today about embryology. Believing the child gains a soul at the "quickening" when a mother can feel her fetus moving is superstitious and something we can't prove. But we know, scientifically, that a day-one zygote has all the necessary characteristics of life, including responding to stimuli, cellular organization, and growth. Just because you can't feel your child moving doesn't mean there isn't a lot of activity going on. If a woman had a cryptic pregnancy and didn't know she was pregnant until she was about to give birth, her denial or unawareness wouldn't make the child any less alive.

The soul is immaterial, so our idea of "personhood" should be made up of more than physical markers our body achieves throughout normal development.

When asked, "How would you feel if your mother aborted you?" Pro-choice advocates normally respond, "I wouldn't know. I would be dead." Mind you, they'd "be dead" if they were killed, regardless of their age and development. Some of them incorrectly claim they wouldn't exist. But that's not true. You exist at the moment of conception, and nothing can change that. And who is to say you wouldn't know? Your body may cease to grow and begin to decay, but your soul isn't destroyed. It will move on. Who is to say you wouldn't be aware of your brutal end?

I've heard some abortion advocates make the case that it would be better to be aborted because it would be a "free pass" to heaven. This idea is from the concept "age of accountability." Even though a child may not be sinless, they may be too young to truly grasp good and evil in the sense that they would be guilty and held accountable for their sins.

For example, Romans 14:12 says, "Each of us will give an account of himself to God." How can an infant or toddler do that? Also, After David's child (conceived in adultery) passed away, he held the belief his child had moved into heaven, and that he would have to reunite one day.

However, not all denominations believe in the age of accountability. Dr. Leighton Flowers remarked on his website, *Soteriology 101*, that he grew up believing in the concept, but when he got to college and became a Calvinist, he was convinced this was a manmade concept to "help ease the pain of those who tragically lost a young child."[23] Dr. Flowers is no longer a Calvinist and believes there is biblical evidence for this doctrine, but many Calvinists do not. There are also Calvinists who accept the doctrine.

I also once had a conversation with a fellow religious pro-life friend. They were truly grieved about the fate of the unborn, believing they were being sent to hell without a chance to know God. I was surprised he had never heard of the age of accountability, and I shared the doctrine. He was relieved.

But even if you do believe an aborted child is on their way to heaven, simply getting to heaven is not the point of our existence. It's a nice goal to have. It's the destination you obviously want to aim for, but heaven is an amazing place because we're going to be glorifying God for eternity. If God purposed us with a life on earth, it's our duty to glorify God here with our lives. To fear God and keep his commandments is "the whole duty of man," (Ecclesiastes 12:13).

God commands us to give him thanks at all times, through the good and the bad. What struggles do you have in heaven to persevere through, to show the world God is good despite your trials and tribulations?

Jesus had an agonizing mortal death. Not only was he mocked, beaten, spat on, whipped, had to carry his cross, and then was nailed to it; he had to endure 33 years of humanity. The Pharisees constantly questioned, plotted to entrap Jesus, and even implied he was an illegitimate child (John 8:41). Jesus was crucified for literally being who he is. He was betrayed by Judas, and he knew Judas was going to do it. He had to minister and uplift Peter, knowing good and well he was going to deny him. His disciples were often frustrating. He was rejected multiple times; he was even run out of town. Jesus got hungry and thirsty like the rest of us, and he certainly felt pain.

His sacrifice was not solely the cross. His purpose was not solely to die on the cross. He performed miracles, transformed lives, and raised disciples to continue his work and perform even greater works. And he never promised them their lives would be easy. He told them the opposite. Most of the disciples were martyred. Their deaths served a purpose, but their ministries required them to live their lives.

We have no right to rob God of his creation. We are meant to glorify God while on earth, just as Christ did.

> When Jesus had spoken these words, he lifted up his eyes to heaven, and said, "Father, the hour has come; glorify your Son that the Son may glorify you, [2] since you have given him authority over all flesh, to give eternal life to all whom you have given him. [3] And this is eternal life, that they know you, the only true God, and Jesus Christ whom you have sent. [4] I glorified you on earth, having accomplished the work that you gave me to do. [5] And now, Father, glorify me in your own presence with the glory that I had with you before the world existed. (John 17:1-5, ESV)

I have also heard abortion defenders, sadly, claim they would have been better off if their mothers had aborted them. This is always particularly disturbing. Their admission is if you take the total of their life—accomplishments, experiences, family, friends, and relationships—it results in an ultimate negative. Instead of wishing to never exist, they wish they had been killed via suffocation/starvation, ripped apart, or by lethal injection. Who would wish that sort of violence against themselves or want that mark on their mother's soul?

Have you ever spoken with women who live with regret, every day, for taking the life of their child? Even if a woman has the revelation that the abortion industry manipulated them, even if she was in a sympathetic and desperate circumstance, and even though they believe God is a redeemer, women still find it hard to forgive themselves. Abortion is nothing to take lightly. It is not something you should wish for yourself, and certainly, not something you should wish for someone you care for.

And if a woman does not repent of that grave sin, she'll have to answer for that crime on Judgment Day. Each abortion will be accounted for and written down, and God will judge us according to our works (Revelation, 20:12-13).

Genesis 2:7 isn't the only scripture abortion advocates bring up to note breath is required for life. They'll do an internet search and bring up every verse with "breath," regardless of context.

For behold, I will bring a flood of waters upon the earth to destroy all flesh in which is the breath of life under heaven. Everything that is on the earth shall die. (Genesis 6:17, ESV)

Yes, if you cannot breathe, you will die. If an adult is underwater with no source of oxygen, they will not survive. A fetus is submerged in fluid, but as long as they have a source of oxygen, they will not suffocate. To make an argument that we cannot be alive unless we breathe air through our nostrils or mouth is ridiculous. Noah wasn't required to save all animals during the flood because creatures of the sea obviously wouldn't drown. The Bible acknowledges creatures that live in the water are alive (Genesis 1:20-21).

> Then he said to me, "Prophesy to the breath; prophesy, son of man, and say to the breath, Thus says the Lord GOD: Come from the four winds, O breath, and breathe on these slain, that they may live." (Ezekiel 37:9, ESV)

Yes, I have seen people use this passage of Ezekiel prophesying, to prove the Bible does not claim we are scientifically alive without breath.

Most of the criticisms are not from genuine believers who have studied the Bible for any serious amount of time. They also ignore the fact fetuses do breathe in the womb, just a little differently. They do experience a "breath of life." The Bible doesn't say that life starts at first breath. It does, however, mention that the life of a creature is in the blood (Leviticus 17:14). If the pro-choice community wants to go that route, they should consider that through the blood, the preborn receives oxygen. If life does begin at "first breath," then the unborn should be protected in the womb.

If you're going to argue it's not about the literal breath but it's an expression to mean the child is simply outside of the womb and able to breathe on their own, there are circumstances when a born child cannot breathe on their own. If the requirement is that they must breathe air apart from their mother, this would make abortions up until the moment of birth morally permissible. Mind you, this is contrary to what the early church taught and our moral intuitions. If someone purposely beat on a pregnant woman's stomach when she was eight months into her pregnancy, intending to cause a stillbirth, would you honestly make the case that no living human was killed in the eyes of God and man?

When Does Our Value to God Begin?

Upon you I have leaned from before my birth; you are he who took me from my mother's womb. My praise is continually of you. (Psalm 71:6)

13 For you formed my inward parts; you knitted me together in my mother's womb.
14 I praise you, for I am fearfully and wonderfully made. Wonderful are your works; my soul knows it very well. (Psalm 139:13-14, ESV)

Thus says the Lord, your Redeemer, who formed you from the womb: "I am the Lord, who made all things, who alone stretched out the heavens, who spread out the earth by myself." (Isaiah 44:24, ESV)

Listen to me, O coastlands, and give attention, you peoples from afar. The Lord called me from the womb, from the body of my mother he named my name. (Isaiah 49:1, ESV)

And now the Lord says, he who formed me from the womb to be his servant, to bring Jacob back to him; and that Israel might be fathered to him—for I am honored in the eyes of the Lord, and my God has become my strength— (Isaiah 49:5, ESV)

"Can a woman forget her nursing child, that she should have no compassion on the son of her womb? Even these may forget, yet I will not forget you." (Isaiah 49:15, ESV)

"Before I formed you in the womb I knew you, and before you were born I consecrated you; I appointed you a prophet to the nations." (Jerimiah 1:5, ESV)

³Blessed be the God and Father of our Lord Jesus Christ, who has blessed us in Christ with every spiritual

blessing in the heavenly places, [4] even as he chose us in him before the foundation of the world, that we should be holy and blameless before him. In love [5] he predestined us for adoption to himself as sons through Jesus Christ, according to the purpose of his will, [6] to the praise of his glorious grace, with which he has blessed us in the Beloved. (Ephesians 1:3-6, ESV)

Many of these scriptures are repeatedly quoted in the Christian pro-life community. We believe that we serve a God of purpose. He is thoughtful, and he is meticulous. We belong here for a reason, and God intimately knows us.

Some critics argue that abortion is not murder because preborn children do not meet the criteria for moral personhood, even in the Bible. But how would you define it? If God knowing us and calling us—we, his image bearers—isn't a proper definition, then how can anything truly measure up? If God's acknowledgment and duty are irrelevant, then how could any standard by man be acceptable?

In the case of Jeremiah, who was called before the foundations of the world, one could argue his statement is a demonstration of God's foreknowledge and not an acknowledgment of the moral status of a fetus. God knew Jeremiah, but God knows everyone and everything. God knowing when each blade of grass will grow and when it will be cut on your lawn does not infer moral personhood. But God doesn't make rocks and grass in his image, nor does God treat humans the same as rocks, plants, and animals.

In the very first book of the Bible, it is established that God created man in his own image (Genesis 1:27). After the flood, God tells Noah to reproduce and that he has dominion over the earth. He can eat plants and animals, but God explains that when a human's blood is shed, a "reckoning" is required. He tells Noah, "Whoever sheds the blood of man, by man shall his blood be shed, for God made man in his own image," (Genesis 9:6). If we can gather any sense of "personhood" from the Bible, it is simply held within our human nature itself. Humans may look at each other and discriminate based on gender, race, age, and ability, but humans cannot erase the fact that we are made in his likeness. Our sons and daughters in the womb are also image bearers of God.

As an embryo or fetus, you may be unable to recognize yourself or be aware of God's love for you, but our love from God predates, includes, and extends beyond our physical lives on earth. The love my mother and father had for me predated my understanding, yet that didn't make it any less real. Even if my parents hadn't loved me, God's love was still present. Before we have the capacity to form an identity, God already knows who we are and who we're meant to be. Even as a man, Apostle Paul did not know his purpose until Jesus Christ revealed himself. He used to persecute Christians. "But when he who had set me apart before I was born, and who called me by his grace was pleased to reveal his Son to me, in order that I might preach him among the Gentiles..." (Galatians 1:15-16, ESV). To dismiss a fetus for not having an identity prior to their birth is strange, if you believe we all must deny ourselves, slay our former lives, and be born again anyway. You cannot truly know yourself until God gives you the revelation of your identity.

Michigan Congresswoman Hillary Scholten (D) calls herself a "pro-choice Christian" because of passages like Jeremiah 1:5.[24] "It doesn't say the 'government's womb' or the 'Speaker's [of the House of Representatives] womb.' It says, 'the mother's womb.'" The grotesque reality is Scholten misused the scripture to justify voting against the Born Alive Survivors Protection Act, which would require medical care for babies who survived abortion. 210 out of 212 Democrats rejected the bill. So, in this instance, the mother's womb is irrelevant because the child has already survived the attempt on their life.

But Scholten also misunderstands the point of the passage. It's not meant to highlight the authority or the relationship of the mother. The passage highlights the intimate relationship the individual has with God even in their mother's womb. God's relationship with an individual supersedes all others. Jesus says, "If anyone comes to me and does not hate his own father and mother and wife and children and brothers and sisters, yes, and even his own life, he cannot be my disciple," (Luke 14:26, ESV). Jesus didn't say this because he literally wants you to hate the people in your life or yourself. Jesus followed up with an illustration explaining his point; there is a cost to following after him, and you have to be willing to give up *everything*. Sometimes, relationships are strained with unbelievers or Christians who don't understand your calling. God wants you to still treat them with the love of Christ, but you still have to be willing to forsake them and follow after God.

If Scholten were a Christian, she should understand a child's relationship with Christ outranks their relationship with their mother. A woman's obedience to God should also outrank her desire to have an abortion. And even though Scholten has chosen life herself, she certainly should not proudly boast her encouragement of sin for others.

Before the foundations of the world, God had a plan for you. Within the womb, God knows us. And before we are born, God will call us. Perhaps your destiny is to prophesy to the nations or speak a word of encouragement to the right person at the right time, changing the outcome of their entire life. Maybe you are meant to change your community, nation, or the world.

If God has such grand and intimate plans for our lives, who are we to tell God our children deserve the death penalty? As the scripture noted in Isaiah 49:15, even if the mother forgets or has no compassion for her child, the Lord will never forget them.

Does God Value a Fetus?

Pro-choice skeptics accuse God of not valuing a fetus due to a passage in Exodus about injuring a pregnant woman:

²²When men strive together and hit a pregnant woman, so that her children come out, but there is no harm, the one who hit her shall surely be fined, as the woman's husband shall impose on him, and he shall pay as the judges determine. ²³ But if there is harm, then you shall pay life for life, ²⁴ eye for eye, tooth for tooth, hand for hand, foot for foot, ²⁵ burn for burn, wound for wound, stripe for stripe. (Exodus 21:22-25, ESV)

Two men are fighting, and a pregnant woman is caught in the crossfire. The critics argue if the mother has a miscarriage due to the fight, the punishment is only a monetary fine. But if the mother was harmed, it would be "eye for an eye." Therefore, God values a fetus less.

Frankly, this is a very strange passage to try and justify abortion. Unlike an induced abortion—which is a premeditated homicide—these men caused an accidental death. They are instructed to pay a fine like you would in a civil wrongful death suit. Could it be possible that the judgment is based on the circumstances of the case rather than the value of the child? Is it plausible that men should be more cognizant of grown women rather than expecting them to watch out for hidden fetuses who may not have even lived long enough to exit the womb alive anyway? Unequal status or punishment doesn't automatically equate to no moral value. Even if God valued the fetus less than the mother, there is still no free reign given to women to deliberately end the lives of their children.

Critics will also claim the fetus is treated as property in this passage. Specifically, the fetus is the father's property. This point especially cuts against the modern abortion narrative. How can a woman have an abortion because it's "her body, her choice" if the child in her womb belongs to the father? She should have absolutely no right to terminate the pregnancy. There shouldn't be any more sad stories of fathers grieving their dead children, after begging mothers not to kill their heirs. It's also important to note that the Bible also doesn't grant free reign to murder other human beings who are treated as property. There's also a difference between someone belonging to another person (our children belong to us, as opposed to strangers) and property such as a chair, shoe, or an animal. Even if the father's heir belongs to him, it doesn't mean his heir isn't made in the image of God, isn't fearfully and wonderfully made, and isn't entitled to not be purposely killed by their mother.

The text also does not indicate that the "eye for an eye" only applies if the "harm" is done to the mother. It can be read that if a child is premature and there is no further injury, then there is a monetary fine. If there is further harm to the child, then the punishment is more severe.

Critics argue this is a misinterpretation of the passage because the Covenant Code draws from the Code of Hammurabi, which distinguishes the "harm" is directed toward the mother:

209. If a man has struck a free woman with child, and has caused her to miscarry, he shall pay ten shekels for her miscarriage

210. If that woman die, his daughter shall be killed.

The laws of Hammurabi are similar to other laws of that day in the region, but the Mosaic law is a moral improvement compared to the other law codes of the ancient Near East. For example, the punishment for killing a pregnant woman in the Mosaic law is not to direct revenge against an undeserving party. There's already a big difference here. Perhaps the Bible switches up the language because it's supposed to apply to the mother and child.

Some translations, such as RSV, do use the word "miscarriage," while the NIV says "give birth prematurely." There is a phrase associated with miscarriage (shakal) that is used in passages like Exodus 23:26, but what we see in Exodus 21:22-25 is a description that's associated with birth.

Dr. Paul Copan writes, "Furthermore, *yalad* ('give birth') is always used of a child that has recognizable human form or is capable of surviving outside the womb. The Hebrew word *nepel* is the typical word used of an unborn child, and the word *golem*, which means 'fetus,' is used only once in the Old Testament in Psalm 139:16, which we just noted: God knew the psalmist's 'unformed body' or 'unformed substance.'"[25]

The pro-choice advocates should also consider the repercussions of their argument. If Exodus 21:22-25 can be used to prove a preborn child has little to no value, therefore, they can be deliberately killed by their parents, then they also have no value if someone kills a preborn child who is wanted by their parents. If a drunk driver causes a pregnant woman to lose her child, or if a gang beats a pregnant woman and makes her miscarry, or if a father slips his girlfriend an abortion pill, their deaths cannot be avenged. No one can murder your wanted preborn child if they were never a person. Did David or Isaiah hold no moral value when they were knitted in the womb? If King Herod had slain Jesus Christ while he was in Mary's uterus, would he be guiltless?

But this passage isn't even about premeditated murder. It's about the accidental death of a very fragile human. If God holds these men accountable for an accidental death—even if we accept the interpretation that a child's death equated to a monetary penalty—why wouldn't God hold a woman accountable for purposely destroying an image bearer? Whether the text refers to a premature birth or a miscarriage, the men are still held accountable in some sort of way. If God believes in holding us accountable for accidents, don't you think God cares about the deliberate killing of a baby in the womb?

If God has a purpose for us all and knits us together in the womb, he values us even in our most vulnerable state. But the Bible goes even further. According to an angel, John the Baptist not only had a great calling on his life; he was filled with the Holy Spirit while in his mother's womb (Luke 1:15).

[13] But the angel said to him, "Do not be afraid, Zechariah, for your prayer has been heard, and your wife Elizabeth will bear you a son, and you shall call his name John. [14] And you will have joy and gladness, and many will rejoice at his birth, [15] for he will be great before the Lord. And he must not drink wine or strong drink, and he will be filled with the Holy Spirit, even from his mother's womb. [16] And he will turn many of the children of Israel to the Lord their God, [17] and he will go before him in the spirit and power of Elijah, to turn the hearts of the fathers to the children, and the disobedient to the wisdom of the just, to make ready for the Lord a people prepared." (Luke 1:13-17, ESV)

And when Mary visited Elizabeth, John the Baptist leaped in her womb upon hearing Mary. Then, Elizabeth was filled with the Holy Spirit.

[39] In those days Mary arose and went with haste into the hill country, to a town in Judah, [40] and she entered the house of Zechariah and greeted Elizabeth. [41] And when Elizabeth heard the greeting of Mary, the baby leaped in her womb. And Elizabeth was filled with the Holy Spirit, [42] and she exclaimed with a loud cry, "Blessed are you among women, and blessed is the fruit of your womb! [43] And why is this granted to me that the mother of my Lord should come to me? [44] For behold, when the

sound of your greeting came to my ears, the baby in my womb leaped for joy. (Luke 1:39-44, ESV)

There is no doubt God has a purpose for us before being born, and our relationship with God begins within the womb. Biologists and philosophers may choose to reject personhood because the unborn aren't developed enough for sentience (as we understand it), but we are more than the mind and body. We have a spirit. There is no doubt that as Christians, we should respect life at the moment of conception.

Critics may say John the Baptist's reaction to the Holy Spirit isn't significant because it doesn't show that he had an understanding of what was happening and that the Holy Spirit was making him react, but this reveals a great deal about the critics' perception. Humans are not valuable because we're self-aware of our importance or because some other human acknowledges us. We matter because we matter to God, and mattering to God is all that matters. Christians quote verses like Jerimiah 1:5 and Psalm 139:13 because they showcase our relevance and relationship to God. Humans can discriminate and create unjust laws that run contrary to the dignity that God bestows upon his creation, but mankind falling short doesn't destroy what has always been true. As Frederick Douglass once said after *Dred Scott v Sanford*, "God will be true though every man be a liar," (Romans 3:4).

Chapter Two

God is Sovereign

It is difficult for nonbelievers and even Christians to grapple with the sanctity of life when God himself has taken so many lives during the worldwide flood, the firstborn of Egypt, and sanctioned battles throughout the Bible. If God was willing to allow or cause children—even infants—to die, why wouldn't God be fine with abortion?

If you're going to buy into Christianity, regardless of your denomination, there is one thing you have to accept: God is sovereign. Different denominations believe sovereignty to mean different degrees of God's control or involvement, but God is *always* in control.

You must understand:

- God is the Creator; he has the authority to do what he wills with his creations. We do not.

- God is all-powerful and all-knowing. We are not, and we're incapable of understanding the wisdom of his grand design.

- God is just and will dispense justice when he sees fit.

God's Judgment

How can we judge God? Who sits above him to hold God accountable? No one. There is no punishment for an all-powerful and immaterial being. And even if we wanted to judge him, where would we get that standard of morality to base the judgment? Some may say it's acceptable to use God's own rules against him, but the laws are made for us.

As a parent, when you set the rules for bedtime, would you accept a five-year-old saying, "Hey, it's not fair! You should go to bed at 8 PM like I do!" Of course, not. That child may not be able to understand the importance of rest and how vital it is for their body. That child may not grasp how tired and cranky they'll be in the morning if they don't get proper rest. They just want what they want. And even if you explain it, they may not accept it. They may try to reason with you, claiming they'll be perfectly fine in the morning if they stay up playing video games, watching movies, etc. You can either make them go to bed—in the interest of protecting the child from themselves—or you can concede and allow them to prove you right in the morning.

As a parent, you might not have all the answers, but you have parental authority for a reason. Not only do you have life experience and a perspective a child would not possess; you have authority over their lives, and you must exercise it wisely for their benefit.

Well, God is far above us. We may understand the wisdom of our parents as we become adults or have children ourselves, but we'll never be able to match the wisdom of God. We'll never possess his scope; therefore, we'll always lack proper perspective.

God is also like a farmer. He can plant whatever he wants, and make adjustments as he sees fit. If he sees a weed, he can pluck it out. If he wants to let the wheat and tares grow together, God can do what he wills (Matthew 13:24-43). It's all according to his grand design.

So, when God gave us commandments like "thou shalt not murder," those rules are for us. A murder is an unjust killing, and God cannot unjustly take a life.

Now, God may have the authority and power to snap us all out of existence, but he's not some sort of moral monster. Many of the charges thrown against him by nonbelievers misunderstand him entirely.

Let's take a look at the flood. We know that God flooded the world, killing everyone except one family and a bunch of animals. Did God do this because he's a homicidal maniac? No. And the story lays it out clearly.

Genesis 6 starts off talking about the corruption of the earth. The "sons of God" took human brides. There were giants in the land. Then it goes on to describe the sort of evil that rotted the hearts of man. Before the flood, humans lived nearly a thousand years, but God planned to considerably shrink that lifespan to a little over a century.

When man began to multiply on the face of the land and daughters were born to them, [2] the sons of God saw that the daughters of man were attractive. And they took as their wives any they chose. [3] Then the LORD said, "My Spirit shall not abide in man forever, for he is flesh: his days shall be 120 years." [4] The Nephilim were on the earth in those days, and also afterward, when the sons of God came in to the daughters of man and they bore children to them. These were the mighty men who were of old, the men of renown.

[5] The LORD saw that the wickedness of man was great in the earth, and that every intention of the thoughts of his heart was only evil continually. [6] And the Lord regretted that he had made man on the earth, and it grieved him to his heart. [7] So the LORD said, "I will blot out man whom I have created from the face of the land, man and animals and creeping things and birds of the heavens, for I am sorry that I have made them." [8] But Noah found favor in the eyes of the LORD. (Genesis 6:1-8, ESV)

The Bible describes people who were not only evil; they were nonstop evil. Whatever the condition of man was, God regretted making mankind. The Bible says he was "grieved." Interestingly, modern critics complain that God allows evil to persist on the planet, yet they shriek in horror when God issues his judgment against evil.

But Noah was different. God said he was righteous, blameless, and walked with God. But overall, God saw the earth as corrupt, filled with extraordinarily violent people, and they were living for nearly a millennium. The level of evil was so high, that God made the determination to flood the earth and save Noah and his family. God would establish his covenant with him. Mind you, this is a man who already "walks with God."

God gives Noah a monumental task to create the ark. This was not something Noah could complete overnight. It took decades. A replica of the ark opened in Kentucky in 2016. "Spanning 510 feet long, 85 feet wide, and 51 feet high," according to Ark Encounter's website.[1] It took them two years to build and over $100 million, though they didn't make it to float. The wooden structure and tourist attraction are meant as a reminder.

The earth did flood, but Noah and his family survived. Afterward, Noah presented God with a burnt offering, and God promised to never flood the earth again.

A commenter on social media once brought up the flood as evidence of God's evil. I replied, "I have an answer, but I'm not sure it's one you'll like or accept." I referenced World War II and the battle with Japan. A massive land war was something the U.S. could have done, but at what cost? The people of Japan were being mentally prepared to commit mass suicide for their nation. Not only would an estimated one million American lives have been brutally lost, but the Japanese people would have suffered as well. So, in our limited wisdom, we made a horrific decision that we deemed to be the best one at the time. American troops dropped atomic bombs on the cities of Hiroshima and Nagasaki. This led to the country's unconditional and total surrender. Even though this decision is criticized, it's still widely accepted as the correct one.

If mankind can make such a devastating decision in the interest of ending the war and saving the most lives possible, is it so hard to accept an all-knowing God flooded the earth for the ultimate good of mankind? He could have wiped everyone out and started a new species. Instead, by God's grace, he spared a righteous and blameless man, so humanity could continue. The story of the flood is not a story of a vengeful God who thirsted for murder. It's the story of a just God, who poured out his judgment, yet still displayed his mercy and a chance for humanity's redemption.

Critics will also point to God commanding the Israelites to wipe out their enemies. How can a moral God order the obliteration of an entire people? This isn't the strongest example for pro-choice skeptics to point out. The Canaanites were not an innocent people. One of their transgressions was child sacrifice, which God found to be abhorrent. They also knew of God, so they weren't ignorant. Also, God did not simply wipe them out from the start. When God initially made his promise to Abraham, he explained a timeline of events.

> [13] Then the LORD said to Abram, "Know for certain that your offspring will be sojourners in a land that is not theirs and will be servants there, and they will be afflicted for four hundred years. [14] But I will bring judgment on the nation that they serve, and afterward they shall come out with great possessions. [15] As for you, you shall go to your fathers in peace; you shall be buried in a good old age. [16] And they shall come back here in the fourth generation, for the iniquity of the Amorites is not yet complete." (Genesis 15:13-16, ESV)

God did not decide to punish the Canaanites overnight. God had a quota of evil deeds he allowed them to meet before judgment befell them. Through their judgment, God also fulfilled his promise to Abraham and blessed the Israelites. God is a just God and warned the Israelites not to commit the sins of the Canaanites, which included sexual immorality and child sacrifice.

> [24] "Do not make yourselves unclean by any of these things, for by all these the nations I am driving out before you have become unclean, [25] and the land became unclean, so that I punished its iniquity, and the

land vomited out its inhabitants." (Leviticus 18:24-25, ESV)

God also set up a system of blessings and curses for the Israelites. There are many instances in the Bible when the Israelites did wicked in the sight of the Lord and were delivered into the hands of their enemies. God gave the Israelites the law "for our good always" (Deuteronomy 6:24).

God is often characterized as a cruel deity who delights in taking lives. That is not the case. "Say to them, As I live, declares the Lord GOD, I have no pleasure in the death of the wicked, but that the wicked turn from his way and live; turn back, turn back from your evil ways, for why will you die, O house of Israel?" (Ezekiel 33:11, ESV).

God Kills

Christians openly struggle with passages in the Bible when God kills or orders the killing of a people, including children. When pro-choice critics bring up these passages, it is not a compelling argument for abortion. No, you cannot kill your child just because an all-powerful and all-knowing God ordered a war or released a plague thousands of years ago. God killed a lot of people, yet critics aren't arguing all killings are moral or should be legal. In the book of Acts, Ananias and Sapphira were killed by God after lying about how much they gave in church.

As much as the public disliked actress Amber Heard during her highly politicized trial, with her ex-husband Johnny Depp, no one seriously argued Heard should be executed for not donating $7 million in her divorce settlement to charity, despite pledging to do so.

Nevertheless, let's observe some of the charges laid against God.

> And Samuel said to Saul, "The LORD sent me to anoint you king over his people Israel; now therefore listen to the words of the LORD. ² Thus says the LORD of hosts, 'I have noted what Amalek did to Israel in opposing them on the way when they came up out of Egypt. ³ Now go and strike Amalek and devote to destruction all that they have. Do not spare them, but kill both man and woman, child and infant, ox and sheep, camel and donkey.'" (1 Samuel 15:1-3, ESV)

Now, why would God order Saul to kill everything in verse three? Well, the second verse explains that. The Amalekites attacked Israel, unprovoked, after they finished crossing the Red Sea.

> ¹⁷ "Remember what Amalek did to you on the way as you came out of Egypt, ¹⁸ how he attacked you on the way when you were faint and weary, and cut off your tail,

those who were lagging behind you, and he did not fear God." (Deuteronomy 25:17-18, ESV)

The Israelites battled the Amalekites in Exodus chapter 17, and God made a promise.

[14] Then the LORD said to Moses, "Write this as a memorial in a book and recite it in the ears of Joshua, that I will utterly blot out the memory of Amalek from under heaven." [15] And Moses built an altar and called the name of it, The LORD Is My Banner, [16] saying, "A hand upon the throne of the LORD! The LORD will have war with Amalek from generation to generation." (Exodus 17:14-16, ESV)

This was a divine judgment from God. And the Israelites continued battling the Amalekites. They teamed up with the Canaanites in Numbers, and they joined with the Moabites and the Midianites in Judges. They were a constant enemy. And if the critic continues reading 1 Samuel, they'll see King Saul did not "utterly destroy them" (as it says in the KJV). Saul even left their king alive and took livestock. This caused God to reject Saul for breaking his commandment. Prophet Samuel killed King Agag himself (1 Samuel 15:33).

The Amalekites were obviously not literally destroyed because they went on to be a plague against Israel for generations, for hundreds of years. David's famous battle of

Ziklag was due to an Amalekite raid. They even took women and children captive, including two of David's wives.

In 1 Chronicles, the remnant of the Amalekites was defeated. But in the book of Esther, the main antagonist, Hamon, is a descendent of King Agag, the Amalekite king Saul spared. Hamon conspired to have the Jews in Persia killed, but his plan was thwarted thanks to the boldness of Queen Esther, who stood up for her people. King Xerxes destroyed Haman and his sons instead.

When humans make decisions over life and death, they do so with limited wisdom and speculation. But God is all-knowing, and he is ultimately a just and perfect judge. God grants life and has full authority to take it. God's ways are not our ways, and his thoughts are not our thoughts, but your lack of understanding does not justify your condemnation of God.

Dr. Paul Copan also noted in his book, *Is God a Moral Monster*, that commands such as "utterly destroy" were used as hyperbole, similar to how we proclaim our favorite basketball team "demolished" their competitor, or our favorite political commentator "completely destroyed" their opponent. It's a conversation that merits truly analyzing the scriptures and historical context. Copan spends several chapters devoted to warfare and refuting atheists' claims of God committing ethnic genocide.

For abortion activists to use warfare from the ancient Near East as blanket permission or justification for abortion is absurd. Specific battle commands for specific times were never meant to be an ongoing commission of warfare. God's redemptive plan was to bless all families of the earth through Abraham (Genesis 12:1-3), and Jesus died on the cross for all people: Jew and Gentile as well as mother and child alike.

Another challenging story is the Exodus and God's plague upon the firstborn of Egypt. When a new Pharaoh in Egypt came into power who did not know Joseph, they began to treat the Israelites with prejudice because they were numerous. The Egyptians were cruel to the Israelites and placed them in bondage, but they continued to multiply. So, Pharaoh ordered the midwives to kill the male Israelite newborns.

God's plagues are not a petty tit-for-tat. God wanted to reveal his wonders upon Egypt, not only for the Egyptians and Pharaoh but for the Israelites. Pharaoh's heart continuously hardened and he refused to let the Israelites go. Eventually, Pharaoh reached a point of no return and God solidified Pharaoh's resolve, so he could demonstrate his power and divine judgment.

> Then the LORD said to Moses, "Go in to Pharaoh, for I have hardened his heart and the heart of his servants, that I may show these signs of mine among them, ² and that you may tell in the hearing of your son and of your grandson how I have dealt harshly with the Egyptians and what signs I have done among them, that you may know that I am the LORD." (Exodus 10:1-2, ESV)

The bondage of the Israelites was foretold, but so was their deliverance. God also promised Abraham that he would curse those who came against Israel (Genesis 12:1-3). Pharaoh gave his orders, but the cruelty committed against the Israelites was committed by the Egyptian people. Even still, when God issued the plagues upon Egypt, Moses announced them publicly. During the plague of hail, some of the servants of Pharaoh sheltered their livestock, and they were spared (Exodus 9:18-21).

Some Christians have noted the plagues showcase the God of the Israelites over the Egyptian gods. For example, God had a plague of darkness to show authority over Ra. At first, Pharaoh had magicians who tried to showcase power themselves to dilute the wonders of the great "I AM," but God showed himself to be mighty, repeatedly. "For I will pass through the land of Egypt that night, and I will strike all the firstborn in the land of Egypt, both man and beast; and on all the gods of Egypt I will execute judgments: I am the LORD," (Exodus 12:12, ESV).

It was also important to show his authority over Pharaoh, who was thought of as a god himself. In the end, Pharaoh did not possess the power to protect his people. He could not even protect his own son. The only salvation is in submission to the one true God.

The final plague was not maliciously done against infants like the Egyptians targeted the Israelites. It was all firstborns who are normally the heirs in their families and leaders in their communities. Rabbi Allen S. Maller believes God spared nearly all the Egyptians.[2] While the plagues were taking place,

Egyptians began to speak up for the Israelites and acknowledged God's power (Exodus 10:7-8). The Egyptians even paid what Maller referred to as reparations (Exodus 11:2-3). The reparations were a redemptive measure for the Egyptians, and when they saved their cattle during the plague of hail, it foreshadowed their opportunity for salvation. Then, the Israelites had their Passover in obedience to God. When Exodus 12:27 says God "spared our houses," Maller claims that includes the Egyptians who gave and sided with the Israelites. In the New Testament, Jesus was willing to give up his life, so we can be spared from judgment for our sins. He is referred to as the slain Passover lamb (1 Corinthians 5:7-8).

But even if God did slay many, he is sovereign and able to issue judgment as he sees fit. God told Moses that he "will redeem you with an outstretched arm and with great acts of judgment," (Exodus 6:6, ESV). And when it came time for the final plague, God issued his judgment against man and the gods of Egypt. The Israelites were guilty as well and had succumbed to the idols of the Egyptians (Ezekiel 20:7). That's why they needed the Blood of the Lamb to save them. Whether we are the oppressor or the oppressed, God holds us accountable for our sins, and we must repent and turn to God.

Pro-choice skeptics also bring up the death of David's illegitimate child as justification for abortion. Bathsheba did not deliberately or even spontaneously kill her child in the womb. The child was not stillborn. The child was sick, and despite David's prayers and fasting, God would not heal the baby. David does believe the baby goes onto Heaven after his passing (2 Samuel 12:19-23).

David not only committed adultery with another man's wife; he strategically placed Uriah in a battle to be killed, so he could take Bathsheba as his wife. Now, this was already a grave sin, but to showcase how utterly wrong David was, the prophet Nathan told David a metaphor, and David—unknowingly— passed judgment upon himself (2 Samuel 12:1-15).

David said the man who had done the deed "deserves to die, and he shall restore the lamb fourfold." Nathan also warns, "Now therefore the sword shall never depart from your house." The "fourfold" came to pass. Four of David's sons died. Bathsheba's first son, Amnon, Absalom, and Adonijah. The dysfunction that prevailed in David's house was a fate worse than death. Every individual is responsible for their own sins and receives their own judgments from God, but no action in life is committed in a vacuum.

It is said David is a man after God's own heart, but he was also a man of war who had shed much blood. In 1 Chronicles 22, David notes that God does not want him to build the temple, but he did gather the supplies for Solomon, so he could build it instead.

A skeptic is likely not operating from the same presupposition as believers. God is the ultimate authority on life and death, he has the authority to issue judgment, he has the omniscience that we lack, and he is a just God.

The skeptics also bring up Psalm 137:9, "Blessed shall he be who takes your little ones and dashes them against the rock!" to claim God is happy with killing children. This verse is easily taken out of context. First and foremost, God is not commanding anyone to brutally kill babies. These are the words of a Psalmist, not God. The Jewish people were praying for God to exact revenge against their enemies while exiled in Babylon. The previous verse says, "O daughter of Babylon, doomed to be destroyed, blessed shall he be who repays you with what you have done to us!"

Unfortunately, humans do not always pray or ask God to do moral things, especially when we are grieved or speaking in anger. A friend of mine once asked for prayer, wanting God to remove a difficult person from her life. She thought they were hindering her professional progress. To her surprise, her prayer partner—who was not emotionally compromised—went into prayer and revealed God's hand was upon her rival's life. That proved to be true, and that rival ended up being a great blessing.

Some skeptics have remarked that if all scripture is "God-breathed," then God inspired the Psalmist to want to smash in the heads of babies. The word says, "All scripture is breathed out by God and profitable for teaching, for reproof, for correction, and for training in righteousness, that the man of God may be complete, equipped for every good work," (2 Timothy 3:16-17, ESV).

God does not possess the authors. While reading different books of the Bible, you can pick up different tones and personalities. Why are there any imprecatory prayers or lamentations in the Bible? To know that we can go to God with anything. Thankfully, God does not answer all of our prayers. God can respond, correct, and especially teach us through our frustrations and vulnerability.

The Sanctity of Life

Critics will often say, "The unborn may be alive, but so are plants and animals. Unless you're a vegan, you're a hypocrite."

God does value the life of his creations. There's a famous gospel song, "His Eye is on the Sparrow," taken from Matthew 6:26 and Matthew 10:29-31. Jesus also notes in those passages that mankind is more valuable than those birds. They're brought up by Jesus to emphasize if God cares about these creatures and supplies their needs, then how much more does God care about us! He even knows the number of hairs on our heads.

He cares about the sanctity of life, but chickens were put on this planet for me to put salt, pepper, and Lawry's on them. I once told my father I didn't eat fish, and he was offended. "Jesus ate fish. You think you're better than Jesus?" Of course, he was mostly joking. But in all seriousness, God made man to have dominion over animals. He gave Adam the task of presiding over them, naming them, etc. When his eyes were open to his nakedness, God skinned an animal for Adam and Eve to clothe themselves.

God himself also demanded blood sacrifices. Sin is such an awful thing. It separates us from God, and it's born out of disobedience. When Adam and Eve disobeyed God and partook of the Tree of Knowledge of Good and Evil, he kicked them out of the garden, so they wouldn't partake of the fruit of eternal life and be trapped in their fallen state forever. The wages of sin equal death. God believes sin is so serious, that there needs to be a shedding of blood to atone. So, in the Old Testament, God would accept an animal sacrifice. In the New Testament, Jesus lays down his life to become that ultimate sacrifice for all sins, past and present. When Cain tried to merely give a grain offering, God scolded him. Even a lamb that is set upon an altar serves a purpose.

Just because God has an order in the world—a hierarchy of nature—doesn't mean every creature doesn't possess a level of sanctity to them. That doesn't mean it's a sin to step on a bug, but even bugs serve a purpose. Bees, for example, are crucial to pollination.

To pretend you can't be pro-life if you're not vegan is ludicrous. Pro-life is specifically referring to abortion and euthanasia anyway, but animals do not hold the same value as humans. God gave us dominion over them.

Chapter Three

How Does God Feel About Abortion?

Playing God

What is an abortion? Merriam-Webster's Medical Dictionary defines it as, "The termination of a pregnancy after, accompanied by, resulting in, or closely followed by the death of the embryo or fetus."[1] In 1952, Planned Parenthood said, "An abortion requires an operation. It kills the life of a baby after it has begun. It is dangerous to your life and health. It may make you sterile, so that when you want a child you cannot have it."[2] A miscarriage is technically referred to as a "spontaneous abortion," but it is not the same thing as deliberately going to a clinic with the intention of your baby not surviving. An ectopic pregnancy is not an abortion, and Planned Parenthood's website used to admit that. "Treating an ectopic pregnancy isn't the same thing as getting an abortion. Abortion is a medical procedure that when done safely, ends a pregnancy that's in your uterus. Ectopic pregnancies are unsafely outside of your uterus..." In July of 2022, Planned Parenthood scrubbed its website as the media and abortion activists openly conflated the two. These tactics are needlessly scaring women in a post-*Roe* world, but I suspect that's the intended goal. In our conversation about abortion, we are discussing the deliberate killing of an unborn child.

It's very safe to assume that God hates abortion. Are you going to find the word "abortion" in the Bible? No. But you will find "You shalt not murder," (Exodus 20:13, ESV). You might be saying, "Well, it's not murder where I'm from," because it's legally permissible according to man's law. But man's laws change. If a law was passed to make the world like *The Purge* franchise, and every crime became legal for one night, would you no longer think it was murder if someone killed you? They would get away with it—since it was legal—but it's still an infringement on your right to life.

Just because man's law says something is legal, doesn't mean it's not a violation of God's moral law. We've already established that life begins at conception, and our value to God begins before that. In Proverbs, in a list of things God hates, "hands that shed innocent blood" makes the cut.

I've heard pro-choice advocates claim a fetus cannot be "innocent" because they lack the mental capacity to be good or bad. Technically, no one is good but God (Mark 10:18). But the fetus did nothing to earn the death penalty. If you choose to rob a bank, and it escalates to the point of needing to shoot a woman to make your escape, were they not an innocent bystander? Maybe she was the world's greatest soccer mom or a black widow. Whether she is morally a good person is irrelevant. You didn't have the right to take her life.

Mankind also committed child sacrifice in the Bible, and God expressed very strong opinions about it in Leviticus. God told Moses he wanted any Israelites who participated in child sacrifice to be stoned. And if the Israelites ignored this heinous sin, he would cut them off for being sellouts.

> The LORD said to Moses, [2]"Say to the Israelites: 'Any Israelite or any foreigner residing in Israel who sacrifices any of his children to Molek is to be put to death. The members of the community are to stone him. [3]I myself will set my face against him and will cut him off from his people; for by sacrificing his children to Molek, he has defiled my sanctuary and profaned my holy name. [4]If the members of the community close their eyes when that man sacrifices one of his children to Molek and if they fail to put him to death, [5]I myself will set my face against him and his family and will cut them off from their people together with all who follow him in prostituting themselves to Molek. (Leviticus 20:1-5, NIV)

The Canaanites would sacrifice their babies by placing them on superheated idols, and then they would sizzle to death. They would beat loud drums to drown out their screaming. This, of course, sounds monstrous. It's a lot showier than the neatness of an abortion clinic. Cleverly, so much of the abortion argument is centered around privacy. But just because there's a smaller audience or if you're alone in your bedroom waiting for a dead baby to pass through you, it doesn't erase the fact that abortion is child sacrifice. Instead of setting your child on a golden idol, you sacrifice on the altar of self.

Instead of sacrificing for rain and crops, women sacrifice their babies for bachelor's degrees, finances, or relationships. The vast majority of abortions are done out of convenience, not medical emergencies. Convenience doesn't mean the decision wasn't difficult or that the abortion wouldn't be traumatic, but there were other plausible options that didn't need to result in a child's death.

Celebrities have been opening up about their abortion stories, to keep the choice available for other women. Keke Palmer is a young actress, who has been a leading lady since the age of 11. She's had over 100 credits and is a talk show host. After Alabama passed a law that effectively banned abortion, Palmer was "disheartened." She wrote on social media, "I was worried about my career responsibilities and afraid that I could not exist as both a career woman and mother."

Palmer also said, "Making individual choices is not a betrayal to your faith. Mainly, because God knows your heart and your journey. God never judges."[3] Of course, this is blatantly false. God judges all of the time, and he's a righteous judge. Keke Palmer's abortion has been recorded, and God will judge her for it. God does know our hearts, and he knows they're "deceitful," (Jeremiah 17:9). That's why we are supposed to live according to God's standards, not our own. We're supposed to hide the word of God in our hearts, so we might not sin against him (Psalm 119:11). And the choice to have an abortion is a betrayal of God's commandments. The moral laws are very clear and still apply. It's still a sin to murder. And God will forgive our sins, but our hearts need to be repentant. How can you do that while leading others down a path of sin?

Palmer isn't the only woman in show business to feel as though they couldn't manage both. Cecily Strong, from *Saturday Night Live*, did a very distasteful skit in full clown makeup. "Here's my truth: I know I wouldn't be a clown on TV here today if it weren't for the abortion I had the day before my 23rd birthday."

On *Piers Morgan's Life Stories*, Joan Collins explained she had an abortion in her younger days. "It would have been the death of my career, and I was by then 26."[4]

Sanya Richards-Ross, 4x Olympic gold medalist, opened up to Christian influencer Emmanuel Acho, during an episode of *The Uncomfortable Conversation: Roe v Wade*. Ross found herself in an "impossible situation" because she was carrying the child of the man she wanted to spend the rest of her life with, yet she had the opportunity to compete for gold. She had an abortion just before leaving for the Beijing Olympics. Despite feeling unworthy of gold and crediting her guilt to losing the race she wanted to win the most, Richards-Ross still can't imagine her life without the Olympic victory. "I don't know if I would've been who I am today."

Acho proposed a question to her: "So, then, would you say, or submit in the figurative sense, your abortion also saved your life?"

"Yeah."

It was an egregious question for Acho to even ask. Richards-Ross didn't need to give up her life for her child. Perhaps she might have needed to sacrifice her dream, but that is a part of life. It was not strange for Jesus to challenge those who sought after him to lay down their careers. Jesus told Simon and Andrew if they came after him, he would make them fishers of men. So, these fishermen cast their nets aside and followed. To the rich young ruler, Jesus told him to sell all of his possessions. He refused and walked away from Jesus sorrowfully.

Besides, Richards-Ross wouldn't have needed to make any sacrifice if she brought her flesh under submission. She claimed, "I never ever thought that I would be in that situation," yet she was fornicating. God does not issue purposeless commandments. Nearly all abortions wouldn't exist in the U.S. if sex was refocused on the covenant of marriage and family-building.

Is a career worth someone else's life? When you're eighty and looking back on your life, are you truly going to wish you had clocked in one more billable hour? Your job in a law firm is replaceable. The role in your movie can be recast. There's always an extra athlete waiting on the bench. These careers are very important to us at the moment, but someone can always run faster and jump higher. You'll always be a mother, and our children are not replaceable. They are unique human beings at the moment of conception, and abortion doesn't undo them or blot them from existence. When Abel killed his brother, God said, "The voice of your brother's blood is crying to me from the ground," (Genesis 4:10, ESV). This is not something God takes lightly, nor does God forget. Cain killed his brother out of jealousy, because Abel brought forth the proper sacrifice, and Cain was scolded for the one he brought forth.

> [6] The LORD said to Cain, "Why are you angry, and why has your face fallen? [7] If you do well, will you not be accepted? And if you do not do well, sin is crouching at the door. Its desire is contrary to you, but you must rule over it." (Genesis 4:6-7, ESV)

God wants us to please him and follow his commandments. When we do not, sin is waiting for us. We have the power to resist, and God expects us to. Our fleshly desires are contrary to our spirit man, yet God commissions us to rule over our sinful impulses.

Pro-choice women have an interesting saying: "No woman dreams of having an abortion." There's a handful of trolls on social media who say otherwise, but most people would agree with that statement. Regardless, some women know within themselves that if their birth control fails or if they have an unplanned pregnancy, they plan to have an abortion. But not all women are like that. They make the difficult decision while in the moment or mull it over for days or weeks. Whether you're grieved about it or not, it doesn't erase the sin. It's your job to resist.

Who is to say that the plans we set aside for ourselves are the plans God has ordained for us? We treat God like our co-pilot when he's supposed to be operating like our GPS. He's not just "along for the ride." We have control and free will, but we can't blame God when we get lost after rejecting his direction.

Eugenics was used to breed out suffering, and the same ideology is repeated today. Women claim they need abortion because they can't afford it, and it's not ethical to bring a child into this world while financially unstable. Well, that's a better argument to practice abstinence, use condoms, and faithfully track your fertility; it's not a good reason to terminate someone else's life. Life is also not linear. Children who are born in poverty don't have to permanently live that way. It's not reasonable that Christians who quote, "With God, all things are possible," are so afraid of poverty, that they create stepping stones from the bones of their children while climbing to the top of the mountain. Mind you, many of these Christians believe they can figuratively cast mountains into the sea through their faith. Well, faith without works is dead. Your fear and insecurity are not worth someone else's life, and God has not given us the spirit of fear.

Life, even a hard life, is worth living. We do not possess God's omniscience to know whether someone will ultimately live a good or bad life. Whether you are fostered, adopted, or in a single or two-parent home, you're going to face trials and tribulations. Even if your parents turn out to be dreadful, that doesn't mean you won't purpose within yourself to make a better life for yourself and future generations. You can have a family of degenerates, and then one person finds Jesus and starts a shift. After applying biblical principles to their lives, they could live a blessed life and become a witness to many others.

It's not your place to play God. You lack the qualifications.

God's Commanded Sacrifices

Some critics have noted God told Abraham to sacrifice his son, Isaac. Therefore, they believe this is somehow equivalent to a woman having an abortion. Obviously, Abraham didn't have an abortion, and Isaac wasn't a baby. And here's a little spoiler alert if you've never read the story: Abraham didn't kill him. An angel of the Lord stopped him.

It would have been a very hard thing for Abraham to take the life of his son, who was more than just a mere child. He was a promise and a fulfillment of a covenant that God made, technically to himself, on behalf of Abraham. It's one thing when we have a dream. It's on a different level when we know God himself gives us a dream. What would you be willing to do to prove that God still comes first? Can you lay your dream on the altar and slay it?

We can only speculate what was going on in Abraham's head the whole time, but when Isaac noted they had no lamb for the sacrifice, Abraham believed God would provide. Perhaps he believed the angel would always stop him. But we do know that Abraham loved God and trusted in him enough to make the sacrifice. God only required his obedience, not the life of his son.

Abortion isn't a sacrifice to God, and no human is worthy of that sort of worship.

And God proved Abraham correct. God did provide the sacrifice, and then God the Son, Jesus Christ, became the sacrifice. If you are a Christian, why can't you trust Christ's sacrifice is enough?

Skeptics sometimes bring up Jephthah, the Judge born of a warrior and a prostitute. Jephthah made an oath to God that if he won his upcoming battle, he would sacrifice whatever came out of his door when he returned home. Sadly, it happened to be his daughter, who encouraged him to keep his oath. This story illustrates the state of Israel's moral decay. Jephthah was so far removed from God, he treated him like a Canaanite deity. It also demonstrates why you shouldn't make such rash and foolish oaths, especially ones that violate God's word. God condemns human sacrifice multiple times, and he distances himself from Israel's actions when they fell into that wickedness (Jeremiah 7:31; 19:5; 32:35). The most important commentary is God never commanded Jephthah to do such a thing. The book of Judges features very flawed leaders such as Gideon and Samson. Not every action a biblical figure makes is in line with God's commandments. We learn from their faith and their failures. Dennis Prager, the co-founder of PragerU, often says he believes the Torah is divine because it was certainly not written to be pro-Jewish propaganda. Jacob was renamed "Israel" after wrestling with God, and his descendants continued that contentious relationship.

Critics have also said, "If God killed his kid, why can't I kill mine?" Sadly, I've heard this more times than I care to count. Most Christians believe in the trinitarian doctrine. God is one being in three persons. There is God the Father, Son, and the Holy Spirit. The Son spent 33 years in human flesh and then willingly laid down his life, so he could be the lamb slain for our sins.

When many women have abortions, it is a sacrifice for their own benefit. We serve a God who was willing to sacrifice himself for our benefit. The least we can do is live our lives to be living sacrifices for him.

Does God Sanction Abortion

No.

There is a popular narrative going around from abortion defenders that the Bible not only allows abortion; it explains how to perform one. You may be scratching your head, pondering how this can be true. After all, it sounds so horrifyingly unlike anything you've ever heard preached from the pulpit. Well, if the nonbelievers had enough sense and honesty to question their bias, they'd easily discover their misconceptions have already been debunked.

In the past year, Numbers 5 has become the chapter I've had to explain the most. People genuinely believe this chapter is the smoking gun that proves God is for abortions. It's alleged that a jealous husband takes his wife—expected of adultery—to a priest so he can give her a potion that causes a miscarriage. Granted, there is a translation from the NIV that lends to some of this confusion, but it is clearly an error. One very viral TikTok user reads from NIV to make this claim, even though she has two Bibles in the video. She never addresses the other. Even so, if you look at the text and think critically, you can figure out this is not an abortion.

Numbers 5:11-31 is about a husband suspecting his wife of adultery. The punishment for adultery in the Old Testament is death (Leviticus 20:10), for both the man and the woman involved. That is another reason why in the New Testament when Jesus saves a woman from being stoned; the crowd was not following the law. It is also notable, that you must have multiple witnesses for capital punishment (Deuteronomy 17:6-7), and Numbers 5 is speaking to a case where there are none. A human court is unable to make this determination. Therefore, a woman can place her innocence in God's hands. She will say an oath and drink from the "bitter water." If she is guilty, there will be a supernatural sign and she will become barren. If she is innocent, she will be able to bear children.

Let's look at the text from the ESV:

[11] And the LORD spoke to Moses, saying, [12] "Speak to the people of Israel, If any man's wife goes astray and breaks faith with him, [13] if a man lies with her sexually, and it is hidden from the eyes of her husband, and she is undetected though she has defiled herself, and there is no witness against her, since she was not taken in the act, [14] and if the spirit of jealousy comes over him and he is jealous of his wife who has defiled herself, or if the spirit of jealousy comes over him and he is jealous of his wife, though she has not defiled herself, [15] then the man shall bring his wife to the priest and bring the offering required of her, a tenth of an ephah of barley flour. He shall pour no oil on it and put no frankincense on it, for it is a grain offering of jealousy, a grain offering of remembrance, bringing iniquity to remembrance.

This passage about barley flour is very important. Some critics believe that barley flour is the ingredient used in the bitter water that will cause the woman to have an abortion. As you continue reading, you'll discover the woman never consumes it at all. Barley flour is a grain offering. The practice is talked about in

Leviticus 2. It's an offering to God and for the priests, certainly not an ingredient to kill a baby.

> [16] "And the priest shall bring her near and set her before the LORD. [17] And the priest shall take holy water in an earthenware vessel and take some of the dust that is on the floor of the tabernacle and put it into the water. [18] And the priest shall set the woman before the LORD and unbind the hair of the woman's head and place in her hands the grain offering of remembrance, which is the grain offering of jealousy. And in his hand the priest shall have the water of bitterness that brings the curse. [19] Then the priest shall make her take an oath, saying, 'If no man has lain with you, and if you have not turned aside to uncleanness while you were under your husband's authority, be free from this water of bitterness that brings the curse. [20] But if you have gone astray, though you are under your husband's authority, and if you have defiled yourself, and some man other than your husband has lain with you, [21] then' (let the priest make the woman take the oath of the curse, and say to the woman) 'the LORD make you a curse and an oath among your people, when the LORD makes your thigh fall away and your body swell. [22] May this water that brings the curse pass into your bowels and make your womb swell and your thigh fall away.' And the woman shall say, 'Amen, Amen.'

[23] "Then the priest shall write these curses in a book and wash them off into the water of bitterness. [24] And he shall make the woman drink the water of bitterness that brings the curse, and the water that brings the curse shall enter into her and cause bitter pain. [25] And the priest shall take the grain offering of jealousy out of the woman's hand and shall wave the grain offering before the LORD and bring it to the altar. [26] And the priest shall take a handful of the grain offering, as its memorial portion, and burn it on the altar, and afterward shall make the woman drink the water. [27] And when he has made her drink the water, then, if she has defiled herself and has broken faith with her husband, the water that brings the curse shall enter into her and cause bitter pain, and her womb shall swell, and her thigh shall fall away, and the woman shall become a curse among her people. [28] But if the woman has not defiled herself and is clean, then she shall be free and shall conceive children.

[29] "This is the law in cases of jealousy, when a wife, though under her husband's authority, goes astray and defiles herself, [30] or when the spirit of jealousy comes over a man and he is jealous of his wife. Then he shall set the woman before the LORD, and the priest shall carry out for her all this law. [31] The man shall be free from iniquity, but the woman shall bear her iniquity."

The bitter water amounts to dusty temple water. It probably didn't taste very good, but it is harmless. If it were simply a medicine to make a miscarriage happen, there wouldn't be an option of success. God would supernaturally have to make this curse affect this woman. The curse of the bitter water is believed to be barrenness, considering how the curse affects her womb and that if she's innocent, she shall conceive children.

The New International Version, better known as NIV, states the word "miscarry" rather than having a variation of "thigh falling away," but it's different than the other major translations.

There is no indication in the passage that the woman is even pregnant. But even if she were pregnant with another man's baby, and God caused her to have a miscarriage, that would be an example of exercising his judgment on his creation. This does not set a standard for women to have the full authority to take the life of their children, for whatever reason they please. In 2020, 86.3 percent of abortions were carried out by unwed women [5], and the woman in this passage is married and accused of adultery. If we're going to argue this is a biblical abortion, then have it done *biblically*. Have your husband bring you before a Levitical priest with an offering, drink dusty temple water, and see if God pours out his judgment. No more pills, forceps, and abortion clinics. Do it "God's way."

Of course, no one would go for that. In my experience, critics who bring up this passage will dismiss the entire Bible as a silly fairytale as soon as you simply explain the verses. It's been debunked repeatedly.

And even after going through the verses, some critics will contend nothing supernatural happened and the priests merely poisoned the women themselves with the ink from the curse. It's interesting that if the priest did rig the game, the skeptics assume the priests would poison the woman instead of offering her harmless water to ease the husband's mind. The worst-case scenario is always assumed. While I can understand it's difficult for nonbelievers to wrap their minds around the supernatural, the supernatural exists regardless. And even if it didn't and religious people merely *think* it does, the authors of the Bible certainly did or at least wrote about supernatural occurrences. God spoke through a burning bush, sent the 10 plagues in Egypt, split the Red Sea, and provided manna from heaven, but a supernatural adultery test is where we have to draw the line? If you are going to use the Bible as the point of authority on this topic, you've got to operate from the presumption that God is sovereign. If you can't grant that concept for the sake of the conversation, then don't use the Bible as your point of authority.

Chapter Four

Does God Value "Choice?"

Free Will

"Respect a woman's choice," is also a curious talking point in the abortion debate. It's so enormously dishonest. A woman is not such a holy creature that her "choices" are not wrong or always respected. During the COVID-19 pandemic, were women respected if they chose not to be vaccinated? Even at the beginning of the pandemic when women reported their periods were being affected, their concerns were largely ignored and suppressed. It was a full year before the mainstream media began to admit the impact on menstruation. How many politicians who support the "right to choose" don't extend that attitude toward school choice? When President Donald Trump was elected in 2016, former First Lady Michelle Obama said the women who voted for him, "voted against their own voice."[1] When a white woman has a fit in a store, are her choices respected, or is she called a "Karen?" If you caught another woman sleeping with your husband, would you respect her "choice?"

Simply because someone "chooses" to do something, doesn't mean it's moral, legal, or should be respected. No one cares if a man "chooses" to accept his role as a father. He has to pay child support. But if a man wants a woman to keep her baby, he may be left crying and begging outside of an abortion clinic. There is no consistency of respect with this issue.

When the pro-choice movement says, "We hate abortion, but we respect a woman's right to choose," they are talking about the woman's choice to choose abortion.

If a woman has an abortion because she thinks it will be a clean slate, that's her choice. If a woman has an abortion to spite her boyfriend for leaving her, after he found out he's not the father, that is also her choice. If a woman wants to have an abortion because she wants to have an out after a one-night stand, that is her choice. Do you stand by all these choices? Are these justified abortions to you? How can they not be if you support the "right to choose?"

If one were to argue women should have all the say because she is carrying the baby, we have to ask the obvious question: how did the baby get there? Did she choose to have sex? If so, how can our society expect a man to be on the hook for at least 18 years of his life, yet the woman doesn't have an expected parental responsibility of at least nine months?

Women do not need to be infantilized. Women have survived the Great Depression, and the Dark Ages, exploring the wilderness, wars, famines, and plagues all while continuing to be mothers. Women in their twenties claim they can't accept the responsibility of motherhood while women their ages have been queens of nations. We are not building a better society. Abortion breeds weak women.

If we are to respect "choice," we must respect that a woman made choices leading up to her pregnancy. Did this young college student sleep around with a financially unstable partner? Did this career woman slip up and have unprotected sex? Did she sleep with someone else's husband or boyfriend? The Bible doesn't address sexual immorality because God was bored, throwing darts in heaven, and whatever sticky note it landed on ended up on a stone tablet or parchment. To nonbelievers, God may seem like a tyrannical control freak. To Christians, it should be evident that God's love is demonstrated by his commandments, his works, grace, mercy, and even his judgment. When God makes it clear you shouldn't have sex with anyone other than your husband, it is for your benefit. It's better for you, and it's certainly better for society. The health of civilization is centered around the structure of the family.

Pro-life activists are often accused of "only wanting to control women." It's ironic since abortion is largely about population control. If God wanted to create robots with no opinions and who only obeyed, he could have. But how can you truly have a relationship without choice? How would we worship God without the choice to sacrifice? How can we love without choice? Biblical love isn't simply an emotion. It's a commitment to a list of actions (1 Corinthians 13:4-8). Choice is extraordinarily important to God, but God still wants us to choose righteousness. The Christian position isn't about controlling people. The Christian position is about encouraging self-control.

God grants us free will, and we can choose whether or not we're going to serve him. But just because God permits us to sin, doesn't mean he approves. If God didn't take issue with humanity doing whatever they pleased, he wouldn't have flooded the world or done any other acts of judgment. He wouldn't have the Mosaic laws to separate his people from pagans. He wouldn't have the moral laws that we are expected to follow.

You may say Christians are different, and we can't expect the world to follow God's commandments. That would be ridiculous. When God wiped out Sodom and Gomorrah, he wasn't going to spare them because they were heathens. He judged them based on their sin. He would have spared them if there were any righteous people, but there were not. Just because God may especially care about the transgressions of his people, doesn't mean he's ambivalent about the sins of the world.

Besides, the moral laws are written on our hearts. Internally, we know the difference between right and wrong. We can make all sorts of philosophical arguments to talk ourselves out of it, but we know.

I have heard the argument, "Well, God gave us free will, so a woman should be able to have an abortion. She'll have to meet her maker one day." Yet, no one would dare say, "Well, God gave us free will, so a man should be able to rape a woman. He'll meet his maker one day." No one would argue free will is a good enough reason to plunder and pillage as if we were all pirates. And you certainly wouldn't shrug your shoulders and expect the laws of man to support such brutality.

It should also not be acceptable for Christians to shrug their shoulders as women commit a grave sin that God hates. Penn Jillette is a famous magician and a well-known atheist. Yet, he made one of the most profound statements about evangelism. "I don't respect people who don't proselytize." He went on to ask, **"How much do you have to hate somebody to not proselytize? How much do you have to hate someone to believe everlasting life is possible and not tell them that?**

"If I believed, beyond a shadow of a doubt, that a truck was coming at you, and you didn't believe it, that that truck was bearing down on you, there's a certain point that I tackle you, and this is more important than that."[2] Even if an atheist doesn't want to hear it, why would you stay silent and risk their soul over social respectability?

Abortion is not a normal sin. You can return an item you have stolen. A lie is immoral, but you can correct the record—hopefully—with no major harm done. Adultery is a sin against the body and painful for the betrayed parties, but you can try to make amends, repledge commitment, and work on regaining trust. You cannot bring an aborted child back to life. You cannot undo that harm. You can only seek God for forgiveness, repent, and move forward in an attempt to live a more righteous life. Even knowing God is a redeemer, some women carry the scars of these actions until the day they die. If you love these women, and if you care for them, you will not support this sin. You would scream from the rooftops to try to save the child and save the mother from heartbreak.

A better question for pro-choice Christians is if God allows free will, why are they using theirs to allow evil? They could use their free will to make abortion illegal or help the pro-life activists make it illegal. They could, at the very least, use their free will to keep their mouth shut and be passive. But they aren't doing that. They voice their support for a woman's choice to terminate the life of their child. "I'm a Christian, but..." If you wanted to do the bare minimum, you could at least be silent on the matter.

Just because people have free will, doesn't mean we should support their choice to choose sin. If you have a friend who is fornicating, you can still love them as a human being. You can care about their lives, pick them up when they fall, etc., but you shouldn't encourage them to sin or give the implication that you approve. You don't have to beat them over the head every day with scriptures, but you should be sowing seeds in their life.

Those seeds may fall on good ground, but you'll never reap what you don't sow.

We don't always want to be a witness. Jonah didn't want to preach to Nineveh. Honestly? He thought they deserved God's judgment, and he didn't want God to transform their lives. So, he did the most futile thing you can do: he ran from God. Even though Jonah was someone who knew God and heard his voice, God was still willing to punish Jonah until he submitted. God respects your free will, but he's not above coercion. Jonah had a God complex. He thought he had a say in who deserved God's judgment, but it's God's grace, not your grace. We must come to grips with the fact that we are merely humble servants, meant to serve an extraordinary God.

You can have a personal opinion on the matter, but if your personal opinion doesn't align with God, there's a specific word for that: wrong. You are wrong.

It's alright to question God when you have doubts or you're confused. Job certainly did, for example. But God is the only one who has the whole picture. You do not know or understand more than God. Instead of trying to frame the world around what you think, question if you're aligning with God's will and purpose for your life.

Does God Value Bodily Autonomy?

Growing up in Pentecostal circles, I've always heard the saying, "The Holy Spirit is a gentleman." There may be moments when the power of God may hit someone and they react strongly, but overall, God values the ask. Do you want Jesus to be your Lord and Savior? Do you want to be baptized in water or by the Holy Spirit? Those are decisions you get to make. No one can *make* you be a Christian. A parent can drag you to church. A strict nun may "terrorize" you for not following the rules. But whether or not you choose to believe in Christ and place your trust in him, is entirely up to you.

And once you make that decision, a Christian is expected to be a living sacrifice (Romans 12).

The Bible is not a YOLO (you only live once) mentality book, where men and women are encouraged to live selfishly for their self-gratification. If you want to follow after Christ, you're supposed to deny yourself and take up your cross daily (Luke 9:23).

C.S. Lewis, British theologian and author of *The Chronicles of Narnia*, eloquently wrote about the importance of denying ourselves in pursuit of true joy. It's not that we have to seek self-denial because our desires are too strong, but because they're too weak. "We are half-hearted creatures, fooling about with drink and sex and ambition when infinite joy is offered to us, like an ignorant child who wants to go on making mud pies in a slum because he cannot imagine what is meant by the offer of a holiday at the sea. We are far too easily pleased."[3]

We are often told to follow the desires of our hearts, but the Bible says our hearts are deceitful (Jeremiah 17:9). Humans are unbearably fickle. How many times in your life have you been denied something or even someone you were absolutely certain you wanted or thought you needed, only to be grateful it didn't work out? The job you didn't take? The man you didn't marry? The school that didn't accept you? The role in the play you didn't get and turned out to be a hot mess?

We are like Tinkerbell, a fairy so tiny that she can only experience one emotion at a time, and it's to the max. If she's angry, she's enraged. If she's jealous, she's a violent and bitter terror. If she's happy, she's a delight. In the cult classic film *Hook*, Tinkerbell is able to wish herself big, so she can finally confess her love to Peter Pan, who has grown into a man. She says, "This is the only wish I ever wished for myself. This is the biggest feeling I've ever felt, and this is the first time I've been big enough to feel it."[4]

God is calling us to be more spiritually mature than tiny Tink. Though our flesh can feel insatiable, it's primitive. You can give it a quick fix with sinful desires. Even a lie can make you happy. It doesn't make it real, and it certainly isn't going to last. There's a reason why the "pursuit of happiness" is a right, rather than a "promise of happiness." But God calls us to something beyond that. He calls us to pursue joy, to delight ourselves in him, and *then* he will give you the desires of your heart (Psalm

37:4). And through that lifestyle of joy, you will be able to find a peace that passeth all understanding (Philippians 4:6).

But you do have a choice.

God respects your bodily autonomy enough to grant you free will, and God has such respect that he will judge you according to your works. If God acknowledges a mother's bodily autonomy, he'll also acknowledge her child's. God is more than aware that pregnancy is difficult, and childbirth feels like being ripped in half. He did increase Eve's pain in childbirth because of her disobedience.

Just as our lives are not our own, we should dedicate our children to God. Even though Hannah was greatly loved by her husband, she wanted a child. She prayed so hard for God to bless her, the priest Eli thought she was drunk, and he scolded her. When Hannah explained she was petitioning God for a child, who she promised to dedicate to the Lord, Eli told her God would do it. She then had Samuel, one of the greatest prophets in the Bible. "For this child I prayed, and the Lord has granted me my petition that I made to him. Therefore I have lent him to the Lord. As long as he lives, he is lent to the Lord," (1 Samuel 1:27-28 ESV).

Your relationship with God is your relationship. Your child also has a unique relationship with God, as well as a purpose and a calling. Just because you may not recognize the value in your unborn child, doesn't mean God hasn't. And as a parent, it is your duty to train them up in the Lord (Proverbs 22:6).

¹³ The end of the matter, all has been heard. Fear God and keep his commandments, for this is the whole duty of man. ¹⁴ For God will bring every deed into judgment, with every secret thing, whether good or evil. (Ecclesiastes 12:13-14, ESV)

Chapter Five

Is Abortion Compatible with Christianity?

The Family

I once saw a video from a secular pro-life account stating that Christians should bow out of the debate if they cannot keep other beliefs—particularly on homosexuality and gender identity—to themselves. Their reasoning was their "bigotry" turned people off to the pro-life movement and affirmed insults, such as being pro-control and pro-birth. I, respectfully, disagreed with this statement and found it incredibly shortsighted.

The pro-life movement is driven by Christians. Right to Life was founded by Catholics.

It would be self-defeating to expect Christians to drop out of the movement, and it would be wrong to ask them to abandon parts of their mission when their goal isn't only to save people in this life; they're trying to save them in the next one. Christians are concerned about the well-being of women who may or may not have abortions, and they are concerned about their souls. The same goes for their children.

Christians should see abortion as a symptom of the rejection of God's commandments and design. God made male and female. That is all. You may have a genetic mutation that makes you intersex, but sex is still binary. Only two types of gametes exist. It is God's design that a man will leave his mother and father and cleave to his wife, and they will become one flesh. Men and women possess a complementary nature. We can see that biologically. Two males or two females cannot create a family naturally. It requires the opposite sexes to join as one. God also made Adam a female counterpart because he said it was not good for him to be alone. Before Adam could even fathom the need, God produced a solution. Though men do need other male companionship, God created women to be the helpmeet or helper. The helper doesn't equate to a servant. The Hebrew word "*ezer*" was never used as a subordinate in the Old Testament. Women are meant to strengthen men. From there, God began to establish the roles between the genders and their relation to each other. God wants us to procreate. We're designed to do it, but God desires that a man and woman join together in the covenant of marriage.

When Eve disobeyed God in the Garden of Eden, she was punished for her actions. "To the woman he said, "I will surely multiply your pain in childbearing; in pain you shall bring forth children. Your desire shall be contrary to your husband, but he shall rule over you," (Genesis 3:16, ESV).

It's strange that in 2022, there are so many women pointing out the pain and dangers of childbearing as if it's recently learned information. Some pro-choice women claim becoming a mother made them pro-choice because pregnancy is so hard, it's something you should have to choose. Well, it's been that way since the beginning of mankind. If a woman doesn't want to experience labor, that's a good reason to not get pregnant. It's not a good reason to abort a child. A woman needs to decide whether she loves sex more or not being pregnant. If she can't go without sex, she needs to take precautions. Only about half of women who have abortions reported using birth control in the month they became pregnant.[1] If a woman becomes pregnant, she needs to be woman enough to bear the child.

Complementarians and egalitarians have many debates over these passages and the roles of men and women, but we do know God was displeased Adam listened to Eve and disobeyed his commandments, leading to a curse on mankind.

> [17] And to Adam he said, "Because you have listened to the voice of your wife and have eaten of the tree of which I commanded you, 'You shall not eat of it,' cursed is the ground because of you; in pain you shall eat of it all the days of your life; [18] thorns and thistles it shall bring forth for you; and you shall eat the plants of the field. [19] By the

sweat of your face you shall eat bread, till you return to the ground, for out of it you were taken; for you are dust, and to dust you shall return." (Genesis 3:17-19, ESV)

Now, some would think Eve's punishment is an example of God being a sexist monster. But just as the woman is meant to serve and reverence her husband, the man is meant to serve his family. It doesn't mean a woman cannot work, but it is a man's duty to provide for them. It is a man's duty to put his life on the line and die, if necessary.

²² Wives, submit to your own husbands, as to the Lord. ²³ For the husband is the head of the wife even as Christ is the head of the church, his body, and is himself its Savior. ²⁴ Now as the church submits to Christ, so also wives should submit in everything to their husbands.

²⁵ Husbands, love your wives, as Christ loved the church and gave himself up for her, ²⁶ that he might sanctify her, having cleansed her by the washing of water with the word, ²⁷ so that he might present the church to himself in splendor, without spot or wrinkle or any such thing, that she might be holy and without blemish. ²⁸ In the same way husbands should love their wives as their own bodies. He who loves his wife loves himself. ²⁹ For no one ever hated his own flesh, but nourishes and cherishes it, just as Christ does the church, ³⁰ because we are members of his

body. [31] "Therefore a man shall leave his father and mother and hold fast to his wife, and the two shall become one flesh." [32] This mystery is profound, and I am saying that it refers to Christ and the church. [33] However, let each one of you love his wife as himself, and let the wife see that she respects her husband. (Ephesians 5:22-33, ESV)

Though many women resent the "submissive" assignment, I believe men have a more difficult role to fulfill. With leadership comes responsibility and accountability. When there's danger, they protect and fight if necessary. If the ship is going down, the women and the children get off first. Society accepts that men have a necessary obligation to their families; that's why we have child support and men are mostly on the hook for it. Women may have to submit their will, but men are expected to submit their all. They cannot love themselves more than their family.

And just because men lead, does not mean women cannot advise or speak up. Women can be strong like Ruth and courageous like Esther. Women can lead like Deborah. Women are not merely meant to be incubators for children and servants to men. Read Proverbs 31. Women can be good mothers, faithful wives, pillars of the community, business savvy, entrepreneurs, multi-talented, and so on.

It is the role of the parents to train their children, guide them, and discipline them, but also not provoke them to wrath, and make sure there's something to leave behind for them (Proverbs 13:22). Children are supposed to honor their mothers and their fathers.

God desires to see his children blessed, and just as God made female companionship to fill a need, God designed the structure of a god-fearing family to bring joy.

> [3] Behold, children are a heritage from the LORD,
>   the fruit of the womb a reward.
> [4] Like arrows in the hand of a warrior
>   are the children of one's youth.
> [5] Blessed is the man
>   who fills his quiver with them!
> He shall not be put to shame
>   when he speaks with his enemies in the gate.
> (Psalm 127:3-5, ESV)

Maybe you believe you're not the type who will enjoy a family. Adoption has blessed the lives of many families, especially women who are barren. Don't rob potentially good parents of that blessing, and don't rob your biological child out of their life.

There's also the fact humans are often wrong. The world is full of parents who had unexpected pregnancies. My mother wanted two children. She had seven. When she was pregnant with my youngest sibling, Mom cried because she nearly had all of her children in school. Well, she toughed it out, and Tina is a complete joy in our lives.

In modern society, we also underestimate the profoundness of responsibility. A friend of mine came to a very difficult period of her life right out of high school. She wasn't being kind to herself and her body. But when she discovered her pregnancy, her life changed. She had to pull herself together and be responsible for the life inside of her. She was accountable to someone. She believes that her son saved her life, and he's an imaginative and caring young man. She was the ideal candidate for an abortion: unstable life in a relationship with no future. Instead, motherhood was the jumpstart she needed to get her life in order. She ended up meeting a wonderful man, got married, and continued building her family.

God is a God of purpose. God made man with tasks. He even says if a man doesn't work, he ought not eat. This philosophy saved the lives of Jamestown settlers, who were taking food but not contributing to society. Captain John Smith got this life-saving advice from the Bible (2 Thessalonians 3:10). During the COVID-19 pandemic, congress passed bills that essentially paid workers to stay home. In many cases, even more handsomely than businesses. Predictably, it led to a labor market shortage. Many businesses, schools, and areas where people would gather to engage in social activities were shut down, and the people were isolated. The pandemic led to a rise in opioid addiction, depression, and alcohol use. Men need meaning.

Clinical Psychologist Professor Jordan Peterson often encourages young people to assume responsibility for their own lives. Take ownership and accountability for what is within your control. He often tells his audience to "clean their rooms," in a metaphorical (and literal) sense. "The more responsibility you take on, the more meaning your life has. And the higher degree of responsibility that you agree voluntarily to try to bear, the richer your life will be. And no one is ever told that, and it's the case."[2]

It is not within God's design for men to support abortion. It's a tragedy that men are expected to not stand up against the injustice of child sacrifice. It's unconscionable that men wouldn't stand up for their progeny. Men can't even be brave enough to say, "Don't kill my kid?" And if they are, they're treated as nosey misogynists with no right to even make such a request. I've seen fathers who mourn the loss of their aborted children verbally abused by abortion advocates. Men are expected to be silent, like a rusted and heartless Tin Man. What sort of world are we creating when it's full of fathers who have no right to protect their children?

I was once asked my opinion about a video of a woman who had been conceived in rape. She said her grandparents were Christians and convinced their daughter to keep her. Her grandparents deeply loved and cared for her, but she could tell life was difficult for her mother. There was an emotional drain on her, and she used drugs and alcohol. Eventually, her mother passed away from substance abuse. The woman was grateful for her life and believed she was meant to be on this planet, but she also believed no man should have had a say in how she came to be. Certainly, not her biological father and not even her grandfather.

My heart broke for this woman and at the loss of her mother. I understood where she was coming from, but I could never condone the idea of my father getting no say in my life. My father isn't always right, but he loves me, wants what's best for me, and can hear from the Lord. In times when I feel vulnerable and broken, that's when I need love, comfort, and sound advice from a spiritual leader. Women do not need to be isolated in despair. It may be, ultimately, her choice to make, but why wouldn't someone who loves you, encourage you to make a moral decision? A woman should hear that she has support, so she can be brave enough to do the right thing. She needs to be reminded that she's strong enough to survive and even overcome.

"No uterus, no opinion," is what the pro-choice side claims, but they don't say the same to men who stand up for abortion. If men shouldn't have a say in the abortion debate, then we should have tossed out *Roe v. Wade* decades ago. In my personal experience, pro-choice men are particularly vicious. They say the vilest insults to pro-life women—sexually and graphically violent—and even criticize women who share their abortion regret stories because "it could hinder someone else from getting an abortion." A man once told me he wanted to scoop my eggs out with a hanger.

Irresponsible men have a lot riding on abortion. Vice President Kamala Harris even cautioned Americans about the dangers of *Roe v. Wade* being overturned. "First of all, if you are a parent of sons, do think about what this means for the life of your son and what that will mean in terms of the choices he will have."[3] In other words, if they can't convince their girlfriends and mistresses to have abortions, they'll be saddled with parental responsibility and financial compensation.

Congresswoman Alexandria Ocasio Cortez (NY-14, D) said, "For almost every woman that has gotten an abortion, there's a man who has been affected or liberated by that abortion too."[4] The congresswoman believes men communicating this "vulnerability" will shift the abortion debate the fastest. She is not wrong. Abortion liberates weak men, but men shouldn't desire to live and die in weakness. Our society depends on the strength and courage of men.

Fathers represent the headship. An attack on fatherhood is an attack on order itself. Marxists know this and some of their philosophers argued the Father created the desire to obey and submit to authority. Friedrich Engels wrongly suggested societies originally functioned as promiscuous hordes before capitalism, and the monogamous nuclear family evolved as a response to protect private ownership and property. Of course, patriarchal societies and family units existed long before capitalism. An effective way to tear down society is to take aim at the family, primarily the father figure.

Black Lives Matter, an organization started by lesbian "trained Marxists," said they wanted to "dismantle cis-gender privilege" and "disrupt the western-prescribed nuclear family" on their "What We Believe" page. They also listed many groups they were in solidarity with, but they never mentioned uplifting and supporting the black father. Though the public widely believes their mission is to focus on police brutality, much of their funding is directed at the gay, lesbian, and transgender communities. According to their annual report from 2020, they raised $90 million, kept $60 million for themselves, and split $21.7 million between 30 different groups. 23 of those groups were given to "Black LBGTQIA folks."[5] BLM eventually removed their "What We Believe" page after mainstream figures began pointing out that their lack of love for fathers would cause more harm to black communities.

When good fathers are absent, there is chaos in society. Look at the damage a "fatherless home" can do. In father-absent homes, children are at greater risk of poverty, are more likely to experience drug abuse, suffer from obesity, become pregnant teens, drop out of school, commit a crime, and go to prison.[6] Famous American actor Denzel Washington grew up in the streets and is often asked his opinion on criminal justice. "It starts in the home. You know, if the father's not in the home, the boy will find the father in the streets."

Some push back on the lack of fatherless homes, stating those stats don't always separate fathers who don't live in the home but are still present in their lives. That still speaks to the damage to a father-absent home. Even families that are divorced can have significant negative ramifications on a child. A 2022 study, that collected data across 17 countries, found "parental divorce had a larger impact than parental death" when it comes to educational attainment.[7] Family lawyer Mary Banham-Hall, who helped thousands of couples through their divorces, said "there's no question" that divorce is worse on a child. "People don't generally choose death."[8] Banham-Hall explained divorce not only dramatically alters a child's future, but it can also destroy their perception of the past and the life the family built together. Plus, there's a fight for resources.

The task of parenthood is astronomically important and daunting. Pro-choice activists will argue that's why it's important to "plan parenthood." But you don't need to have an abortion to do that. You can make more responsible decisions about your sexual relationships. From a biblical perspective, you should only be having sex within the covenant of marriage. Though there are married women who have abortions, or some are widowed, divorced, or even abandoned, premarital sex is a huge chunk of abortions.

The Sexual Revolution was pushed to divorce moral connections from sexual encounters. Herbert Marcuse wrote an influential best-seller in 1959, *Eros and Civilization*, that helped kick it off, and influenced the gay liberation movement.

> "The body in its entirety would become . . . a thing to be
> enjoyed—an instrument of pleasure. This change in the

value and scope in libidinal relationships would lead to a disintegration of the institutions in which the private interpersonal relations have been organized, particularly the monogamic and patriarchal family. [9]

Another leader in the sexual revolution was Arthur Kinsey. He was a man who grew up sexually repressed and wanted to radically strip our world of morality involving sex. He once wrote in a letter to an associate, Clarence A. Tripp (who wrote an influential book on homosexuality), "The whole army of religion is our central enemy." Kinsey hypothesized that we are always sexual beings, and he knowingly used data with sexually abused children, collected from pedophiles, to make his case.

After James H. Jones read tens of thousands of letters and interviewed scores of people for his biography of Kinsey, he found a different man than the media portrayed. Jones said Kinsey worked with a "missionary fervor" and loathed Victorian morality. "He was determined to use science to strip human sexuality of its guilt and repression. He wanted to undermine traditional morality, to soften the rules of restraint, and to help people develop positive attitudes toward their sexual needs and desires. Kinsey was a crypto-reformer who spent his every waking hour attempting to change the sexual mores and sex offender laws of the United States." [10]

Sigmond Freud, who is considered the godfather of modern psychiatry, wrote in *Civilization and its Discontents*:

"Man's discovery that sexual love afforded him the strongest experiences of satisfaction and in fact provided him with the prototype of all happiness, must have suggested to him that he should continue to seek the satisfaction of happiness in his life along the path of sexual relations and that he should make genital eroticism the central point of his life."[11]

Freud was wrong. Are people obsessed with gender identity and sexuality happier? Society is told that we have to accept and even celebrate the LGBTQ+ community, or else they might commit suicide. How can the need for such emotional blackmail be an indication of fulfillment or mental health? Men have access to pornography at their fingertips, and it hasn't created a happier society. Pornography victimizes women, some are even sex trafficked and rape victims. The harder the porn and the more men consume it, the harder it is for men to be stimulated by normal sexual pleasure.

Pro-choice women often complain they do not want to merely be "incubators," which obviously isn't the case. Mothers still have dreams, thoughts, aspirations, rights, and opportunities. It is a *biblical perspective* that mothers can be multi-talented and multi-purposed. Motherhood should be a blessing, not a detriment. But it's the *world's perspective* that a woman should be a vessel of pleasure. Women will lay with a man and be angry when all they have to offer her is the cash for the abortion. They keep making soul ties to dead weights.

Pregnancy is treated like a disease. I've, unfortunately, heard many pro-choice activists compare pregnancy to cancer, asking things like: "If you would remove a tumor, why wouldn't you think it's okay to remove a fetus? Cancer is natural." Cancer is the body's cells going into rebellion. Pregnancy is the result of something going right. Our bodies are made to reproduce and bear offspring.

I am often told the best way to prevent abortions is an increase in sex education. According to the CDC, 87.8 percent of abortions in 2020 were for women aged 20-40. [12] They know how babies are made. Some of them are repeat offenders. And with technology at our fingertips, sex education isn't the problem. The problem is the concerted effort to decouple meaning and responsibility from sex. And with pro-choice activists now saying, "Consent to sex isn't consent to pregnancy," they'll continue to push degeneracy and justify abortion. Even worse, they'll paint abortion as a justified moral good because you're removing a foreign invader violating your bodily autonomy. They'll grant no moral consideration to the child. They'll even argue it's irrelevant.

Marriage may be running jokes on sitcoms, but surveys and studies point to married couples being happier and having more sex, and women with few to no sexual partners before marriage are less likely to divorce. [13] If you want a statistical likelihood of not being permanently poor in the United States, all you have to do is graduate high school, keep a job, and don't have children out of wedlock, according to the Brookings Institute. There is power in the family unit and much happiness.

According to Brooking's economist Ron Haskins, their research shows out of the Americans who follow their rules, "only about 2 percent are in poverty and nearly 75 percent have joined the middle class." When Planned Parenthood criticized Mayor Michael Bloomberg of New York for his ad campaigns, drawing attention to the negative impacts of teen pregnancy, Ron Haskins suggested Bloomberg launch a "public campaign about the value of marriage to adults, children, and society." Haskins said even if critics pushed back, at least the media would cover the debate. He was confident the world would see Planned Parenthood's way of thinking as wrong.[14]

As Viktor Frankl, a psychiatrist and neurologist who suffered as a prisoner at Dachau and Auschwitz, said, "Man does not want to be happy; he wants a reason to be happy."[15]

I've already stated this, but it's worth repeating: God is a God of purpose. He made man to protect and provide. He made women to nurture and support. Together, they complement each other. They raise children and create civilizations. The fate of society is built upon the strength of the family.

Climate alarmists and even pro-choice advocates will claim there are enough children already, but that isn't true. The United States is not even meeting its replacement rate. In 2021, the National Center for Health Statistics said, "This is the sixth consecutive year that the number of births has declined after an increase in 2014, down an average of 2% per year, and the lowest number of births since 1979."[16] But even if the earth had been filled to capacity, that would be a reason to make more responsible decisions regarding procreation (as the Bible encourages), not to sacrifice already existing babies in the womb for the collective.

If you don't feel that getting married and having children is for you, that's fine. Apostle Paul enjoyed singleness and expressed so openly in 1 Corinthians 7. However, he said if you cannot exercise self-control, it is "better to marry than to burn with passion."

Trusting God's Plan

Much of the abortion debate revolves around the idea of limiting suffering for either the mother, those around her, or the child. For example, TV analyst MJ Acosta-Ruiz had an abortion after dropping out of college. Her parents had left their careers in their homeland to make opportunities for their daughter. She said her "parents did not do all of this" for her and her child "to be in poverty," and for them to suffer together. She "quickly decided" abortion was the way to go.[17]

Secretary of Treasury Janet Yellen discussed how the end of *Roe v. Wade* would damage the economy, women, and their children. "In many cases, abortions are of teenage women, particularly low income, and often Black, who aren't in a position to be able to care for children, have unexpected pregnancies, and it deprives them of the ability, often, to continue their education to later participate in the workforce."

Republican Senator Tim Scott (SC-R) responded to Yellen: "I'll just simply say that as a guy raised by a Black woman in abject poverty, I am thankful to be here as a United States senator."[18]

Life is not linear. It has ups, and it has downs. We do not know how different life will be in five, ten, fifteen years, etc. There's a scripture in the Bible that says, "Time and chance happen to them all," (Ecclesiastes 9:11). We live in a society where a news report can make you go viral—like the "Bed Intruder" song—or a man can put his hair in a "man bun" and achieve fame. We're living in an age of opportunity. The world may feel like it's ending for a woman staring at the lines on her pregnancy test, but they're a representation of a story yet to be written. There is no permanent fate of poverty stamped onto their existence. And even if there were, poverty is not an acceptable death sentence.

A popular tactic from pro-choice activists is to bring up foster care. They'll ask how many kids you have adopted. Mind you, I've seen pro-life activists respond with a number, and then they were asked why they didn't adopt more. There is no correct number; it's just a distraction. But more importantly, foster care is a reunification process. Children are placed in the care of the state because of some sort of issue with their parents, but many of them still have parental rights. They aren't available for adoption. And it's very difficult to adopt a child because the state heavily prefers reuniting them with their family. Newborns likely do not end up in the foster care system, especially if there is an adoption plan. There are far more parents waiting to adopt than children available. The Adoption Network says, "Experts estimate it is somewhere between one and two million couples." Every year there are about 1.3. million abortions. Only 4% of women with unwanted pregnancies place their children through adoption."[19] Planned Parenthood only reported 1,940 adoption referrals but they performed 383,460 abortions according to their 2020-2021 annual report.[20]

Nevertheless, pro-choice activists will argue there are too many children in foster care, implying that a child would be better off dead. If you ask for clarification, many will insist foster care kids suffer so much trauma and abuse, they'd rather be dead. Other children who survived foster care, find the assertion offensive. I know foster care kids who lived in a nightmare yet grew up to have very successful careers and families of their own. As Ronald Reagan once said, "I've noticed that everyone for abortion has already been born." Everyone expressing their opinions on this matter is exercising their right to life. It's unfair to deny that right to someone else based on assumed suffering. It also doesn't make sense that assumed suffering is justification to kill someone, but known suffering is not. Would it be moral to kill foster kids? Abused kids? Kids who are sexually assaulted? Extremely impoverished? Of course not.

As Christians, we should know there is value in life and our fortunes can—and do—change. In 1 Samuel, Hannah says a prayer exalting God for being in control of man's fate. Hannah herself was barren, and God blessed her with a child.

> [7] The Lord makes poor and makes rich; he brings low and he exalts.
>
> [8] He raises up the poor from the dust; he lifts the needy from the ash heap to make them sit with princes and inherit a seat of honor. For the pillars of the earth are the Lord's, and on them he has set the world. (1 Samuel 2:7-8, ESV)

How can Christians read the story of Joseph and support abortion? He was favored by his father, so much so that his brothers faked his death and sold him into slavery. He found favor serving his master, Potiphar, but was sent to prison after Potiphar's wife falsely accused him of sexual assault, yet Joseph found favor there as well. Eventually, his gift of interpreting dreams led him before Pharaoh. After interpreting Pharaoh's dreams of years of plenty and famine, Joseph was placed in charge. Eventually, famine did come, and Joseph's family came for help. Joseph was initially upset but ultimately saw the design in God's plan. If not for all he had been through, he would not have been able to save his family.

Just because you go through trials and tribulations, doesn't mean God isn't working it out for your good. We all have the choice to choose sin. Joseph's brothers chose envy and deceit. Potiphar's wife chose lust, attempted adultery, and lied. Lives are disrupted when people choose to sin. But we also know "that for those who love God all things work together for good, for those who are called according to his purpose," (Romans 8:28, ESV). Trust that, ultimately, God is working out everything for your benefit and his glory.

How can a Christian know the story of David and support abortion? When Samuel came to Jesse to anoint one of his sons, they didn't even think to call David in to join them. When Samuel saw Eliab, he thought he was certainly the future king, but God corrected him. "Do not look on his appearance or on the height of his stature, because I have rejected him. For the Lord sees not as a man sees: man looks on the outward appearance, but the Lord looks on the heart," (1 Samuel 16:7, ESV). Samuel looked at all the sons before him but knew there must have been one more. Then, they called for David, and he was anointed to be king.

How can Christians look at their present circumstance with their limited scope and vision and judge whether someone should live or die? How can we determine who someone else is meant to be? When God explained his compassion to the prophet Isaiah, he said:

[8] For my thoughts are not your thoughts, neither are your ways my ways, declares the Lord.

⁹ For as the heavens are higher than the earth, so are my ways higher than your ways and my thoughts than your thoughts. (Isaiah 55:8-9, ESV)

We may not be able to understand God's plan, *but it is, nevertheless, God's plan.* He is the ultimate judge. We are incapable of truly seeing someone else's worth. We're incapable of seeing our own worth! When an angel of the Lord appeared before Gideon, calling him a "mighty man of valor," he didn't believe it. He questioned why God allowed the Midianites to conquer them, and he certainly didn't believe God would be able to use him to deliver his people. His clan was the weakest, and he was the least in his father's house. But the angel encouraged him and gave him a sign. Gideon gathered an army together, but God wanted it to be evident that he was working in their lives, rather than the Midianites thinking that Israel won on the merits of their own strength. God weeded out the fearful and dropped the army from 22,000 to 10,000 men. Then he gave instructions to single out more and left them with 300. While this might have looked like a suicide mission in the natural, God imparted fear into the enemy. When Gideon and his men came armed with torches, trumpets, and jars, their enemies fled.

Sometimes, *God doesn't want the world to make sense to you.* **He wants you to lean not to your own understanding.** He wants you to trust him, and he wants the outside world to see the blessings of God rather than the boastings of man. Maybe other people wouldn't choose you. Maybe you wouldn't have chosen yourself. That doesn't mean God wouldn't call you.

> [26] For consider your calling, brothers: not many of you were wise according to worldly standards, not many were powerful, not many were of noble birth. [27] But God chose what is foolish in the world to shame the wise; God chose what is weak in the world to shame the strong; [28] God chose what is low and despised in the world, even things that are not, to bring to nothing things that are, [29] so that no human being might boast in the presence of God. [30] And because of him you are in Christ Jesus, who became to us wisdom from God, righteousness and sanctification and redemption, [31] so that, as it is written, "Let the one who boasts, boast in the Lord." (1 Corinthians 1:26-31, ESV)

Abortion does not simply end the life of one child; it erases the origin of a generation. Imagine if when God gave Abraham his original promise, Abraham backed out of the covenant because future generations would be enslaved. Would it be worth it to wipe out his entire lineage to spare them the bondage of Egypt? Of course, not. It is not for us to determine who should live and die based on our limited understanding of God's design.

Crucifying Ego

I once saw a viral video of a young pro-choice woman explaining how terrible her abortion was and that she needed to set the record straight because pro-lifers had "no idea." Of course, the pro-life community knows how difficult abortions—including the pill—can be. Many pro-life advocates are women who once had abortions. We actively try to warn women all of the time.

The young woman expressed she hated when pro-life people claim abortions are done out of convenience, yet she had a fundamental misunderstanding of what we mean by that. That became evident in follow-up videos. She had an abortion because she didn't feel financially stable enough to have a child. This is a textbook example. It wasn't an emergency; the baby either was inconvenient or came at an inconvenient time.

The young woman went on to say that when she did have a child, she wanted to give that child "the world." This is a naïve endeavor. Even parents who feel extremely prepared come to feel overwhelmed when the baby is crying throughout the night or smearing poop on the walls. And some parents have unexpected babies, learn along the way, and turn out to be tremendous parents. It's admirable to want to set your child up for the best chance of success, but you can't offer your child "the world" if you won't at least offer them life. Your next child after an abortion is not a reset. An inconvenient baby isn't a glitchy video game that you pop out of the system, blow into the cartridge, and fire back up hoping for success. Abortion is the annihilation of a unique person. That child will never exist again.

And what if you never achieve those perfect standards to have that baby? What if you do, but everything falls apart after you have the baby? What if you can never even have another baby? It's arrogant to think you can control everything or that people have to live and die based on your expectations. Plenty of children grow up in poverty and are grateful for their lives, whether they improve their economic status or they continue to financially struggle.

Would-be parents should ask themselves a question before they have an abortion out of "compassion" for their baby: are you trying to spare them a life of struggle or are you trying to spare yourself from the trials and tribulations of a struggling parent?

When I was in middle school, our family lost our home. Though it was difficult to experience that loss as a child, there was certainly a level of pressure my father endured that I couldn't relate to. It's not easy feeling like you've failed your family.

My father used to carry a lot of guilt and shame for his times of lack, mostly because his family struggled alongside him. Now, he can look back and see that we all had our own relationships with God to develop, and we certainly learned to place our trust in God. And I can say, I'm certainly glad to have lived my life. Emotional scars can heal, but abortion is permanent.

Besides, so many children who develop bonds with their parents, dream of being successful for their parents' sake. I've heard so many celebrities say the first thing they did with their big checks was to buy their parents a house. They're driven toward success for the sake of their family. You don't have to give your child "the world." Just give them a world worth fighting for. Coals don't become diamonds without pressure. We cannot be too afraid to face adversity or be too proud to struggle.

Pride focuses on the self. The women Emmanuel Acho selected for his abortion discussion had conversations about *their* lives, *their* experiences, *their* dreams, and *their* expectations, and they never took the time to reflect on God's commandments and what **he would have wanted for them**. They also never address the children who were killed. It was about how we can address *their* hurt, understand *their* decisions, and support *their* lives. Men were only addressed in relation to *their* feelings and needs. There was never a focus on God or the child.

> For by the grace given to me I say to everyone among you not to think of himself more highly than he ought to think, but to think with sober judgment, each according to the measure of faith that God has assigned. (Romans 12:3, ESV)

If a pagan came up to you and said they were going to sacrifice a baby for your success, you'd probably be mortified. It would go deeper than not believing in their deity; you wouldn't want that sort of guilt on your conscience. You'd know, internally, that a political science degree or a job promotion wasn't worth someone else's life. And if that's the case, elective abortion is a practice far beyond your worthiness.

Perhaps you feel as though your pride is under control. Perhaps you feel as though you have the opposite of high self-esteem or self-importance. Insecurity is also a form of pride when it's powered by fear. If a woman has an abortion because she is afraid of her inadequacies as a mother, lack of finances, and so on, she's leaning toward her own understanding instead of God. As I address in, *Slay Your Fear: How to Overcome a Spirit of Fear:*

> God doesn't make mistakes. Stop telling God that you're not good enough. We think we're being humble when we list how unworthy we are off to God. The truth is insecurity isn't humility. It's pride. We are "fearfully and wonderfully made." Everything about you, God made with care and love. He intimately knows you, and if He's purposed you for a task, do not doubt Him."

"My body, my choice," is completely about ego. Abortion isn't solely about a woman and her body. When a child is conceived, a family has been made. There is a mother, a father, and a baby, and each person has a distinct relationship with God. To zone in specifically on the needs and the desires of the woman, and supersede all other parties involved, takes a tremendous amount of pride.

If the father pressures the woman to get an abortion or is even in agreement with the woman, they are still putting themselves above their child and the will of the Lord.

Is the couple so focused on their present and how their life will change that they don't see the generations that will be lost if they choose abortion? On September 3, 2022, I attended the funeral of Mary Reid, the mother to dear friends. In the church of her youngest son, Pastor Marlin Reid, children, grandchildren, and great-grandchildren gathered. Speakers got up in amazement, "Look at her legacy!" The lessons she taught in her home to her ten children have been carried all around the world through her seed. They are preachers, pastors, and ministers; her son, Karl, was in the famous gospel group, Commission.

Her life was not easy, especially by modern standards. She was raised during the Great Depression. When her father passed, she dropped out of school to help her mother with bills. The love of her life went to fight in WWII, and she chose to marry an unsaved man when he returned (which she said was a mistake, but he did eventually receive Jesus). Raising ten children was a big task, but that church was full of the blessings of God.

Jesus had a very specific task in his ministry. Yes, he came to be our savior, but he also came to raise disciples. Ministry isn't about one person. It's a continuation, just as life is. God's first commandment was to be fruitful and multiply. Humanity is not supposed to be a dead end.

And when someone confronts you about abortion, do you defensively push back? Can you have an honest conversation about the procedure and the life of the child, or do you resort to insults like *pro-birthers*, *you just wanna control women*, or do you even go as far as to accuse pro-life activists of killing women? Do you deflect and go to conversations about the death penalty, war, and other topics unrelated or secondary to abortion? Are you reacting or are you pausing and reflecting so you can respond honestly?

Before seeking an abortion, do you ask the crucial question: *"Is this what God purposed for my life?"*

If you can't ask it, answer it honestly, and act accordingly, then you've placed your ego above the will and commandments of the Lord.

The Value in Suffering

Here's an inconvenient truth: there is value in our suffering. Through our loss, tragedies, afflictions, sorrows, and frustrations, God sees purpose through it all. This is not always a comforting thought while enduring a trial; it takes spiritual maturity to appreciate it. And you can't reach that spiritual maturity without the experience of God's constant faithfulness, even through the midst of the storm.

In Acts 3, a man lame from birth was carried daily and laid at the gate of the temple to beg for money. Peter and John got the man's attention, and Peter said, "I have no silver and gold, but what I do have I give to you. In the name of Jesus Christ of Nazareth, rise up and walk!" Strength immediately came to the man's body, so he leaped to his feet and began to walk and praise God. The Bible says, "All the people saw him walking and praising God." They recognized him as the lame man who would ask for alms, so they were "filled with wonder and amazement." His life was filled with suffering. His body was a prison. He wasn't on disability with the pleasure of many benefits we're afforded in a first-world nation. He begged! But his suffering and his appointed time for a miracle served a greater purpose. He was a testimony to the power of Jesus Christ.

Christians love to quote, "I can do all things through Christ who strengthens me," but we often forget the context and how the Apostle Paul came to that conclusion. Christians will often quote this passage in their desire to escape pain, poverty, etc. Paul learned a "secret," whether he was facing plenty, hunger, abundance, or need. Regardless of whatever struggle Paul endured throughout the ministry, he could endure it all because Christ strengthened him.

In 2 Corinthians 12, Paul speaks of receiving a thorn in his flesh, to keep him "from being conceited," after receiving heavenly revelations. Some Christians believe the thorn was a physical illness, others believe the thorn was a demonic opposition. Paul did say it was a "messenger of Satan to harass me." And Paul pleaded with the Lord three times to remove this thorn. But God's reply was, "My grace is sufficient for you, for my power is made perfect in weakness." Paul then said, "I will boast all the more gladly of my weakness, so that the power of Christ may rest upon me. For the sake of Christ, then, I am content with weakness, insults, hardships, persecutions, and calamities. For when I am weak, then I am strong."

No one, generally, likes to suffer. But the older I get and the more trials I overcome, the more I can see God preserving me through it all, making me perfect in my revelation that God is in control, his grace has gotten me through every hardship, and he, undoubtedly, loves me.

> [3] Not only that, but we rejoice in our sufferings, knowing that suffering produces endurance, [4] and endurance produces character, and character produces hope, [5] and hope does not put us to shame, because God's love has been poured into our hearts through the Holy Spirit who has been given to us. (Romans 5:3-5, ESV)

If you are a Christian, it is not acceptable to have an abortion to spare yourself or your child the pain of life. We should work to eliminate the suffering, not the sufferer. It is not a sin to need help and to ask for it, and it is certainly a Christian duty to aid those in need. We take care of widows, and orphans, and provide a hand up for those who can work but need support.

I was blessed to grow up in a home with a lot of love, but we did not grow up in a home with abundant finances. Some years were very lean, but I did learn to trust God for my provisions and favor. At my sister's Fourth of July party, I looked around at the spacious backyard of her home, the playset, and the pool. I told her, "You have a lot of things you can give your kids that we didn't have growing up," and my sister was grateful. I also observed how the children bounced from the pool to the swings, and to the option of so many toys. When the pool was empty, I conversed with other adults, "If I had a pool, I would be in it nonstop." It was mind-blowing to us, but scarcity brought a different appreciation for their many blessings. My sister didn't hit the lotto to change her fortune or marry into an uber-rich family. She's wise with the money that comes in, benefits from having a support system, and definitely gets special attention from being the first to produce grandchildren.

In the West today, we don't place enough value on the benefit of building a family. We should listen to the advice of Ron Haskins and the Brookings Institute: graduate high school, get a job and keep a job, and don't have children out of wedlock. And when you need extra help, there's charity or government assistance.

Sometimes, we have to look around at our tragedies and ask if our sin has led us to a less-than-ideal situation. Sometimes, we're in less-than-ideal situations because of the sins of generations before us. God told Moses in Exodus 34:

⁶The LORD passed before him and proclaimed, "The LORD, the LORD, a God merciful and gracious, slow to anger, and abounding in steadfast love and faithfulness, ⁷keeping steadfast love for thousands, forgiving iniquity and transgression and sin, but who will by no means clear the guilty, visiting the iniquity of the fathers on the children and the children's children, to the third and the fourth generation." (Exodus 34:6-7, ESV)

"Visiting the iniquity of the fathers on the children" is not about God enacting generational revenge. God judges every man according to their own works. But it is a reality the consequence of sin leaves a residual effect within homes, generations, and communities. If your life is difficult because your parents and grandparents engaged in carnal pleasure rather than building a family with stability, that is an example of visiting iniquity. If your household had animosity because your parents were unequally yoked when they got together, and they're not on the same page about following God's moral laws, that's going to cause visiting iniquity. If a parent commits a crime and goes to jail, leaving the child with one parent or in foster care, that is a visiting iniquity.

Can you break the cycle? Of course, you can. You are responsible for your own decisions, and you can choose to live a more abundant life. And that contrast, between a life without God and a life following the wisdom of his commandments, will glorify him. With God, you can endure your hardships. And with God, you can overcome them. It is even God's desire to bless his children because that will also glorify him as well.

But regardless of whatever we experience, we are supposed to count it all joy and praise God through everything. "Rejoice always, pray without ceasing, give thanks in all circumstances; for this is the will of God in Christ Jesus for you," (1 Thessalonians 5:16-18).

Suffering can be a consequence of sin, a means of sanctification, or a test of faith. There's a purpose in suffering, and it is not acceptable to take a child's life to spare them from that purpose. You may believe you're making a responsible decision as a parent, but what you're doing is butting in between God and *his* creation, and you do it with your limited knowledge and vision.

Many abortions are performed on children with Down Syndrome. *CBS* reported in 2017, that the number of children with Down syndrome has decreased in Europe and the US as women choose prenatal screenings. "Since prenatal screening tests were introduced in Iceland in the early 2000s, the vast majority of women—close to 100 percent—who received a positive test for Down syndrome terminated their pregnancy."[21] *The Washington Post* reported that 98 percent of babies with Down syndrome in Denmark face termination. In the UK, it's 90 percent. In the U.S., 85 percent. In France, 77 percent. If this is to spare them the pain of being different or going through life with a disability, 99 percent of people with Down syndrome are happy with their lives.[22]

After *Roe v. Wade* was overturned, political commentator Ana Navarro, who claimed to be a "very passionate woman of faith," went on to justify abortion, using her family as an example. She has family members with "special needs kids," a "brother who's 57 and has the mental and motor skills of a one-year-old," and a step-granddaughter who was born with Down syndrome. "There are mothers, and there are people who are in that society, or in that community will tell you that they've considered suicide because that's how difficult it is to get help, because that's how lonely they feel because they can't get other jobs, because they have financial issues, because the care that they're able to give their other children suffers. And so why can I be Catholic and still think this is a wrong decision? Because I'm American." [23]

As a Catholic and an American, Navarro should believe all human beings, despite having a disability, deserve equal protection under the law and shouldn't be discriminated against. Navarro said she's a "Catholic inside the church," but God needs Christians to be Christian 24/7. She should be moved to help women in need, rather than using their suffering as justification for their genocide.

Navarro later claimed, "some have twisted my words," on Twitter, claiming it's hypocritical to be pro-life yet not give more funding to these people in need. Yes, it would be, and Navarro is a woman of means who can be part of the solution. She did not walk back her belief that women should be able to have the choice to end the lives of their children, especially for eugenics.

We, unfortunately, live in a fallen world and there is no guarantee to live life without sickness, challenges, persecution, or death. But if we abide in Christ, we can find joy. And through our joy, God can grant us peace.

[4] Rejoice in the Lord always; again I will say, rejoice. [5] Let your reasonableness be known to everyone. The Lord is at hand; [6] do not be anxious about anything, but in everything by prayer and supplication with thanksgiving let your requests be made known to God. [7] And the peace of God, which surpasses all understanding, will guard your hearts and your minds in Christ Jesus. (Philippians 4:4-7, ESV)

Self-Sacrifice

[9] As the Father has loved me, so have I loved you. Abide in my love. [10] If you keep my commandments, you will abide in my love, just as I have kept my Father's commandments and abide in his love. [11] These things I have spoken to you, that my joy may be in you, and that your joy may be full. [12] This is my commandment, that you love one another as I have loved you. [13] Greater love has no one than this, that someone lay down his life for his friends. (John 15:9-13, ESV)

I've often heard atheists make the case that Jesus didn't sacrifice anything because he was already going to win. When he died, he was always going to be resurrected. Even though he was betrayed, sentenced to death (for being exactly who he is, mind you), ridiculed, beaten, spat on, whipped, had to wear a crown of thorns, carried his cross, and was crucified, they still don't see the value in it because he rose again in three days.

Well, there aren't many people in this world who would be willing to suffer such persecution. The disciples and early church Christians were willing to die for the gospel. That's one of the reasons why it's so compelling. Why would so many fraudsters brutally die for their cause? And modern-day Christians are willing to die for Christ. Read about the accounts of Christians in communist nations, like in *Tortured for Christ*. But Jesus suffered persecution while having the full power to call twelve legions of angels to save him. He truly laid down his life, so we could be saved from the wages of sin.

But I'm also tickled by their assertion. The benefit of Christianity is that we have victory the entire time. In the end, there's nothing Satan can do. God has already won, and we're on the winning team. Perhaps that's hard to grasp from the outside looking in, but it feels good from the winning side.

They underestimate the sacrifice of doing the work leading up to the cross. Jesus, being God, decided to live a human life for 33 years. That isn't long in the span of eternity, but it's all the time I've been here on this earth. That's long to me. He suffered from the limitations of the human body, like hunger and tiredness. When he began his ministry, he had to deal with people. As an introvert, I can see that as a cross all on its own. He had to deal with the Pharisees, who were constantly nagging him, trying to set him up for failure. Jesus could barely heal someone without it turning into a controversy. Even his disciples were frustrating at times. "O faithless and twisted generation, how long am I to be with you? How long am I to bear with you?" (Matthew 17:17, ESV). Mind you, Jesus was annoyed because they couldn't cast a demon out. Even when Jesus was interceding in the Garden of Gethsemane, until sweat fell like great drops of blood, they fell asleep on him.

In our lives, we gear ourselves up for acts of heroism and grand gestures of love. If I had to fight to the death to defend my family, I would. But if I have to pick someone up from the airport, it's the worst thing in the world. If a sibling announces they need to be picked up from work, the family group chat becomes a game of pointing fingers with gifs. You may be that church member willing to drop a hundred-dollar bill in the offering bucket, but would you vacuum the floors? Would you serve church dinners? Would you wash someone else's feet as Jesus did?

Love is not simply a feeling or a deep affection for another person. Love is service. Jesus explained to his disciples that if they loved him, they would keep his commandments. God desires that the disciples bear good fruit, and God would receive glory in this. And in turn, God also desires to bless us. And God expects us to love one another.

Love is work, its duty, it's sacrifice.

4 Love is patient and kind; love does not envy or boast; it is not arrogant 5 or rude. It does not insist on its own way; it is not irritable or resentful; 6 it does not rejoice at wrongdoing, but rejoices with the truth. 7 Love bears all things, believes all things, hopes all things, endures all things. (1 Corinthians 13:4-7)

The truth of the matter is the abortion argument has mostly moved beyond the question of whether an embryo or fetus is alive. The debate is, "At what point is it acceptable to discriminate against another human?" We base the legitimacy of the baby's humanity and personhood on how vulnerable and dependent they are. If the child needs their mother, then the child does not deserve to be protected against violence.

It is simply not Christlike for a woman to slay her child, whether it be to advance her ambitions or out of fear of her deficiencies and current circumstances. God has not given us a spirit of fear. Instead, he's given us power, love, and a sound mind (2 Timothy 1:7).

Many pro-choice activists focus their compassion on mothers, but it's shortsighted and destructive. They think easy access to abortion and not guilting her out of it, is kindness. They think driving her to a clinic is support, or minding their business is best. But when that mother is alone in her room, maybe five or twenty years later, contemplating the due date of a child she never got to hold, those friends and chanting activists won't be with her. That mother will have to carry the scars of what she's done. She will stand before God alone and be held accountable for her sins unless she gives those burdens to Christ.

If you loved someone, and they were about to walk blindly off a cliff, would you not be willing to tackle them to the ground to keep them from harm? If you are a Christian, supporting sin or being apathetic toward it is not an act of love. You should do your best to persuade them from an evil action.

We should have compassion for both mother and child. That's why pregnancy crisis centers will help with appointments, parenting classes, diapers, cribs, strollers, counseling, babysitting, school, etc. Parenthood is not an easy transition, but it makes an extraordinary difference when the community rallies behind a mother.

Judging

"Who am I to judge?" Pro-choice activists who identify as Christians will often say they don't want to judge others, or skeptics will judge Christians for judging in general.

The Bible never says a Christian cannot judge. Frankly, that wouldn't make any sense. Before establishing a kingship, God set up a governing system of judges. There's a book in the

Bible called "Judges," as a matter of fact. What God calls us to do is judge righteously. God tells us in Proverbs to open our mouths and speak for those who cannot, to stand up for their rights, and "judge righteously," (Proverbs 31:8-9).

The go-to passage on judging is Matthew 7, "Judge not, that you be not judged." But people normally stop there instead of continuing with the rest of the passage.

> [2] For with the judgment you pronounce you will be judged, and with the measure you use it will be measured to you. [3] Why do you see the speck that is in your brother's eye, but do not notice the log that is in your own eye? [4] Or how can you say to your brother, 'Let me take the speck out of your eye,' when there is the log in your own eye? [5] You hypocrite, first take the log out of your own eye, and then you will see clearly to take the speck out of your brother's eye. (Matthew 7:2-5, ESV)

George W. Bush had a great quote at a funeral for Dallas police officers in 2016. "Too often, we judge other groups by their worst examples—while judging ourselves by our best intentions. And this has strained our bonds of understanding and common purpose."

Jesus wants us to not be too quick to judge others, and not be too harsh over small things (the speck) while committing such blatant wrongs ourselves (the beam). Instead of getting right with God, we'll overcompensate our sense of righteousness by condemning the offenses of others. It wasn't the intention of Jesus that we don't address the sins of others, but it's not appropriate to feel everybody else needs to live right except for you.

But more importantly, you don't have to judge what is right and wrong. God already made that assessment. If you tell a woman it's wrong to kill her child, that's already aligned with God's word. It's no judgment to tell her that. She has to take that up with God.

But Christians shouldn't condemn her to hell. That's not your place. She can get right with God. You shouldn't assume to know her thoughts or her heart unless God supernaturally reveals it to you; you're not a mind reader. But the Bible does say, you can know a tree by its fruit. So, God does expect us to have a level of discernment for one another, we can observe each other's actions, and we can make assessments. There's nothing sinful about stating it's wrong to have an abortion and telling women they shouldn't do it.

If you lack the courage to speak on what God already stated, that's a different issue.

The Golden Rule

When I was in high school, a teacher asked the class what the golden rule was. A friend of mine said, "Whoever has the gold makes the rules." Some chuckles filled the room, but my friend was confused. She heard that saying from somewhere and believed that was the answer. We had to tell her the golden rule was the principle that you should treat others how you want to be treated, which is found in Matthew 7:12.

Many abortion activists can concede that abortion is wrong or at least not ideal after consciousness is achieved, but I've seen many "philosophy bros" ask why abortion is wrong in the first trimester. The answer is simple. I would never advocate that it is moral to conspire to unjustly end my life at any point. It would be wrong to kill me tomorrow, yesterday, when I was a toddler, six minutes after birth, or six minutes after being settled in the womb. At no point, would I grant my mother the green light to kill me.

I am not currently an embryo in my mother's womb, so I've, thankfully, escaped the danger of being aborted. Praise God, my mother would have never done such a thing to me. But why would I advocate that another human being shouldn't be protected against such violence just because I escaped unscathed? Imagine if this were the 1800s and I was a slave who escaped a plantation, and then I went on to advocate that it was perfectly acceptable for the masters to enslave other unfortunate negroes.

Human beings in the womb, like myself, are made in the image of God and worthy of protection. They are a living member of my species with a future like mine, on a self-determined path to maturity and rationality. No one has to call Amazon and have consciousness delivered and installed to be made whole. From the moment of conception, we are whole human organisms. Every parameter critics claim is necessary for personhood is in our nature, and the capacity is present—even if not yet manifested—at conception.

We must consider the two greatest commandments according to Jesus Christ. The first is to love God with all our heart, soul, and mind. The second is, "You shall love your neighbor as yourself. On these two commandments depend all the Law and the Prophets," (Matthew 22:36-40). When activists dead set on protecting abortion claim it is no one else's business if a child in the womb is being slain, our response should be: you are killing my preborn neighbor. It truly should be as simple as if you do not want to be killed, you shouldn't kill someone else. If you do not want someone to kill you, you shouldn't want someone else to be killed. If you don't think someone should be allowed to unjustly kill you, then you shouldn't find it permissible for other living humans to be unjustly killed.

Justice

Fathers shall not be put to death because of their children, nor shall children be put to death because of their fathers. Each one shall be put to death for his own sin. (Deuteronomy 24:16, ESV)

We are responsible for the actions we choose to take. I've seen pro-choice activists take offense to, "If you have sex, you have to deal with the consequences." They, perhaps insincerely, sneer at the implication that a baby is a consequence. Well, "consequence" may have a negative connotation, but that doesn't make it a negative word. It's simply the result of your actions. I wrote a children's book, *Superkid*, that explained this quite well. But you don't have to think of a baby as a consequence; a baby is a blessing from the Lord.

But a consequence of sex may be pregnancy at a time you didn't consciously decide and is terribly inconvenient. It's going to cost some of your body (a woman still has bodily autonomy and a life of her own, even if she's renting out her uterus), time, and money, and could impact your health (sometimes positively, but also negatively). You may be tied to the father for at least 18-25 years. It's going to result in sleepless nights, tears, and filthy diapers. Motherhood will put a serious dent in your social life. It's going to cost you what's left of your adolescence because there's nothing more grown-up than being responsible for another human being.

It doesn't make sense that a woman's choice must be celebrated and respected, yet we ignore the actions she takes leading up to her pregnancy. To reject these possible consequences would mean forcing your son or daughter to pay with their lives. We know this would be unjust in the sight of the Lord, and God hates hands that shed innocent blood.

The prophet Micah famously said, "He has told you, O man, what is good; and what does the LORD require of you but to do justice, and to love kindness, and to walk humbly with your God?" (Micah 6:8, ESV).

Some "pro-choice Christians" cite free will as an excuse to allow women to choose abortion, and they say God will sort this all out on judgment day. God still calls his people to justice. God gave us laws to follow and created a system of judges in the Old Testament before moving to a kingship. But if a king and the people did evil in the sight of the Lord, he would punish them. Because Solomon did not keep the covenant and allowed evils such as idolatry and child sacrifice into his kingdom, God raised an enemy against him (1 Kings 11:14). Will God pour out his judgment on a country that allows between 800,000 to 1,000,000 abortions per year?

Many times, before calamity came, God sent prophets to warn the people. That's what Micah was doing. The people were wicked and unjust, so he warned that Assyria and later Babylon would bring destruction. "But as for me, I am filled with power, with the Spirit of the Lord, and with justice and might, to declare to Jacob his transgression and to Israel his sin," (Micah 3:8, ESV).

Would a just God not warn people of their accused crimes and warn them of their coming judgment? Why would Christians choose to not speak up? Feckless Christians today are much like Jonah, but instead of refusing to preach to Nineveh because their salvation would be imminent, Christians are choosing destruction for nations due to social respectability. You don't want to rock too many boats, hurt feelings, or make anyone uncomfortable, so instead of preaching the word of God, you allow judgment to fall.

What is the point of being a Christian if you do not seek to save others from damnation? Jesus died on the cross to bear God's wrath upon himself (Isaiah 53). We don't have to bear that judgment. How selfish is it of "believers" that they would rather stay silent and even support others in their sin, dooming them to condemnation?

A big talking point within the pro-choice community is that if a woman has an abortion, it does not affect you. This is not a biblical way of thinking. But justice in the Bible is not merely about retribution, meaning one gets what they deserve. The Bible also deals with restoration. The Bible Project describes it as "seeking out vulnerable people who are being taken advantage of and helping them." They say, "mishpat," the Hebrew word for justice, goes beyond charity. It's "taking steps to advocate for the vulnerable and changing social structures to prevent injustice." They say, "Righteousness and justice are about a radical selfless way of life," and these examples are all over the Bible. [24]

> [8] Open your mouth for the mute, for the rights of all who are destitute. [9] Open your mouth, judge righteously, defend the rights of the poor and needy. (Proverbs 31:8-9, ESV)

If you are a believer, you should speak up for the unborn, who cannot advocate for their lives. They should not be killed due to reasons like financial lack. Believers should be advocating for cultural changes that will eliminate the injustice of abortion. Some will automatically think of government intervention: government-funded childcare, enforcing companies to pay for maternity leave, free college, etc. I strongly caution against that; the more government is involved in your life, the more control they have over you and your family. Christians should be charitable and help women in need. But if Christians pushed the restoration of God's intended family structure, the perceived need for abortion would quickly dissolve. Two married people working together, to benefit their family, is far more beneficial than the average woman going at it alone or with an unstable and undependable lover.

The solution is always God: his standard of morality, his design, and his truth.

Chapter Six

Separation of Church and State

U.S. Senator "Reverend" Raphael Warnock (GA-D) once tweeted, "As a pro-choice pastor, I've always believed that a patient's room is way too small for a woman, her doctor, and the United States government. I'll always fight to protect a woman's right to choose. And that will never change."[1]

Warnock's post bothers me for several reasons. The first is the assertion this Democratic senator is for small or limited government in any way. Many of the pro-choice Americans screaming about bodily autonomy and getting the government out of their uteruses, didn't stand up against government lockdowns, mask mandates, or vaccination mandates. President Joe Biden tried to use OSHA to enforce a vaccine mandate for businesses with over 100 employees. If an employee did not get the vaccine, they had to wear masks and submit for weekly testing (likely out of the employee's pocket). This was pushed regardless of natural immunity and despite the fact, the vaccinated can still catch and spread COVID-19. If they had a true libertarian or anarchist approach to life, I could at least respect their position, but the government proved it does not care about bodily autonomy.

Secondly, it is not the position of the Democrat Party that abortions should only be between a woman and her doctor. Senator Bernie Sanders (VT-D) pushed on the 2020 campaign trail to get rid of the Hyde Amendment, which forbids federal dollars from being used for most abortions. President Joe Biden used to strongly support the position, but he flipped. Now, more leaders are openly calling for its removal. New York Governor Kathy Hochul (D) urged President Biden to use federal lands to protect abortion facilities, and she allotted $35 million to protect abortion providers.[2] California Governor Gavin Newsom (D) wants his state to be an abortion sanctuary. If taxpayer dollars are involved, your abortion is no longer private. "My money, my business." It's as simple as that. Politicians used to agree abortion was such a controversial issue for Americans, they could at least try to keep federal dollars out of it. Now, they want to evangelize it around the world with the hard-earned money of Christians and non-Christians alike.

Thirdly, Warnock mentioned the woman, her doctor, and the U.S. government, but there was no mention of the future victim (the child) or the father. Men should not willingly take the backseat when a woman says she's going to destroy their heirs. If the child is born, the fathers get no say in child support.

The state doesn't care whether a man is ready to be a parent. They do what's in the best interest of the child. So, why do we push fathers aside while that very same child is in their mother's womb?

And lastly, Warnock ignored the fact God is in the doctor's office. God is big enough, powerful enough, and loving enough to deliver her from whatever despair that led her to that abortion clinic. As a "reverend," you'd think he'd have some words of encouragement or that he'd want to inspire hope.

When Warnock says he's a "pro-choice pastor," he's using his authority to soften the idea of abortion, even though his position has no bearing on being pro-choice at all. It would be like me announcing, "As a minister, I can attest that pineapple goes on pizza." One has nothing to do with the other. Warnock is pro-choice because he decided the Christian faith should not inform his position.

But is it possible for Christians to be thoroughly against abortion, personally, yet allow women to support it? Most Americans find abortion to be a terrible thing, and many still believe it's, ultimately, up to the woman to decide.

This is a foolish and dishonest position. We would not apply this sort of logic to any other violation of human rights. We wouldn't say, "Well, I'm personally against slavery, but I don't want to impose my beliefs on other people." Perhaps Americans did once upon a time ago, but the idea of slavery became morally abhorrent. We only allow the unborn to be killed because we have chosen to justify it in our own minds, not because it is a morally justifiable position.

Imposing One's Beliefs

Let's assume that as a Christian, you concede abortion is abhorrent and not what God intends for his creations. Does that mean we should impose our beliefs upon other people? What about the "separation of church and state?"

People of faith are not the only human beings who have "beliefs." Atheists don't have a lack of belief. They have a very strong belief there is no God. They will evangelize this belief with such conviction. They'll write books, create entire social media platforms, and hold conferences. They'll debate or troll Christian pages, hoping to validate their position and destroy the faith of someone else. Some atheists have more passion for their cause than many Christians.

The truth is everyone is religious. It's just a matter of who you worship. Perhaps it's a god. Perhaps it's your ego, nature, sexuality, celebrities, politics, etc. Rush Limbaugh used to say liberalism is a religion and abortion is their sacrament.

There's such a push to remove "beliefs" from politics, but we make laws based on what we believe to be moral and just. We have laws against murder, for example. That's one of the Ten Commandments. Yes, we want to protect the rights of human beings. In the U.S., we recognize we are endowed by our Creator with unalienable rights, such as life. Because of that, no one should be able to infringe upon that right.

Secular people also want to use their beliefs to push legislation. People like Senator Bernie Sanders believe no one should have to work without making a "livable wage." His supporters believe the minimum wage should be raised, and no one should have to work more than one job to provide for themselves and their families. All of these positions are based on belief. They want to use the arm of the government to control what businesses and employees voluntarily agree to because they believe allowing the free market to have total control is immoral. Whether you agree or disagree with their political assessments, you cannot say it's not rooted in a belief.

When Senator Sanders grilled Russel Vought on Capitol Hill during a confirmation hearing for the director of the Office of Management and Budget, he did so based on his belief. Vought had written a paper defending his college's position on the centrality of Jesus Christ, and Sanders was offended because Vought didn't think Muslims "knew God" or were getting into heaven. Vought said he believed everyone was made in the "image of God and are worthy of dignity and respect, regardless of their religious beliefs."

Sanders still did not believe Vought was respectful because non-Christians are "condemned." He eventually said, "This nominee is really not someone who is what this country is supposed to be about. I will vote no." [3] This was a very discriminatory action by Senator Sanders, based on his belief and bigotry toward Vought. Sanders did receive backlash, as many Americans saw this as a "religious test" that should not be permitted by the government. But some media, like YouTube's darlings, *The Young Turks*, labeled Sander's shameful display: "Bernie Sanders Destroys Religious Bigot During Confirmation Hearing."

California Senator Scott Weiner (D) is a gay man who believes it's pointless to lecture gay men about their sexual behaviors, even if diseases like monkeypox are almost exclusively spread by promiscuous gay sex.[4] It would be good public health policy to strongly discourage orgies and kinky festivals, but he disagrees. That's interesting, considering Weiner wanted a nationwide mask mandate during the coronavirus pandemic and mocked anti-maskers, anti-mandates, and anti-vaxxers. He believes lectures, coercion, and blatant force is okay for COVID-19, but we have to shrug our shoulders when gay men want to have orgies? He's operating off of belief, rooted in his bias.

Abortion is completely centered around belief. It is an objective scientific fact that when women are pregnant, they are carrying humans who are alive. If they die, it's a miscarriage or "spontaneous abortion." But there are about a million induced abortions meant to kill living humans in the womb in the U.S. every year. The way to make these facts more palatable is to push a belief that the baby is not truly "alive," or even an "actual baby." A belief is pushed that the woman's bodily autonomy is more important than their "potential life." And because of these beliefs, they push policies to violate the human rights of a vulnerable child.

And women are not simply asking for a "right." They want blanket immunity for hitmen who execute the order and access to make it happen. They're going to want it to be affordable, subsidized, and perhaps even "free" one day, meaning paid by the taxpayer. Our neighbors to the north in Canada have taxpayer-funded abortions.

There is no such thing as "mind your business" when it comes to sin. Satan is a devourer. Just because you want to keep your faith in a corner doesn't mean evil won't spread. In 2014, Hobby Lobby, a major arts and crafts franchise owned by Christians, went to the Supreme Court in a fight over the Affordable Care Act—better known as Obamacare—and their insurance regulations for employees. There were certain contraceptives they could not provide in good conscience; in case they caused a fertilized egg to not implant. But no one let them off the hook for their religious convictions. They were forced to participate, and they had to fight.

The Little Sisters of the Poor is a group of nuns who bring comfort to the elderly. They would have very much wanted to be left alone to do their work, but the Obamacare mandate required them to violate their faith by providing birth control, including ones they thought could terminate a life. They won an exemption in 2016, and the Supreme Court told the government to find a solution to work for everyone. After President Donald Trump won his election, they issued exemptions to religious objectors. However, states still decided to sue to force their compliance. In 2020, they won their case.

After Joe Biden defeated Donald Trump in the 2020 election, he nominated Xavier Becerra to lead Health and Human Services, who sued the Trump Administration and the nuns. Curiously, Becerra holds no particular expertise in health.

It's unfair to expect a secular society to operate off their beliefs and ask everyone else to check their convictions at the door. Everyone fights for what they believe in, and part of politics is making arguments for the best way to exercise our liberties. When Christians argue against abortion, they're not saying, "Pass a ban because abortion makes Baby Jesus cry." They say it's immoral to rob a human being of their right to life. From there, we can debate.

It is also important to note just because religious people widely agree with a political position or law, doesn't mean it should be tossed. Christians believe in property rights, it's wrong to steal, commit libel, or slander someone. Should we remove all laws and legal protections regarding these matters? The idea of needing to be proven guilty beyond any reasonable doubt comes from Blackstone's ratio, from English Jurist William Blackstone, which largely contributed to Anglo-Saxon law philosophy. "It is better that ten guilty persons escape than that one innocent suffer." An early example of this principle appears in the Bible when Abraham bargains with God to spare Sodom and Gomorrah.

You don't have to be a believer to acknowledge that Judeo-Christian values have greatly benefited our society. The beauty of America is that so many people can simultaneously hold so many values, yet peaceably live together. That balance can only survive if there is mutual respect for each other's rights and religious liberty.

Besides, as a believer, I cannot separate my faith from who I am. My identity isn't in my race or gender; it's in Christ. My moral values align with God's moral laws. I don't follow the gospel because I'm bored and need club activities, at least three times a week. I follow the gospel because it is the truth. I believe God has left behind a blueprint for a better life. I'm willing to debate how those morals shape policies and their validity, but Christians shouldn't be willing to surrender.

In reality, secularists are asking Christians to not participate in society unless their Christianity can be so absolutely meaningless, that they won't interfere with their legislative ambitions. After all, when politicians on the left side of the aisle invoke religion—largely out of context—you don't see a big call on the left to shut them down. No, they love it when Christians lose their flavor and become clumps of useless salt.

Christians may argue they have to obey the laws of the land, and that is true, but that doesn't mean people of faith shouldn't participate in government or advocate for certain issues. We should be bold and give non-believers the reason for the hope that lies within us. The Bible is a blueprint for a more abundant life, and it should be evident with empirical data that God's moral laws make sense. Christians should not shirk the responsibility of persuading non-believers to embrace Godly principles. And if there are immoral laws, citizens must stand up and try to get them changed. Slavery was legal and considered a right, but Christian abolitionists campaigned to change the laws. Christians must remember we are *in* the world but not *of* the world. We live among unbelievers, but we must not conform to the world, but be transformed by the renewing of our minds (Romans 12:2).

It's also important to note that being "pro-choice" is not a neutral stance. If a woman was pregnant and everyone did nothing, a baby would be born in nine months, unless there is a medical complication. Abortion is an initiation of force. Being "pro-choice" isn't necessarily saying you approve of the mother's "choice" or her reasoning, but you are telling the government they have no right to protect that child from violence. It's not a passive position. Imagine if there was a group of Asians being attacked every day, and nothing could be done about it because everyone else in the country decided it was a "fundamental right." The authorities won't get involved because the attackers can't be prosecuted. Now, imagine if lobbies formed to make everyone fund the attackers—even people who found it immoral—and discouraged any sort of narrative that opposed the beatings.

If you are pro-choice, you are imposing your beliefs and morality. The pro-life position maximizes the liberty of both parties involved. The pro-choice position grants the executioner their axe.

Freedom "of" Religion, not "from" Religion

It has been my experience that when someone quotes "separation of church and state," nine times out of ten, they have no idea what it means and where it originated from. It's brought up in political debates, like abortion, implying Christians have no right to interject their beliefs into policy. Politicians inject their beliefs into politics every day, regardless of their faith.

For example, the 2020 Democrat Party platform embraces the idea that we can no longer have neutral laws that treat everyone equally. They "recognize that race-neutral policies are not sufficient to rectify race-based disparities."[5] This isn't so far-fetched once you remember they embrace critical race theory. Some defenders claim critical race theory is a legal theory only taught in college, while knowing people like the Superintendent of Detroit Public Schools, Dr. Nikolai Vitti, openly admitted it was incorporated in nearly all their subjects. Also, in *Critical Race Theory: An Introduction*, Richard Delgado and Jean Stefancic make it known that "Unlike traditional civil rights discourse, which stresses incrementalism and step-by-step process, critical race theory questions the very foundations of the liberal order, including equality theory, legal reasoning,

Enlightenment rationalism, and neutral principles of constitutional law."[6]

They don't believe we can live in a post-racial world because we're too damaged, and white oppressors benefit from the system and don't truly want to fix it. The same book also says, "Unlike some academic disciplines, critical race theory contains an activist dimension."

So, the next time someone tells you that your Christian faith shouldn't shape your values and has no place in the government, remember the sort of philosophies they ascribe to and how they want to change the world.

But where did the "separation of church and state" come from? Many Americans believe this is a line within the Constitution, but that's not the case. It originated from Thomas Jefferson.

The Danbury Baptist Association penned a letter to Jefferson. They were concerned with the Constitution because it wasn't clear enough. They feared since the Constitution mentioned the freedom of religion, that it was the document and lawmakers themselves who granted it. And if men could grant it, they could take it away.

> Our sentiments are uniformly on the side of religious liberty—that religion is at all times and places a matter between God and individuals—that no man ought to suffer in name, person, or effects on account of his religious opinions—that the legitimate power of civil

government extends no further than to punish the man who works ill to his neighbors; But, sir, our constitution of government is not specific. Our ancient charter together with the law made coincident therewith, were adopted as the basis of our government, at the time of our revolution; and such had been our laws and usages, and such still are; that religion is considered as the first object of legislation; and therefore what religious privileges we enjoy (as a minor part of the state) we enjoy as favors granted, and not as unalienable rights; and these favors we receive at the expense of such degrading acknowledgements as are inconsistent with the rights of freemen. It is not to be wondered at therefore; if those who seek after power and gain under the pretense of government and religion should reproach their fellow men—should reproach their order magistrate, as a enemy of religion, law, and good order, because he will not, dare not, assume the prerogatives of Jehovah and make laws to govern the kingdom of Christ.[7]

When Jefferson replied, he alleviated their fears:

Believing with you that religion is a matter which lies solely between Man & his God, that he owes account to none other for his faith or his worship, that the legitimate powers of government reach actions only, & not opinions, I contemplate with sovereign reverence that act of the whole American people which declared that their legislature should "make no law respecting an establishment of religion, or prohibiting the free exercise thereof," thus building a wall of separation between Church & State. Adhering to this expression of the supreme will of the nation in behalf of the rights of conscience, I shall see with sincere satisfaction the progress of those sentiments which tend to restore to man all his natural rights, convinced he has no natural right in opposition to his social duties. [8]

The Danbury Baptists were especially concerned because in England, the Anglican denomination was favored, and others were discriminated against by the government. Even colonies and early states favored certain denominations, and Baptists were a minority. Jefferson made it known the federal government could not make anyone Catholic, atheist, Anglican, Lutheran, Quaker, etc.

The more the government gets involved with religion, the more the church is absorbed into the government and becomes an arm of the state. That's one reason why churches are tax-exempt. Chief Justice John Marshall famously said, "The power to tax is the power to destroy." In 1970, in *Walz v. Tax Commission of the City of New York*, the Supreme Court upheld in a 7-1 decision that tax exemptions created a "minimal and remote involvement between church and state and far less than taxation of churches." If the government began taxing churches, do you not think they'd favor mega-churches that rake in bigger bank than tiny storefronts, especially if those storefronts were preaching the unfiltered gospel and mega-churches watered down their sermons to maintain membership and government perks? Perhaps tax breaks for community outreach if they're good boys and girls? Many small churches wouldn't even take in enough money to survive.

American Christians don't want to take the risk of ending up like China, which has state-sponsored churches that meet their standards. The churches that preach the entirety of the Bible have become the underground church, and Christians risk their lives to spread the gospel.

When Secretary of Transportation Pete Buttigieg (D) was on the 2020 presidential campaign trail, he invoked religion to push his ideals, though out of context. He even alleged Democrats don't mention religion as much out of respect for all faiths, but that's not accurate either. Did Senator Bernie Sanders (VT-D) snap at Russell Vought at his confirmation out of respect? Did Senator Cory Booker (NJ-D) grill multiple candidates in confirmation hearings on their opinions of gay sex out of respect? Did New York Governor Kathy Hochul (D) show respect for religious people when she attended a mega-church and called them the "smart ones" for being vaccinated and said others "aren't listening to what God wants?" Hochul asked them to be her apostles and said getting vaccinated was an act of love.[9] Mind you, this happened at a time when Hochul was fighting against religious exemptions for the COVID-19 vaccine.

If Christians don't stand up for their liberty to freely exercise their religion, either a perverted version of Christianity will prevail to empower government, or it will be snuffed out in the interest of tyranny. We live in a world where people have different beliefs, so we aren't always going to agree. We're going to bump heads and make each other uncomfortable at times. We'll need to have vigorous debates amongst ourselves, which isn't a bad thing. Barring people of faith from participating in civil society would be discrimination in favor of secular beliefs.

Law of the Land

You may live in a state with very radical abortion policies, like California, New York, Vermont, Maine, Illinois, Rhode Island, Michigan, etc. Many believers are tempted to or have thrown their hands up and said, "Well, that's it! That's the law!" There are also many Americans repeating lines about *Roe v. Wade*'s repeal, "Oh, this was a right for so long! How could they take it away?" They think it's so mean that the Supreme Court doesn't blanketly protect killing the unborn nationwide.

The United States of America has repealed heinous laws that people felt very passionately about. Slavery easily comes to mind. If Frederick Douglass could still be optimistic after the *Dred Scott v. Sanford* decision, how can Christians roll over and accept defeat? He said, "Such a decision cannot stand. God will be true though every man be a liar. We can appeal from this hell black judgment of the Supreme Court, to the court of common sense and common humanity. We can appeal from man to God. If there is no justice on earth, there is yet justice in heaven. You may close your Supreme Court against the black man's cry for justice, but you cannot, thank God, close against him the ear of a sympathising world, nor shut up the Court of Heaven."

Douglass believed, "Slavery lives in this country not because of any paper Constitution, but in the moral blindness of the American people, who persuade themselves that they are safe, though the rights of others may be struck down."[10] The abolition movement was resilient, and Douglass determined if he could open up the eyes of Americans to the horrors of slavery, they would demand we live up to the promises made in the Declaration of Independence, for all people. But it certainly wasn't an easy task. Douglass even had to call out Southern churches that were in support of denying human beings their rights. And though it seemed impossible to change so many hardened hearts and stir the apathetic Northerners, the abolition movement was successful.

If we don't wake up and be the change, that change will never happen. But it *can* happen. We have to be courageous enough to fight for it.

As of now, many will say abortion is the law of the land. After Prop 3's passing in Michigan, abortion is a "fundamental right." That's true, but the abortion lobby fought to make it so. It's not unreasonable for the pro-life movement to fight to undo it.

If you're being told to "obey the law of the land" to dissuade you from trying to abolish abortion, you should know that our government exists because it operates with "the consent of the governed," to secure our rights. So, the question is, what are you consenting to?

"Obeying the law of the land" has been used as a political football. During the pandemic, the passage was used widely on the political left as a critique against Christians who were told not to worship in person. Not too long before that, Jeff Sessions, who was the Attorney General under President Trump, cited Romans 13 to condemn illegal immigration.

Christians should be making an impact on the world and proactively changing it for the better, but God is also a God of order. Even if we feel strongly about the evils going on in the nation, we don't have to be unruly and instigate violence like Antifa or Roe's Revenge, who attacked pregnancy crisis centers after the *Dobbs v. Jackson* decision was made known to the public. We can be peaceful and proactive. You can change the system without creating chaos. Having structure is a good thing.

God wants and expects us to care for our leaders. We're supposed to pray "for kings and all who are in high positions, that we may lead a peaceful and quiet life, godly and dignified in every way," (1 Timothy 2:2, ESV). We're not supposed to mentally check out and allow the world to devolve into a dystopian or apocalyptic nightmare. Pray good people are elected into high positions of authority, work for good people to get into good positions, and even if someone you dislike gets in, pray God deals with their heart and that you find favor.

Government is also supposed to be a good thing, but they aren't always. Romans 13 instructs believers to be good subjects to governing authorities, pay taxes, etc., but it also says, "For rulers are not a terror to good conduct, but to bad." A good government is not supposed to terrorize its people or be active agents of evil.

God does not call Christians to give mindless obedience to the state. In Acts chapter 5, when the apostles were arrested, an angel of the Lord opened the prison doors and told them to preach in the temple. When the high priest reminded the apostles they were not allowed to teach, Peter answered, "We must obey God rather than man," (Acts 5:29). Their lives were spared, but they were beaten and counted it an honor to suffer for the gospel.

If you are lucky to live in some sort of democracy or republic where you can be represented, be grateful and use your power as a citizen. At the very least, you can vote for legislators who will secure God-given rights. Christians in free nations like the United States of America are blessed to be able to petition and vote for positive change. It's well within our rights to do so.

Chapter Seven

The "Exceptions"

Abortions in the Case of Rape

Rape is a horrific tragedy that no one should have to experience. Any victim of rape deserves the support of their community and should be met with love and dignity. They deserve swift justice, and every rapist should be prosecuted to the fullest extent of the law.

In the Old Testament, rape was punishable by death (Deuteronomy 22:23-27). The crime is even equated to a man attacking and murdering a neighbor. It is nothing God takes lightly. (It is important to note the following verses, 28-29, do not deal with rape. Some English translations, such as the NIV, mistakenly use that word. Analyzing the Hebrew translation and context of the previous verses implies it's a consensual encounter, leading to a "shotgun wedding" scenario. Sandra Richter, Ph.D., who specializes in the Hebrew language and Deuteronomistic history, sits on the NIV committee and is "confident" the translation is wrong. Richter publicly stated her plans to convince the committee to change it. [1] Dr. Paul Copan also addresses this in his book, *Is God a Moral Monster?*)

Too often, rape is used as a "gotcha" argument by the pro-choice side, and pro-life activists jump through hoops to avoid the conversation. Many plainly say they do not wish to argue such fringe cases because rape accounts for less than one percent of abortions. That may be true, and I find many pro-choice activists insincerely bring up rape to guilt pro-life people out of their positions. After all, most of them still support abortion outside of rape.

But it still deserves to be addressed.

If you are pro-life and make remarks blaming the victim for not reporting or going to the hospital, minimizing their experience, or even questioning if it was "real rape," you are doing a disservice to the victim and their unborn baby. Women *need* to know the pro-life community cares for them and not simply the fetus. Lives are literally dependent upon your compassion.

Rape is an exception a majority of Americans agree with, including many Republicans. It was the position of President Donald J. Trump, George W. Bush, and President Ronald Reagan. Trump even blamed much of the

Republicans' underperformance in the 2022 midterms on pro-life candidates who believed in "no exceptions, even in the case of rape, incest, or life of the mother," on his Truth Social website. The truth is, that many candidates Trump endorsed, and even handpicked, had very hard-right stances on abortion.

I understand why people want an exception for rape. In this instance, the mother was not responsible for how the child came to be in her womb. This stance makes sense if you hold bodily autonomy in equal regard to the right to life. However, if your position is, "An innocent child has a right to be protected from being killed," the rape exception undercuts the right to life.

Pro-Life advocates, particularly within the Republican Party, will not be able to hide behind their exception forever. It is becoming more mainstream for pro-choice activists to point out the inconsistencies of that position. If it's wrong to kill babies, why is it permissible to kill this particular kind of baby? Steven Kenneth Bonnell II, known online as Twitch streamer "Destiny," challenged Jedediah Bila about this on her podcast.[2]

If you make an exception for rape because the mother didn't willingly engage in the act of procreation, you're making the case women should be held accountable—or even punished—for their sexual activity, rather than being rooted in the protection of human rights.

Bila admitted to struggling with this issue, and many pro-life advocates do. They sympathize with the victim and don't wish to place a larger burden on them. But we need to truly ask ourselves if abortion is the best way to alleviate that burden for the mother and child, why we are so conditioned to jump to this "solution," and if it does more harm than good.

When someone asks for an exception for rape, they are asking for you to discriminate against a certain group of people. Do women like Kathy Barnette deserve a right to life? Barnette's mother, who had her daughter at the age of 12, said, "It wasn't a choice, it was a life."[3] While Barnette was on the 2022 primary campaign trail in Pennsylvania for Senate, she said her family clawed their way out of poverty. Barnette didn't live an easy life, but she's blessed today with a family of her own. We need to have compassion for the women who endured the violent act, but we cannot and should not ignore the humanity of the person who would be violently killed.

When talking about the subject of rape, both sides of the aisle need to be mindful of the fact people are walking around today who are products of rape. The mother of Valerie Gatto (who won Miss Pennsylvania 2014) was raped at knifepoint. Her rapist was going to kill her, but a bright light from an unknown source scared him off. She often calls Valerie her light. Though she never considered abortion; she was going to give Valerie up for adoption until her grandmother encouraged her to keep the baby. "We are always given the grace to sustain us."

Gatto was inspired by her mother and grandparents and lived her life giving back, whether it was giving gifts to sick children in hospitals, clothing drives, or writing letters to soldiers. She also uses her platform to help sexual assault survivors and prevent more from being created. Gatto told the press during the Miss USA campaign, "I believe God put me here for a reason: to inspire people, encourage them, to give them hope that everything is possible, and you can't let your circumstances define your life."[4]

Eartha Kitt was a famous actress and singer. You may have heard her rendition of "Santa Baby" or seen her in Adam West's *Batman* series. Younger generations may know her from her brief role in *Harriet the Spy*, Yzma from *The Emperor's New Groove*, and *Holes*. Kitt is believed to be conceived in rape, born on a cotton plantation in 1927.

When addressing the nation about abortion rights after *Roe v Wade* was overturned, President Biden didn't acknowledge the unborn until he referred to them angrily as the "rapist's child."[5] This was horrific. I've heard young women, who were sexually abused and impregnated, heartbroken and enraged at such derogatory language. Pro-choice activists talk about the stigma of having to live with a "rapist's baby" or being a "rapist's child," not realizing they are pushing that cruel stigma.

The "woman with the issue of blood" was known only as a woman with a problem, until she met Jesus. He addressed her as "Daughter," and by her faith, she was made whole (Mark 5:25-34). If you feel all unborn children should be equally discriminated against and have no right to life, there is no need to bring up any exceptions at all. But anyone conceived in rape is just as human as everyone else. They are created in God's image, loved by him, and deserve to be protected from violence.

I've heard abortion advocates argue children conceived in rape will experience abuse and neglect. They say these children will walk around with the pain of what their father did. I've even heard adults conceived of rape share their struggles and explain how their mothers couldn't connect emotionally or abused them. You don't lose your right to be protected from violence because you do or don't suffer. And children who are consensually conceived—even by couples with deep affection for each other—may end up abused. We can't kill people based on how they *might* suffer. Though children conceived in rape carry the weight of their father's crime, that doesn't mean they won't experience love and find a fulfilled life.

Let's say a mother decides to keep her child conceived in rape, which is a choice women decide to make all of the time. But when the child turns two years old, they begin to resemble their father. The pain of that traumatic experience begins to creep in or even flood back. Would the mother be justified in taking the life of her child? This is a question the Equal Rights Institute often poses in lectures and conversations across the country. The answer is usually, "No," or, "That's different! They're human." Well, that same child has always been human, and they were alive at the moment of conception. If emotional trauma isn't a good enough reason to kill a two-year-old, how can it be reason enough to kill them five minutes, three months, or thirty weeks before they're born?

We do need to also consider the mother, and how we can best serve her. As Josh Brahm, President of the Equal Life Institute says, "If you're going to use violence, you had best make certain there are no other options on the table."

When I am asked about exceptions for rape, I ask 5 questions:

- Do you believe abortion will undo the rape?
- Do you believe abortion will bring healing to the trauma?
- Do you believe a child should be punished for the crimes the father committed?
- Do you believe a rapist deserves more rights and dignity afforded to them than an unborn human baby?
- Is adoption an option?

Will Abortion Undo the Rape?

Again, rape should never happen. No person should have to suffer through such a heinous action. But we live in a fallen world where people choose to do evil against one another. I've had women tell me they've had abortions because they thought it would be a blank slate, only to find they had to carry that loss with them for the rest of their lives. Abortion is not a cure for rape. Renowned abortionist, Dr. Warren Hern, who wrote the textbook *Abortion Practice*, recognized this. "Victims of sexual abuse and rape deserve special care. However, the abortion counselor should recognize that the emotional trauma experienced by the rape or incest victim cannot be treated adequately, if at all, in the abortion clinic setting. All rape and incest victims, as well as victims of physical abuse, should be referred for appropriate psychological counseling and support."[6]

If you do not allow abortion in the case of rape, pro-choice activists will claim you are "forcing" a woman to carry their pregnancy to term. The only act of force was committed by the violent aggressor. Though it's understandable for conversations around sexual assault to be highly impassioned, it's disingenuous to accuse a pro-life activist of force, when their goal is to prevent another victim from being harmed. Abortion is a second act of force and violence. Regardless of how a child is conceived, birth is inevitable. The child will either pass through the mother alive or dead. If laws against murder are "force," then we're all being oppressed by the government for not being allowed to kill one another.

Even if a woman terminates her child, that rape and the abortion will stay with her for the rest of her life.

When we face a tragedy or a trauma, the unfortunate truth is, we don't always have an easy answer. Abortion is not an easy answer, and neither is carrying a child after being abused in such a horrific way. When we watch our loved ones suffer, we feel helpless and as if we have failed. We'd do anything to make it right. That's why you see so many parents dead set on defending abortion if their child was raped. But the child killed would be their grandchild. Snuffing out their life won't erase their existence, nor will it erase the trauma of the victim. It's always going to be something that happened. Maybe you can't help them get over their trauma, but you can help your loved ones get *through* it.

We should build a community of support around mothers and let them know they are strong and capable, even when they don't believe they are. I've heard so many stories from women who opted to keep their baby, just because someone encouraged them and said, "You can make it."

Women do not need to be treated as perpetual victims of circumstance for the rest of their lives. They are beautiful, courageous, and more than overcomers.

Will Abortion Heal the Trauma of Rape?

No. An abortion will not heal the trauma of rape. Pro-choice activists may argue a woman will at least be healed from the trauma of her pregnancy, but licensed mental health counselor Robin Atkins, says it's wrong to assume a woman's pregnancy is inherently traumatic. Some women even see their pregnancy as a way of taking back their agency and power by offering sanctuary to their children. While Atkins notes pregnancy itself can be traumatic, trauma from rape and trauma from pregnancy are addressed differently. The techniques used to help women in either circumstance are not the same.

Atkins specializes in helping women through reproductive trauma, and she experienced rape, has had an abortion, and a traumatic pregnancy (to the point of being near suicidal). Medical practitioners should address the individual needs of their patients and enact treatment suited for them. If pro-choice activists are going to resort to violence as a cure, it had better be the best solution. "If we're going to be compassionate, we need to be compassionate for all parties involved."[7]

Rebekah Berg knew all too well aborting her twins would not bring healing for her rape, even though it was the option immediately offered to her by medical staff at John Hopkins in Baltimore. Berg worked at the hospital herself, and a friend offered a "free, hush-hush, and legal abortion to end her pregnancy." Berg, unfortunately, had experience with abortion, back when she was "young and dumb." The first was a D&C (dilation and curettage surgery) at nine weeks. About a year later, she had a partial-birth abortion at 18 weeks. "It has been 18 years—and no one can tell me different—that I heard my baby scream." Berg said, "How could I heal that violence of rape with more violence?"

Berg decided to keep her baby and was helped at the local level by churches and religious associations with furniture, food, cars, etc. She lived at a woman's shelter for two years, and an abortion recovery program in Alabama helped Berg recover from post-abortion stress syndrome. On a state level, her children's medical bills were taken care of as well. Berg urges women to seek out resources because they are available.

Most importantly, Berg says her twins are "the best things that ever happened to me. I would have died over, and over, and over again if they weren't there for my reason to live." Berg and her children resent offensive rhetoric that dehumanizes, devalues, and gives the impression her children didn't deserve the right to exist. "But they do! I didn't save them. They saved me. Who here had the choice of their conception? They turned my night of horror into a blessing, and they are the less than one percent who have been demonized and exploited." [8]

Kathleen DeZeeuw knows what it's like to raise a child conceived in rape and feels "personally assaulted and insulted every time" she hears that abortion should be legal because of rape and incest. She and other rape victims feel as though they're being used as pawns to advance the pro-abortion agenda while never asking to hear their side of the story. [9]

A group of women who've been pregnant through sexual assault signed an open letter and petitioned Congress and state legislators to hear their stories, after Senator Barbara Boxer (D-CA), wanted to authorize federal funding for military personnel impregnated from sexual assault.

> Every year, legislators, judges, and other policymakers discuss the problems of women who have become pregnant as a result of sexual assault. These discussions take place without ever first soliciting our input. In most cases, it is only in the context of highly divisive debates over abortion that we are discussed. In virtually every case, those people who claim to be defending our interests have never taken the time to actually listen to us to learn about our true circumstances, needs, and concerns.
>
> We are deeply offended and dismayed each time our difficult circumstances are exploited for public consumption to promote the political agenda of others. This is a grave injustice. In pursuing their political agendas, these exploiters have reduced our concerns, needs, and circumstances to a crude caricature.

The 38 signatories go on to say:

Our experiences are varied. Many of us carried our pregnancies to term. Some of us raised or are raising our children, while others placed our children in adoptive homes. Others of us had abortions. In many cases, we felt pressured to abort by family members, social workers, and doctors who insisted that abortion was the "best" solution. For many, the abortion caused physical and emotional trauma equal to or exceeding the trauma of the sexual assault that our abortions were supposed to "cure."[10]

Robin Atkins notes there isn't a lot of data on rape victims and pregnancies, but there is data to suggest pregnancy from sexual assault isn't inherently traumatic, and we need to "separate the two."

Dr. Sandra Mahkorn published a report in 1979, studying 37 pregnant victims. Dr. Mahkorn found that between 75 and 85 percent of pregnant rape victims chose to keep their babies. Granted, the sample size is small (and the study is old), but their stories shed light on a real issue in society: our feelings toward victims and their children. Women noted situations that made it most difficult to continue their pregnancies were attitudes and opinions of loved ones, whether they would be believed or blamed, and their level of culpability.

[This study indicates] that pregnancy need not impede the victim's resolution of the trauma; rather, with loving support, nonjudgemental attitudes, and empathic communication, healthy emotional and psychological responses are possible despite the added burden or pregnancy.[11]

Atkins says, "If we tell people abortion is treatment for pregnancy from rape, then we're telling people who don't have abortions after pregnancy from rape they're not healed? Their treatment was somehow invalid? No. And abortion isn't a mental health treatment."

Though abortion can bring relief, it comes and goes in waves, just like grief and shame. Women deserve better than being made to feel it's necessary to remove a child as if she were erasing a stain. Women deserve more, and their children deserve more.

Should a Child Pay for the Crimes of Their Father?

To be abused in such a horrific way is unacceptable, but why is it socially acceptable to pass on more abuse to another victim? Abortion is a continuation of violence. We know the Bible says in Deuteronomy 24, that children should not be put to death for the sins of their fathers.

A woman may not think of it that personally, but abortion is personal. It's admittedly complicated. A woman has bodily autonomy, but it has been violated. If she tries to reclaim it through abortion, it will cost a human being their life. Does the child deserve the death penalty? Perhaps it's not a matter of "deserve." The mother doesn't deserve to be placed in this brutal predicament. They are both innocent, and their rights are colliding because of the aggression of a terrible man. It still does not change reality or the gravity of her choice. If a woman chooses an abortion, her son or daughter will be killed.

Some pro-choice activists will reject the notion of a baby being "killed," especially if you take the abortion pill and simply "deny them your resources." Imagine for a moment you were kidnapped and placed in a cold and dark dungeon with a newborn baby. Your captor assures you will be released in nine months, as long as you care for the newborn. But he gives a second option. He'll immediately allow you to go if you leave the newborn on the floor, to cry alone and starve to death.

Which option would you take? Because the only difference between a newborn and the unborn is a few inches of skin. And the difference between that newborn and a fetus, who would be normally killed by an abortion pill, is 30 weeks.

Sometimes, there are no ideal options, but we have the opportunity to make moral choices. Sometimes, they supersede what we believe we're able to handle. There's a famous gospel song from Kirk Franklin, "More Than I Can Bear," about how God won't put more on you than you can handle. However, this scripture is misquoted.

> No temptation has overtaken you that is not common to man. God is faithful, and he will not let you be tempted beyond your ability, but with the temptation he will also provide the way of escape, that you may be able to endure it. (1 Corinthians 10:13)

Paul is referencing the children of Israel and the many challenges they faced in the wilderness, and how they chose idolatry, tested God, committed sexual immorality, and grumbled. We all may be tempted to choose sin, but we are always capable of choosing a righteous path. And God will provide a way to escape and endure that temptation without sinning against God.

When it comes to trials we face in life, God wants us to lean on *him*. Jesus referred to the Holy Spirit as "the Comforter." God wants to save us, to help us. "The LORD is near to the brokenhearted and saves the crushed in spirit," (Psalms 34:18, ESV). I do not believe a woman should have to handle the burden of her sexual assault on her own. God does not want her to. And God wants Christians to be encouraging, compassionate, and useful to women who are hurting beyond belief. God calls Christians to bear each other's burdens. If

Christians want abortion to truly be unthinkable, they have to be a part of the solution.

> "Brothers, if anyone is caught in any transgression, you who are spiritual should restore him in a spirit of gentleness. Keep watch on yourself, lest you too be tempted. [2] Bear one another's burdens, and so fulfill the law of Christ." (Galatians 6:1-2, ESV)

Does a Rapist Deserve More Rights and Dignity than the Unborn Child?

In a just world, after a rapist commits such an egregious act, he would be caught by law enforcement and charged. He would be tried by a jury of his peers, have legal representation, and be sentenced. After the rapist has due process, his rights can be removed from him.

In the United States of America, considered to be the freest country in the world, an unborn child can be killed simply because the mother does not wish to carry them to term. Some states have outright bans, some make exceptions for rape, but some allow abortions for up to nine months.

As an Illinois state senator, Barrack Obama opposed legislation that would give care to children who survive abortion. When Obama spoke against Senate Bill 1663 in 2002, he thought the bill was unnecessary. Obama had "confidence" the abortion doctor would look after the child (which is foolish if you consider abortionists like Kermit Gosnell), but he also complained the bill was "really designed to burden the original decision of the woman and the physician to induce labor and perform an abortion."[12]

Why do we allow an abuser of women to have more moral consideration and justice than a child who has committed no crime? They merely exist, due to no fault of their own. Even if abortion had to be treated as a necessary evil, wouldn't it be better if abortion was permissible because it was *proven* to be a necessity, rather than granted access for any reason? The unborn deserve justice and protection.

Journalist Sally Kohn on *CNN Crossfire* once accused Live Action founder Lila Rose of "saying, in effect, the rapist should have more rights than the woman to decide what happens in that womb."[13] This, of course, is blatantly offensive and false. A rapist has no right, whatsoever, to violate a woman. If he had a right, he wouldn't be arrested, tried, and placed in prison. You don't have a right to violently aggress upon another person. Period. Pro-choice activists will throw accusations at women like Lila Rose, claiming they are supporting rapists by pointing out that no one has a right to kill anyone. Protecting a child from harm doesn't mean you're protecting an abuser.

And the reality is if you believe the unborn have no right to life in the case of rape, but you believe a rapist should have a process to be tried and convicted, **you do believe he** *deserves more rights than a fetus.* Many pro-choice individuals don't believe a rapist should get the death penalty, yet they believe the unborn should automatically qualify.

Adoption

I have spoken with many women who have kept their children conceived from rape, have expressed tremendous love *for* them, and experienced abundant love *through* them. But I have also talked to women who have concluded they could not bear to raise that child. They, heroically, carried their children to term and put them up for adoption.

States have safe harbor laws. You can leave babies at the hospital or take them to fire and police stations. Someone will find them love and care. There are waiting lists for parents who want to adopt. There is no shortage of love. But you can also set up an adoption plan before their birth. You can have little or no contact. One survivor told me her daughter's adoptive parents raised her to be a talented gymnast. I congratulated her, and she wouldn't take credit. But the brave mother was satisfied she made the right decision.

It can be tremendously difficult to live with the curiosity and pain of knowing your child is somewhere out in the world without you, and adopted children can also experience growing pains and trauma from being separated from their birth mother, along with a whole list of questions. But your child still deserves a chance at life.

If you attend an event like the March for Life, you will see many adults and young people who are pro-life because they were adopted. They are grateful for their lives and believe other children like them deserve the same.

Too often, abortion is pushed as an option. Some women who go into clinics like Planned Parenthood claim they were never given adoption referrals. Adoption is even attacked today. Pictures of pro-life activists holding signs with statements like: "We will adopt your baby" are viciously ridiculed. Actor Mark Hamill, who has voiced Joker for years in Batman cartoons, compared pro-life couples to the clown prince and his girlfriend, Harley Quinn.[14] Of course, Joker is the main villain of Batman, who was orphaned after his parents were murdered. In Tim Burton's *Batman* (1989), Joker was the man who pulled the trigger. Bruce Wayne also took care of his Robins. Dick Grayson became his legal ward, and he formally adopted Tim Drake. Mark Hamill also played one of the most famous adoptees in the galaxy: Luke Skywalker. Hamill is "pro-choice," yet allegedly pressured his son's baby mama to abort her child. Maegan Chen told *The New York Post*, "Mark Hamill told me that I shouldn't bring a child into the world that nobody wants."[15] Chen's abortion pills failed, and she kept baby Autumn, even though Mark and his son, Nathan, allegedly continued to pressure her.

During oral arguments for *Dobbs v. Jackson Women's Health Organization,* Justice Amy Coney Barrett suggested safe haven laws and adoption addresses the "burdens of parenthood," that are emphasized in *Roe* and *Casey.* Justice Barrett has adopted two children herself. Immediately, *The New York Times* published a piece countering her argument, "I Was Adopted. I Know the Trauma It Can Inflict." The author, Elizabeth Spiers, is a democratic digital strategist and a successful adoptee with two pro-life religious mothers (adopted and birth), who lamented her struggles and the pain of her birth mother's separation. Honestly, it was a very strange article, unless Spiers' point is she regrets being alive. That doesn't appear to be the case, since Spiers said she had a "wonderful childhood," and her birth mother made the right decision.[16] Then *The Washington Post* wrote an article, citing the challenges of adoptees who end up adopted by different races. "I know my parents love me, but they don't love my people."[17] Leonydus Johnson is a political commentator who has had to go through "transracial adoption training," since he and his wife are doing an international adoption. Johnson, who is an adoptee himself, rejects "transracial adoption" and believes it is "contrived nonsense." He says the class is full of "woke, CRT [critical race theory] garbage," and is about creating victims. "But you are sorely mistaken if you think we're going to treat them differently or encourage an identity of victimhood because of where they came from, which is what people like this are telling us to do."[18]

Many pro-choice activists note that adoption is not a solution to abortion, and I agree. We need to address why women want an abortion and meet each woman at an individual level. If we can assure a woman that she will receive care and support, the list of impossibilities may dwindle to nothing. If women are encouraged and empowered instead of infantilized and stigmatized, they may choose to keep their child or at least endure nine months of pregnancy. Adoption is merely an option, not the solution.

But abortion is certainly not a solution to rape.

Medical Complications

Illness of the Child

Joel Kurtinitis, who owes his life to a pro-life billboard that convinced his mother to keep him, said as soon as his son received a death sentence, he was "unpersoned" by medical staff and offered an abortion several times. Like many parents in his position, Kurtinitis saw his son treated as a burden, the effects of a post-*Roe* world that pushes eugenics as a virtue.

"We heard stories of parents having to fight for critical tests, NICU procedures, and even basic comfort care for little ones who weren't expected to live long. We were told that many Trisomy babies die of malnutrition because they cannot yet nurse, and hospital staff don't want to bother with a feeding tube."[19]

Kurtinitis said he could point out the doctors can be wrong (which is true), or the baby could survive. "But that would undercut the universal moral principle at stake here: our son deserves the best care we can give, *even if he is going to die.*"

Everyone is going to die. It's all a matter of time. Some of our lives are long like my great-grandmother and grandmother from my mother's side—who both made it beyond a century—or my siblings who miscarried in my mother's womb. Our existence doesn't begin when we are held in our mother's arms. Our lives begin in the womb, and that is when our relationships with our children begin as well.

Before my sister had confirmation that she was pregnant with her first child, Angelina discerned she was pregnant. She felt something was wrong and asked the Lord to protect her baby. Not too long afterward, she took a pregnancy test and shared the news of Daniel's life with us. I recall the rush of love that flooded my heart when I first saw his sonogram. I couldn't imagine how deep my sister's connection must have been if staring at Daniel's picture could move me to tears.

We would feel him kick and speak to my sister's belly as if he could understand our hopes and dreams for him. We certainly prayed and sang over him. When I finally got to hold Daniel in my arms, I sang Phil Wickham's song, "Beautiful." I still remember his newborn scent and how pink and gangly he was. Now, he's seven; he's learning how to play basketball and loves tinkering on the instruments after church.

Two daughters later, Angelina became pregnant with another boy. Far into her pregnancy, she was very late for a Sunday afternoon service. We learned Angelina couldn't feel the baby moving, and the family was hit with a tornado of complex emotions. I was worried—devastated at the possibility—yet I did my best to fight off doubt with faith. My brother, the pastor, had to keep himself composed to continue with the service. Angelina came in, and she looked so miserable. We prayed for her as a church before she went to the hospital, and hoped for good news.

When people insist life or human value doesn't begin until after we exit the womb, I share my family's collective pain in those hours and ask if they think we would have been irrational to mourn Angelina's baby if he didn't survive. They always say of course not, because human beings absolutely know our offspring hold value before passing through the birth canal.

The baby still had a heartbeat, but Angelina had to make more visits to the doctor to monitor him. She already had much anxiety over her scheduled C-section, so this was an added pressure. But Noah arrived on schedule and was welcomed into a world that already had much love for him.

Parents experience the highs and lows of pregnancy, and they weather those storms not merely out of a matter of biological reality, but because of love and parental obligation. What Joel Kurtinitis understood was he became a parent the moment his son was conceived, *"and the only choice left to us now is what kind of parents we will be."*

When you have an ill child, are you having a conversation about abortion or euthanasia? Maybe the doctors are wrong. Dr. Christina Francis is an OB-GYN who has cared for countless mothers, and her experience makes it evident doctors are only *practicing* medicine. "I can say that we never have absolute certainty about the outcomes of these diagnoses. All we have are statistics."[20]

One of her patients received a grim diagnosis at 12 weeks: cystic hygroma, which is an indication of Down Syndrome and/or a congenital heart defect. A few weeks later, the diagnosis became hydrops fetalis, meaning there was too much fluid in her cavities and likely heart failure. The baby's chance of living to birth wasn't even 5 percent, and there was no chance of surviving afterward. Even though a high-risk specialist suggested termination, the mother decided to carry her child and give her "every possible chance at life."

Then at week 24, the hydrops was miraculously gone.

When Dr. Francis worked for three years in Kenya, women faced dire diagnoses more commonly but had fewer abortions. The atmosphere was different than in the US. Instead of doom and gloom scenarios and statistics, the community rallied around the woman to help carry her grief. The mothers and children are both treated with humanity, and health care is centered around the best options for both patients. There is prenatal hospice and palliative care in the United States, but these options are relatively unknown.

Studies have found about 9 percent of adverse fetal diagnoses on ultrasounds are incorrect, and women make decisions to abort based on these grim predictions. [21] Dr. Francis says, "In some cases, depending on the method, false positives for fetal abnormalities are as high as 50%."

NBC News reported in 2014:

> "But positive results can be wrong 50 percent or more of the time. And an investigation by the New England Center for Investigative Reporting published in *The Boston Globe* found that "likely hundreds" of women are aborting fetuses based on this new generation of testing. One company reported a 6.2 percent abortion rate based on screening results alone—and without further testing, there is no way to know how many of those may have been due to a false positive." [22]

Beth Daley led the investigation and told *NBC News*, "Companies are charging $1,700 or more for each prenatal test, creating a competitive industry that is projected to be $3.5 billion by 2019."

When my sister had her second child, her doctor asked if she wanted a prenatal test for Down syndrome. She said, "For what? I'm not gonna kill my baby." The doctor was taken aback, but she certainly saved on her medical bill.

Genetic testing is done for five reasons, according to retired genetic councilor Bob Resta: preventing the economic and medical burden of genetic disease through selective abortion, informing parents so they can avoid raising a child with a disability, avoiding suffering for the child, providing reassurance to the parents when the results are normal, and to prepare the parents for medical complications of their children.[23]

As already noted in a previous chapter, 99 percent of children with Down syndrome report being happy. You can't know how happy a family will be based on a child's medical possibility. There are plenty of families who learn to cope with a condition—despite how difficult it is—and truly value their relationships for whatever time they have together.

If you're having genetic testing to determine whether or not you're going to terminate the life of a disabled child, that is eugenics. Whether the intent is to end the suffering of the parent or child, it's premeditated discriminatory violence. Whether we can empathize with the parents making the decision doesn't change the ethical implications.

Potential mothers often hear glib stories of suffering and hardship when it comes to raising children with disabilities, yet support, resources, and civil liberties for children with disabilities have increased steadily over the years. Kristina Artukovic, a mother to a child with Down Syndrome and master's degrees in philosophy and philology, said she and her husband were repeatedly told "almost every parent eventually leaves their child with Down syndrome in an institution," which was not the case.

In contrast, they were not informed of available support. Artukovic wrote an article on Secular Pro-Life's blog, criticizing the eugenic nature of prenatal testing as promoting "disability-selective abortion."[24]

For example, a Chinese biotech firm drew outrage after a video emerged of a spokesperson stating they were "screening out" babies with Down syndrome.[25] The BGI Group representative also revealed the tests were a "cash cow." BGI co-founder Wang Jian also drew alarm when he said it would be a "disgrace" for any of his employees to have a child with a birth defect.[26]

If the medical industry has a financial incentive to profit from discrimination, and young minds like Bronte Remsik are being trained by the medical community to selectively value human life based on a patient's desires rather than the inherent value of human life, shouldn't we be suspicious of pro-choice-minded professionals and how they influence their potential patients? When doctors go on television or social media to promote abortion-on-demand legislation in the interest of protecting their patients' well-being, they are doing a disservice to the general public, who place their trust in them. Medical professionals could, instead, work with legislators to craft protections for patients in potential or life-threatening circumstances. Instead, they use their authority as medical professionals to mask their blanket and naked partisanship on the issue. They simply support abortion, so they fight to protect abortion. That's why you see medical professionals try to blur the lines between what a fetal heartbeat is, and Remsik tried to convince Michael Knowles' million YouTube followers that a nine-week fetus has no value because it looks like exploded tissue after they've been sucked through a tube and placed in a Petri dish.

There's also a very compelling talking point that women only have a late-term abortion because of serious fetal abnormalities, but this isn't true. Women have late-term abortions for all sorts of reasons, and abortion activists often want to protect access for reasons outside of medical issues anyway. But even if a woman does discover a fetal abnormality, that doesn't mean the abnormality was life-threatening, would dramatically shorten the lifespan of the infant, or guarantee the child a poor quality of life. Chloe Savage, a mother of an amputee toddler from the UK, admitted her doctor suggested abortion after discovering a deformity in her baby's leg and foot. Doctors feared her baby had a chromosomal disorder at 22.5 weeks, but later discovered it was Fibular Hemimelia. She was told to abort her child at 23.5 weeks anyway.[27] Savage's doctor constantly mentioned she was a young student and said mothers aborted for less serious issues. Even though Chloe was a single mother, she delivered Ollie. After amputation surgery and receiving a prosthetic, Ollie can walk, climb, and play like most other children. But Savage describes her interaction with her doctor as coercive.

Not only can doctors be wrong, but children can also have miraculous recoveries. A few years ago, my father picked me up from a holiday craft show when a woman from a reservation video-called him. He recently had a great revival in Calgary, Alberta, Canada, a place he visited several times. The people have a vast love for him, and he loves to pour into their lives.

The mother wanted prayer because the doctors didn't expect her baby to live very long. She had a genetic disorder, wasn't taking any liquids, and was despondent. My father told the mother to hold the phone up to the baby, so she could hear his voice as we prayed. The baby found the strength to turn her head toward the phone as we prayed for a miracle. She had an immediate turnaround and left the hospital soon after, to the doctor's surprise. The precious baby is now a toddler and doing well.

Sometimes, doctors are correct, and the reality is children will have to live with abnormalities. That doesn't mean God can't or won't heal your child. One of Reverend A. A. Allen's most famous miracles was of a six-year-old boy who had never walked because he had no bones in his legs. The child had a sunken face, and a tiny head, and Allen marveled in horror as he twisted the boys' limbs for the crowd to see. Doctors who have seen the video footage speculate the child was a victim of fetal alcohol syndrome. The ministers and congregants all joined together in prayer, reaching their hands toward heaven, as Allen cried out to God for the boy's healing and the salvation of his parents. Then, Allen asked them to return to their seats. As the tent joined together in a rendition of "In the Sweet By and By," Allen helped the boy to stand and guided his walking, like an infant making their first steps. By the end of the song, the boy ran into Allen's arms. Reverend Allen swept the boy up, and the tent raised their hands in praise to God. Then, the six-year-old mimicked the crowd and did the same.

But there is still the reality that God doesn't heal everyone. Christian women have been traumatized by being told to pray and believe for the healing of their baby, yet then give birth to an unviable or stillborn child. Families have left the faith and been filled with resentment toward God and believers over fetal death.

It's a reality that infants may die. David's son, who was conceived through his adultery with Bathsheba, did not live. David was told by a prophet that his baby would die, *yet he still prayed*. As a father, what else can you do but love your child until the end? David was so grieved; his servants were afraid to tell him when the child passed. But when David found out, he washed and anointed himself, knowing his life had to continue, and he would see his child again in glory.

Christians must have the balance of the three Hebrew boys who were thrown in the fiery furnace. They were absolutely certain God *would* deliver them. But at the same time, they were content with God *not* delivering them. They knew he could, but even if God didn't, they weren't going to bow to Nebuchadnezzar, not even to save their lives. This is not an easy lesson or perspective for even seasoned Christians to grasp. Christians in such desperate need of a miracle cannot afford to possess such a wild naivety that comes off more like desperate clutching for a miracle, rather than the assuredness of faith. Meshach, Shadrach, and Abednego had confidence in God because they respected his sovereignty and divine judgment over their lives and deaths.

"Now faith is the assurance of things hoped for, the conviction of things not seen," (Hebrews 11:1, ESV). My father affectionately calls Hebrews 11 the "Hall of Fame of Faith." And as the Bible talks about Abel, Enoch, Abraham, Moses, etc., it is evident faith is not a "belief." Faith is trust. And when we pray, we pray for God's will to be done—not ours.

There aren't always happy endings in this life, at least not from a secular perception. Those are reserved for our life in the next. The question is, are you going to offer your child the love and care they deserve until their natural death?

Just because we love to rejoice on Sunday mornings singing, "We're blessed in the city," doesn't mean we are only blessed during the high of our abundance. Through our lack and our pain, God is still faithful. Even through our suffering, God is still worthy of our trust and our worship. It is through these times of pain, that our relationship with God is the most crucial.

One story that taught me that, and deeply touched my heart, was that of Ember. Joe Baker is the founder of Save the Storks, and he shared his story of love, heartbreak, and hope with the world. Joe and his wife, Ann, already had three boys and were ecstatic to find out they were carrying a baby girl. Unfortunately, Ember was diagnosed with anencephaly and wasn't expected to live very long. The family chose life and

225

embarked on the "Ember Tour" across the country, visiting places they wished to take Ember before her passing. The Bakers received many prayers around the world, but also artwork to decorate Ember's delivery room. They wanted it to be the most beautiful space possible.

Ember was born on November 4, 2021. She lived peacefully for one hour and six minutes. The Bakers said, "We loved her well, and it was life-changing for our whole family."

I don't know if there is a pain in this life worse than losing a child, but for whatever amount of time we have with our children, *do we love them well?* We are not only called to love our children as parents in the natural, but we are children of God, called to love them as beings who are also loved by God.

We all met the beautiful Ember Moonlight Baker at 11:05 this morning after 26 hours of very intense labor. She was a dainty little thing weighing only 4 lbs. 14 oz. and was 15.75 inches of pure joy. Ember was prettier than anyone could of ever imagined. And that is likely why Jesus took her home so quick. She lived for a precious 1 hour and 6 minutes out of the womb. When she went to Heaven Ann's words were clear: "you were so worth it." I've never cried so hard. I've never fought so intensely. I've never prayed so deeply. I am no longer the same. My family has forever been changed. The world will not forget our blazing Ember – so tiny, so bright, so powerful.

And the whole world saw a girl who could make heaven a little brighter for us all.[28]

Joe Baker said, "I find hope when I remind myself how long eternity is. I will forever have a daughter. We will forever have four children and will forever be a family of at least six. The best is yet to come."[29]

To know a life so small and so short-lived can still minister to so many people is extraordinary. There is a value to all of our lives, whether you live to be 102 like my grandma, Myra Davis, or if it's only for 1 hour and 6 minutes. Whether our lives are bright flames gradually dimming to the end or they're blazes of beauty that extinguish quickly, it matters that we flickered with God's divine purpose.

Life of the Mother

Almost all pro-life activists agree that exceptions should be made when it comes to the life of the mother. This is not a controversial opinion at all. However, some say, "No exceptions."

How can that be? Don't pro-life activists care about the woman and the child equally? Don't we have the right to preserve our lives? How can anyone disagree with that? "No exception" pro-life activists likely do not disagree with those statements. They simply have a different perspective.

Neonatologists like Kendra Kolb deny that "abortion is sometimes medically necessary to protect the life or the health of the mother."[30] She often consults difficult pregnancies and has had two high-risk pregnancies herself. If she has a pregnant patient who is in a life-and-death situation, the pregnancy must end by delivering the baby. These situations can occur from high blood pressure, heart disease, diabetes, cancer, and other medical conditions. If a baby needs to be delivered before they are viable, a preterm delivery will take place which is not considered an abortion. Kolb notes an emergency C-section can be performed in less than an hour. An abortion after 24 weeks takes days. A baby is considered viable at this time because it is medically possible for them to survive. If a mother's life was in danger, why not give them their best shot at life instead of ending it? Why delay a woman's life-saving treatment in favor of abortion?

In a triage situation, medical professionals may have to *prioritize* one life over another. That is not the same as *intending* to harm one life to save another.

Other OB/GYNs such as Omar L. Hamada, MD, MBA have echoed beliefs like Dr. Kolb. "There's not a single fetal or maternal condition that requires third-trimester abortion. Not one. Delivery, yes. Abortion, no."[31]

But is this true?

American College of Obstetricians and Gynecologists believes "induced abortion is an essential component of women's health care," but they share this belief generally. When it comes to the mother's literal health, "Pregnancy complications, including placental abruption, bleeding from placenta previa, preeclampsia or eclampsia, and cardiac or renal conditions, may be so severe that abortion is the only measure to preserve a woman's health or save her life."[32]

Let's just say, there's a difference in professional opinion. While I can understand why some pro-life activists push no exceptions, it's best to concede the argument. If a woman is in a life-or-death situation, doctors do not need to feel like their hands are tied. Besides, the ethics are completely different, and it *rarely* ever happens.

It's also important to note that there are no states, even with strict laws on abortion, that do not have carve-outs for the life of the mother.[33] Doctors and hospitals should know their state laws, so they do not commit medical malpractice. And when mothers don't receive proper care, abortion activists should hold the proper parties responsible instead of trying to repeal laws that protect the unborn. It's been very disheartening to see pro-choice physicians advocate for broad abortion laws rather than focusing on how to best maximize the safety of the mother and her child.

Many people are under the impression that women only get late-term abortions for medical reasons, but this is a myth. In 2022, would-be-grandmother Jessica Burgess was charged in Nebraska for obtaining abortion pills for her 17-year-old daughter, Celeste, who was more than 23 weeks pregnant. The most common abortion pills are not recommended after 10 weeks. This was very dangerous for her daughter. Instead of going to a clinic, they had the abortion at home. They falsely reported to authorities that Celeste gave birth to a stillborn baby. When investigators dug up her baby, there were thermal wounds on the body.

After receiving a search warrant, investigators obtained their conversations through Facebook Messenger. The daughter talked about how she couldn't wait to get that "thing" out of her body. "I will finally be able to wear jeans."[34]

Initially, the two women were charged with a felony for removing, concealing, or abandoning a dead human body. They were also charged with two misdemeanors for concealing the death of a person and falsely reporting.[35] After discovering their Facebook messages, two additional felonies were added to Jessica, pertaining to the abortion.

Katrina Kimport released a study following 28 women who obtained abortions after week 24 of pregnancy. While some women received abortions due to fetal abnormalities, some women aborted because they discovered their pregnancy late. Other women dragged their feet due to the stigma surrounding abortion or lacked the resources to obtain one earlier. One mother obtained an abortion for her healthy child after her (now ex) boyfriend received a signing bonus.[36] Besides, the reasons why women might want an abortion early can certainly still occur later in the pregnancy. For example, you can break up with a partner or your economic circumstances may change. Abortion advocates may claim late-term abortion only or mostly occurs in life-threatening situations, but they still advocate for abortion on demand because they view it as a right that should not be restricted.

We can also consider notorious serial killer and doctor, Kermit Gosnell, who ran an abortion clinic for decades. The Women's Medical Society in West Philadelphia was in deplorable condition. The walls appeared to be splattered in urine, it smelled horrid, cats roamed the halls, medical waste was not properly discarded, staff was not certified, and Gosnell kept jars of fetal remains. In Pennsylvania, abortion was illegal after 24 weeks, but he performed multiple abortions later than that. According to one of Gosnell's employees, around 40 percent of the abortions at the clinic happened after week 24.[37] They would induce labor and snip the spines of the infants. In 2013, Gosnell was found guilty of three murder charges of infants born alive. One of the staff took a picture of "Baby Boy A," who was estimated to be 32 weeks old. Gosnell even joked, "This baby is big enough to walk around with me or walk me to the bus stop."

It is often said abortion is health care, but Gosnell was clearly not offering health care. He was even found guilty of Karnamaya Mongar's death, a refugee who died in 2009 during a botched abortion. As horrific as Gosnell was, he had clients. He is not the type of man you would turn to for a medical emergency.

But what would God allow?

In Judaism, abortion is permissible if the mother's life is in danger. In Catholicism, the church opposes abortion with the direct purpose of destroying the life of the child, even when it is a zygote. You cannot intentionally cause evil against the baby or the mother. However, if there is a situation that would have the unfortunate side effect of the baby dying, such as removing a uterus filled with cancer, that would be permissible. For protestants, ideology is much less uniform because there's such a wide range of denominations.

Regardless of what denomination you're in and what church you sit up under, the child in a mother's womb is human, alive, made in the image of God, and deserves to be treated with dignity.

You may wonder, "What does it matter if the child still dies? Does intent mean that much?" Intent means a great deal. Intent can mean the difference between being found "not guilty" on a murder charge. *Mens rea*, translated from Latin to mean "guilty mind," heavily plays into criminal trials. Some pro-life activists, like popular conservative commentator Ben Shapiro, believe only abortion doctors should be criminally charged with abortions because he doesn't believe women would fit the *Mens rea* criteria for a criminal conviction. He doesn't believe women truly understand they are taking a life. Of course, that is certainly debatable (and will be addressed later), but major pro-life organizations believe women should not be criminally charged, and new abortion laws tend to single out doctors and facilitators.

Your actions certainly matter to Christ, but so do your intentions. God judges us in a manner that man cannot. I'm certain you've heard the phrase, "God knows my heart." Well, he does. In Matthew 6, Jesus talks about not practicing righteousness to be seen, and how there will be no reward from the Father in Heaven for such behavior. Jesus says when you give to the poor, don't make a big deal for the purpose of being praised by others. He says don't pray on street corners to be seen by people. He also says when you fast, don't give the appearance of fasting. God still wants you to pray, give, and fast but you're not doing those things for kudos from the world or fellow church members. Some skeptics have pointed to this chapter to condemn things like corporate prayer, but that's not the purpose. The purpose is that Jesus wants our actions to be about pleasing God and glorifying him, not our flesh.

It was not required for Abraham to literally sacrifice Isaac. God did give Abraham instruction, but God only needed the intention of his servant's heart to be proven. He wasn't trying to prove that Abraham would kill his son for him, but that Abraham trusted and loved God above all things. And, of course, God knows all. But it was proven to Abraham that he did trust in the Lord and that he *could* trust in the Lord.

The most important thing to do in any dire situation is to pray. Seek God for wisdom and understanding. When my mother had my brother, she had a complication. My father talks of finding her in a bathtub filled with blood. The doctor told him they should consider not having any more children. My father took the doctor's words seriously, but when he prayed about it, God told him not to worry. This was a bold step of faith, and he already had a daughter and a new son. But he heard from God and trusted in him. My mother had five more daughters, all-natural and without complication. The last was a whopping ten pounds and four ounces.

But not all Christians know how to hear from God. Not even all Christians believe you *can* hear from God. Regardless of what one may think of that theologically, it's simply the reality, and medical complications will happen. So, when they occur, and the doctor has to preserve one life over the other, I still recommend prayer. Ask for God's wisdom, mercy, healing virtue, etc. Then, a mother and father will have to decide in the best interest of the family. I pray God gives you the assurance to make the best judgment. Many mothers will choose to take a risk and prioritize the baby over their life, but that decision can be more difficult if they already have little ones who depend on them.

Imagine if a mother and father were driving with three small children in the backseat, and an accident caused them to dangle off a cliff. Would the parents usher themselves to safety first or would they prioritize their children? Most parents would save their children. Depending on how the car was sitting and the positions of the passengers, it might be necessary for one parent to get out and pass the children on. If the car falls before all children can be saved, a parent would not be guilty of murder—despite the guilt they'd harbor.

If you find yourself in a triage situation, please, do not carry the guilt of murder with you. I've seen many women who had medical emergencies use their experiences to defend blanket abortion, and they're simply not equivalent. Even women who have had miscarriages, like actress Hilarie Burton from *One Tree Hill*, described her miscarriage as an abortion. She had a dilation and curettage, also known as a D&C procedure, to remove the fetus. Her child was already dead. Just because you have a D&C does not mean you had an abortion. It's used to scrape abnormal tissue from the uterine lining. It can be used to treat endometriosis as well. Perhaps Burton's paperwork noted she had an abortion that was "spontaneous," but it certainly was not "induced" to cause the death of a fetus.

Model, TV host, and social media influencer Chrissy Teigen shared the loss of her son, Jack, after suffering a miscarriage at 20 weeks. In 2020, Teigen was diagnosed with a partial placenta abruption. She originally wrote on Instagram, "We were never able to stop the bleeding and give our baby the fluids he needed, despite bags and bags of blood transfusions." Teigen and her husband, John Legend, even shared pictures of them crying and holding their child in bed together. After *Roe v. Wade* was overturned, Teigen revealed at a social impact agency summit that Legend informed her it was an abortion. Legend and Teigen are retconning the tragedy of a late-term miscarriage and inserting themselves as abortion heroes for political purposes. There's a lot of groupthink and social pressure to accept abortion and even push for it. Some abortion activists even conflate *any* ending of pregnancy as an abortion. They'll do anything to ignore the immorality of deliberately ending the life of a child, for no legitimate medical reason.

But what do we do in situations when we can safely assume a woman may be facing a high-risk pregnancy? For example, if a woman has a disease or injury that would make pregnancy very dangerous or even unbearable? I would say, you don't have a free license to take someone else's life, so not getting pregnant—at all—better be a high priority for you. If you are unmarried, you should be celibate. If you love sex more than not being pregnant, you should deal with being pregnant until you're certain the medical situation is dire. If pregnancy could cost you your life, are you seriously going to rate sex higher than your well-being? Your sex certainly isn't worth a blanket pass to take someone else's life.

If you are married, you can track your cycle (if it is normal). You can use contraceptives (even the Catholic church allows exceptions), make certain your partner is wearing a condom, or become sterilized. What would you be willing to do to save someone's life or, at the very least, not put yourself in the position to contemplate taking someone else's life?

And if you are impregnated, doctors will monitor the pregnancy. If a crisis arises, you'll have to make decisions accordingly. But the ethics of terminating a pregnancy in life-threatening situations—to preserve life—is not the same as getting an abortion because ending a life is the intention.

Lastly, before activists use the maternal mortality rate as justification for abortions, I ask you to put things into perspective. According to the U.S. CDC, there were 871 maternal deaths in 2020. The CDC quotes the World Health Organization's definition: "the death of a woman while pregnant or within 42 days of termination of pregnancy, irrespective of the duration and the site of the pregnancy, from any cause related to or aggravated by the pregnancy or its management, but not from accidental or incidental causes."[38] In the same year, there were 3,605,201 births. Each death is tragic, and we need to do more in society to prevent maternal deaths. Technological advancements will continue to help with this, but doctors need to be more attentive to their patient's needs, women should try to be physically healthier when getting pregnant, try to start their families earlier in life (since risk increases with age), and so on. There are risks associated with pregnancy, and I believe in self-defense, but there needs to be a reasonable risk to your life. Every woman is unique, and each pregnancy is different. But pro-choice activists don't need a guaranteed right to nine-month abortions for any reason, because of fringe cases.

Incest

If incest is the result of rape, it's redundant to mention incest specifically. If you believe abortion should be permissible because relatives consensually engage in intercourse, possibly resulting in a genetic mutation, abortion would be specifically used as eugenics. Killing someone based on the possibility of a disability is immoral.

Chapter Eight

The Necessity of Moral Absolutes

Dennis Prager is an American conservative talk show host and writer, responsible for popular internet videos from Prager University. He's also a Jewish man and has convinced many Christians to retain their faith. Prager has an interesting philosophy: he doesn't waste time trying to prove the existence of God but rather proves his necessity.

> "If I convince you that God exists, I have done nothing. Because the number of people who believe in God who are moral idiots is very large. However, if I can convince you that God is morally necessary, and is necessary for meaning of life, the greatest urge a human has—even more so than sex—then I have changed your life."[1]

In the past, when an abortion activist accused me of pushing religion, I would defensively say, "My argument is based on science and rights." I can make secular pro-life arguments, but I don't think that's the best approach anymore. When someone lodges this accusation against a pro-life Christian, we should ask: "What specific position of my argument, that you believe is influenced by religion, do you disagree with?"

I bet most pro-choice activists haven't thought beyond their reactionary statement, and they merely vomited their bigotry on instinct. Some have reflected more deeply on the matter. Whatever camp they fall into, this line of questioning will get to a lot of core moral principles. While I understand many pro-life activists simply want to stick to "settled science" and take the easiest route to win a debate, Christians must also minister. If we can truly convince an unbeliever of the wisdom and love of God, we should take the long road.

Objective Morality

I'm often told this topic is too nuanced because, *"Abortion is a moral issue, and we'll never agree. Morality is subjective."*

Christians do believe in objective morality. Our morals are centered around what God has dictated them to be. And even for people who do not know the word, we believe the law is written on our hearts (Romans 2:15). Human beings can have different opinions on right and wrong. Our perception can change, and so can our laws. But that doesn't mean it was ever moral. We didn't wake up and suddenly make chattel slavery immoral. It was always immoral; we just had to be courageous enough to admit it and fight for abolition. If we changed our laws and made all murders legal, it wouldn't make it moral.

I've heard pro-choice activists state abortion isn't "wrong," because morality is subjective, then watched them spiral into a committed justification of stealing, rape, and murder if it's deemed normal in another culture. This is horrific. But it begs the question if morality is subjective, why is it wrong to ban abortion?

Overall, it will save millions of lives. The U.S. had almost a million induced abortions in 2019 alone. Imagine if every person in Detroit was wiped off the face of the earth. That still wouldn't equate to the number of children killed. You'd have to add in Grand Rapids and my hometown of Pontiac. It wouldn't lead to "unwanted" children being born. There are always parents waiting to adopt.

Pro-choice activists would claim we need access to abortion or else women will die in "back-alley" abortions, and the legalization of abortion has made women safer. But the data never truly supported this talking point. Pro-abortion group NARAL lied about the number of back-alley abortions to dupe feminists into supporting their cause. Bernard Nathanson, the co-founder of NARAL, admitted abortion activists "sensationalized the effects of illegal abortion and fabricated polls which indicated that 85% of the public favored unrestricted abortion when we knew it was only 5%." He also said, when NARAL spoke of illegal abortion deaths, "it was always 5,000 to 10,000 a year. I confess that I knew the figures were totally false."[2] And the term "back alley" doesn't mean women have abortions with coat hangers in alleys. It means they went to clinics, after hours, through the alley. And the deaths of women significantly dropped through medical inventions like penicillin, not the legalization of abortion. When former Planned Parenthood President Leana Wen claimed, "Thousands of women died every year pre-*Roe*," *The Washington Post* gave her four Pinocchios. By 1972, fewer than one hundred women died from legal and illegal abortions.[3]

Some women did, horrifically, perform abortions on themselves. Whoopi Goldberg, for example, confessed to being one of these women. But if women have illegal abortions today, they will most likely use the abortion pill. The abortion industry swears up and down that it's safe for women to take these drugs. If it's not and will lead to hundreds of women dying, they have a lot to answer for.

And data also supports that if abortion is banned, women get pregnant less. They will be more selective about who they choose to have sex with, when, and how. A European study found an increase in the financial cost of abortion or even modest restrictions "reduced abortion rates on the order of 25 percent, but also reduced pregnancy rates on the order of 10 percent with little net effect on births."[4] They also found that "Medicaid funding restrictions and parental involvement laws in the United States have been found to reduce abortion and pregnancy rates."

Women on social media sites like TikTok are already talking about going on sex strikes, and news sites like *The Guardian*, *CBS News*, and *The Washington Post* reported men are rushing to get vasectomies after *Roe v. Wade* was struck down. That would suggest the obvious: people make more responsible decisions with pregnancy when they know abortion cannot be their safety net.

But even if that weren't the case, and there are potentially hundreds of women—thousands even—who are desperate enough to risk hurting or killing themselves to have an abortion, that means these women are near-suicidal. If women who have abortions are mentally distressed, is it the benefit of society that we send them to an abortionist rather than a pregnancy crisis center, a counselor, or even a church? Why would we allow these vulnerable women to be herded off to a butcher who profits off of killing her baby?

They don't believe in true informed consent; their goal is manipulation. Planned Parenthood even stealth edited their website that once admitted between week five and six of fetal development, "a very basic beating heart and circulatory system develop." Sometime after July 2022, it was changed to say, "It sounds like a heartbeat on an ultrasound, but it's not a fully formed heart—it's the earliest stage of the heart developing."[5] Georgia Democrat Stacey Abrams repeated this talking point at Morehouse College. "There is no such thing as a heartbeat at six weeks. It is a manufactured sound designed to convince people that men have the right to take control of a woman's body."[6] Of course, there is no grand conspiracy of doctors and medical technicians inventing a heartbeat sound, so men can control women's bodies. There isn't a group of evil men, twirling their mustaches, in the back room of hospitals and clinics. Rhetoric like this makes it clear the abortion lobby cares about protecting abortion, not protecting women.

Regardless, we cannot hold millions of people hostage because of what women might **choose** to do to their bodies.

Most importantly, even if morality was subjective, that's an even greater reason why we need clear and consistent standards when life should be protected. If you can believe Adolf Hitler wasn't immoral for the genocide of millions of Jews, I don't want you to decide when my life may hold value. The only thing between you and another mass genocide is the power of persuasion in your tongue.

The clearest standard is conception. That is the origin of our lives. It is at that point we should come to at least respect we have a right to not be killed. Without life, we can possess no other rights. And if our right to life is decided based on the whims of the mother, *no one* has unalienable "God-given" rights.

We fight about the "right to life," thinking it's only a dispute between each other. But our rights are not only meant for us; they protect us from the government. The Constitution exists to limit the power of the federal government. But women are marching in the streets, telling the federal government their children have no right to life in the womb. They're angry because *they want the federal government to recognize their unborn children **don't have a right to not be killed***.

Never fool yourself into believing they won't take women up on their offer, and they won't exercise their authority to commit tyranny.

If you believe a woman's bodily autonomy will stop them, you weren't paying attention during the COVID-19 pandemic. The Supreme Court ruled that medical workers had to be vaccinated to keep their jobs, as long as federal dollars were attached (*Biden v. Missouri*), yet many politicians and their constituents want the government to pay for health care, childcare, education, etc. The threat of losing your job and the reality of not being able to participate in society without a vaccine passport forced many to comply. Before the days of COVID-19, the government conducted syphilis experiments on black Americans. Before that, Americans were forcibly sterilized after the Supreme Court ruled women deemed "feeble-minded," like Carrie Buck, could be. In reality, Buck was a young woman impregnated after being raped by her foster parents' nephew. Margaret Sanger, the founder of Planned Parenthood and feminist icon, praised the court's decision.

I don't need pro-choice activists to acknowledge objective morality or state where theirs comes from if they don't serve a being higher than themselves. It better serves the pro-life position because we cannot trust the subjective judgment of each other. It's in everyone's best interest to simply respect each other's natural rights from when we objectively begin our existence.

Intrinsic Value

I was once told by an atheist, *"It seems as though you are under the impression that all humans possess intrinsic value. Does that opinion come from religion?"*

I have also seen pro-life activists convert to being pro-choice, after concluding intrinsic value cannot be argued without religion.

Intrinsic value means we possess value naturally, simply for being. As a Christian, I do believe human beings possess intrinsic value. We are made in the image of God, and it is indisputable that he has a purpose and a plan for all human beings, even before we are formed in the womb. But if you're a nonreligious person who believes we're all meat sacks, who will live, die, and then no longer exist, perhaps it's difficult to believe in the bigger meaning of it all.

It still shouldn't matter. Even if you don't believe in intrinsic value, it's in everyone's best interest to pretend that we do. If we don't simply possess value for being human, that means our value has to be earned or someone has to grant it. Who has such power, and why should they possess such authority to grant it?

It wasn't too long ago that slaves were thought of as less valuable, even though they were human. It's not as though legislators crafting the Constitution didn't acknowledge they had value, other than monetary. The southern states valued slaves enough to want them counted in their population numbers, to grant them an advantage over the northern states. The North could not allow that to happen. They bargained and ended up with the Three-fifths Compromise. Was it moral to acknowledge a human being enough for your political advantage, yet deny them enough humanity to free them from the bonds of enslavement? Most today would think not. Back then? It was just good business.

In the Zong trial of 1783, the court had to decide whether throwing at least 142 African slaves overboard, in an attempt to save the crew during a storm, would be covered by insurance. These were human beings, but it was argued they were "cargo" and "was the same as if horses had been thrown overboard." This trial helped to highlight the inhumanity of the slave trade and fueled abolitionists to end it. The insurance companies were not ordered to recoup the losses, but those responsible for the massacre were never brought to justice. Justice

John Lee, Great Britain's solicitor general, didn't think it warranted criminal charges. "What is this claim that human people have been thrown overboard? This is a case of chattels or goods. Blacks are goods and property; it is madness to accuse these well-serving honourable men of murder. They acted out of necessity and in the most appropriate manner for the cause. The late Captain Collingwood acted in the interest of his ship to protect the safety of his crew. To question the judgement of an experienced well-travelled captain held in the highest regard is one of folly, especially when talking of slaves. The case is the same as if wood had been thrown overboard."[7]

Today, we view these statements as monstrous, but they sound awfully familiar to me. "What is this claim that abortion takes a human life? This is a question of bodily autonomy. Fetuses are clumps of cells, and the property of the mother until they reach viability. It is madness to accuse women of murder. They act out of necessity for what is best for their physical, mental, and emotional health. To question their judgment and their choice is wrong, especially when talking about a parasite. Treating a pregnancy is the same as treating cancer."

Every sentence in that paragraph is taken from multiple conversations with pro-choice activists, even equating pregnancy to cancer. Instinctively, we know that abortion is a terrible thing. Rationally, we know abortion is a terrible thing. But the horrible truth about humanity is we can rationalize our way into justifying insidious horrors and train others to be numb to them. If you've studied anything about fetuses, you'd know they are not clumps of cells (no more than you and me), they're not the mother's body, and they don't have much in common with parasites. These regurgitated talking points exist to dehumanize the unborn. Abortion activists fight against mothers seeing sonograms. They claim they don't want to bother women who are already making a difficult decision. It's unconscionable that anyone wouldn't want to persuade a woman to change her mind. Senator Elizabeth Warren (D-MA) even rallied against pregnancy crisis centers that help women in need. She's furious they outnumber abortion clinics "3-1" in her state.[8] Governor Gretchen Whitmer of Michigan has also come against them as well. She vetoed $3 million for pregnancy-resource centers and $10 million for adoption promotion out of the 2023 budget.[9] If you fight against informing women, offering them hope, and giving them options, it's not about protecting them. It's about protecting the business of abortion.

And you could rationalize the need for it. Captain Collingwood could argue he did what he had to, to save his crew. If someone had to be sacrificed, why not the slaves? After all, abortion activists argue it's better to be dead than live a life of suffering anyway. Of course, the Zong was overpacked, and that contributed to the crew's predicament. Shouldn't the captain have at least been held accountable for the choices leading up to that horrible decision?

Shouldn't women?

Since more than 99 percent of abortions are enacted through consensual sex, asking, "How did the baby get there?"

will defeat a vast majority of bodily autonomy arguments. Nowadays, you'd likely hear, "Consent to sex isn't consent to pregnancy," but the consent is at least implied. If you don't know procreation can lead to creation, you're certainly too young to have consensual sex. Besides, pregnancy isn't something you can willfully control. You can try to arrange it, but your "consent" doesn't guarantee fertilization and implantation. You either are or you aren't pregnant. Announcing your child—who cannot respond—doesn't have your permission to live, doesn't do anything but make you feel better. But society certainly has no obligation to consent to participating or allowing the killing of that child. There are millions of reasons for society to reject abortion on demand, and each one has their own distinctive set of DNA.

Some activists argue it doesn't matter and will go further beyond bodily autonomy. They'll argue the mother isn't even technically killing a fetus if she takes an abortion pill. She's simply denying resources, and the fetus is dying due to its lack of development. This logic would be the equivalent of Captain Collingwood throwing a slave to the mercy of the ocean and claiming the lack of body temperature regulation, stamina, and skill killed them. After all, viability is your ability to survive in your environment.

Can women take an abortion pill, intending on the result being a dead embryo or fetus, have the intended effect, and then not be culpable for the action? No honest person can believe that, but guilty minds can delude themselves into the most glorious falsehoods. Anything is on the table when you permit yourself to "other" another person and openly discriminate against them.

We'd like to believe killing another human being is difficult, but our "feet are swift to shed blood," (Romans 3:15). Call a human a savage like they did the Native Americans, property like they did the slaves, and rats like they did the Jews. It makes atrocities more palatable.

In *Dred Scott v. Sandford*, it was argued when the Declaration of Independence said, "All men are created equal," they weren't talking about the negro. They said, "It is too clear for dispute, that the enslaved African race were not intended to be included." They believed other laws, particularly dealing with interracial marriage and mixed children, had proven a "perpetual and impassable barrier was intended to be erected between the white race and the one which they had reduced to slavery."[10] The court decided American citizenship didn't apply to anyone of African descent, whether you were free or not. *Dred Scott* has been panned as the worst decision the court has ever made. It was overridden by the 13th and 14th Amendments to the U.S. Constitution.

It's unfathomable that we could have treated other human beings so poorly back then, but it was just as evil back in the 1800s, to anyone willing to open their eyes and see. Frederick Douglass addressed some of the inconsistencies in his speech, "What, to the Slave, is the Fourth of July," written in 1852. "Must I undertake to prove that a slave is a man? That point is conceded already. Nobody doubts it. The slaveholders themselves acknowledge it in the enactment of laws for their government."

It is already a conceded scientific point that the origin of unique human life begins at conception, yet our laws are inconsistent. Why does it make sense that if a pregnant woman were driving to an abortion clinic and was killed by a drunk driver, he would be charged with vehicular manslaughter for killing two people? As President Ronald Reagan pointed out, why does it make sense that the law will respect the property rights of a fetus if a father writes a will to his unborn child, yet the mother can rob the beneficiary of their life? Does anyone doubt Scott Peterson should have been convicted for the murder of his wife and unborn son? Does anyone doubt that Remee Lee's six-week fetus deserved justice after her ex-boyfriend tricked her into taking pills to kill their baby?[11] The death penalty is being sought for Hunter James Tatum for shooting his wife, who was six months pregnant, in the head. The doctors performed an emergency delivery, but Baby Everett did not survive.[12]

I have never had a conversation with an abortion advocate who does not believe the violent aggressors in cases like these should be charged for the deaths of the unborn. But if Baby Everett was aborted on the last day in his fifth month, they would claim he wasn't alive because Everett was not viable or sentient, and it was his mother's right to dismember him. How can what happened to Remee Lee be a grave injustice or miscarriages be a great tragedy, while any other woman who chooses an early abortion is exercising "freedom?"

It is the pro-life position that a mother and her child are both equally valuable, worthy of dignity, and have a right to not be killed. Pro-choice activists argue only the woman is relevant, and they'll base that belief around the baby's vulnerability. "They can't survive outside the womb, they're not sentient, they're not conscious, etc." The fetus can't think for itself or comprehend, therefore, it's permissible for them to be aborted. But why doesn't this make women more accountable? She could comprehend her actions and they resulted in a baby. And if all of her life decisions led her to a place where taking the life of a blameless child is the best option, she's drastically failed. The majority of women who have abortions are adults, not hapless teenagers who made an oopsie. Why not prioritize a new child, who is virtually a blank slate? Again, *this is not the pro-life position*. It is *not my position*. But when you get to pick and choose who is valuable, why choose the woman conspiring to commit homicide?

If it truly is based on the child's vulnerability, why would you assume that logic wouldn't extend outside of the womb? Euthanasia could be the next craze, voluntarily or not. Canada has euthanasia, and it is becoming a human rights concern. Roger Foley, a man with a degenerative brain disorder was so alarmed when the doctors brought up euthanasia that he began recording them. The hospital's director of ethics said it would cost "north of $1,500 a day" to treat him. Foley said he felt like he was being coerced. Other patients, in a country with "free health care," are considering being killed because of medical bills. In Ontario, medical authorities "explicitly instruct doctors not to indicate on death certificates if people died from euthanasia."[13] According to the Canadian government, 3.3 percent of their deaths are from medical assistance in dying.[14]

If vulnerability disqualifies you from intrinsic value, why have social safety nets funded by taxpayers? Taxed income is acquired by labor produced with their bodies. How is it not a violation of bodily autonomy, and why is it that so many people feel we have a moral obligation to strangers outside of the womb, but parents have no moral obligation to their child in the womb? And if parents deserve the choice of parental obligation, why are men forced to pay child support if they are born? He doesn't have a say in whether they *are* born. Yet we're satisfied making men pay, even at the threat of jail, because it's in the best interest of that vulnerable child.

There is no question that the unborn are alive. Whether you value that life, is completely subjective—which remains true in and out of the womb. If you disqualify the unborn from "life," you do so with the foreknowledge of what they lack, for the purpose of actively discriminating against them. Would you justify taking the life of anyone else outside of the womb based on their size, level of development, environment, and degree of dependency (S.L.E.D.)? These humans are treated as though they are the women's property, instead of beings worthy of dignity and moral consideration. Frederick Douglass probably hoped we'd move beyond this sort of archaic thinking, yet here we are again.

Perhaps you can never get to the point of seeing no difference between an unborn baby and a newborn. Perhaps you can't bring yourself to care in general. It's still in everyone's best interest to pretend or at least act as if they do. If you can justify or allow the discrimination of the unborn, in order to deny them basic human rights—the right to not be killed—someone can do the same to you, just as we've done to others.

Christians believe humans possess intrinsic value, but let's be honest; we don't always act like it. We can be unkind, petty, and spiteful to one another. We can be like Jonah and wish for swift judgment rather than mercy. We can wish for tit-for-tat, like the Israelites lamenting to God, praying for revenge against Babylon. We can be too selfish or even too lazy to remember to pray for neighbors and strangers. I'm an introvert. Being around people is not my desire.

But Christians have to crucify their flesh and pray for a burden for the lost. Paul wanted his Jewish brothers and sisters to receive the gospel so desperately, he was willing to give up his salvation for them. That is an extraordinary love and a dedication to the cause, but I have not observed much of that sort of devotion in modern Christianity, especially in the West. While Christians in communist and Muslim countries suffer daily persecution and threats of death, American Christians are too afraid to pick up the phone and invite a friend to church.

Human life is intrinsically valuable, but our value of human life is fickle. It takes discipline. If it were natural to love thy neighbor as thyself, Jesus would not have needed to command it.

Life itself is also intrinsically valuable. Pro-choice activists argue it's acceptable to terminate the life of an embryo or fetus because they are not sentient or conscious. To that, I ask, what does it matter? If someone kills you, you won't be conscious either. The response is normally, "There's a difference. The fetus never knew it was alive." It doesn't matter. Once you are dead, you don't feel one way or another about it. Is the awareness of your death what makes murder immoral? If a serial killer made it quick, painless, and without your knowledge, we would still charge them for murder. We'd still seek justice for your life. Your friends and family would probably be in the courtroom to hear the conviction.

Is it sadder because the people you leave behind will mourn you? If acknowledging your life and grieving your absence is what makes your death tragic, it makes the pro-life cause far more important. We are told to mind our business but mourning and reflection are how we reverence one's existence. To not speak and not care about the millions of children slain in abortion would allow them to fade into obscurity, leaving the door open for more gruesome deaths.

Why do you think we repeat lines like "Never Again" when talking about the Holocaust? It is not only to remember the people who died but to reflect on how such an evil was committed, and to prevent such atrocities from happening again. John Farmer Jr., the Director of Eagleton Institute of Politics said, "Because 'Never Again' is a profession of faith as much as it is a statement of policy; like the plea for universal peace that closes the Kaddish, it is a prayer-like invocation of an as-yet unrealized world, a world in which humanity's moral progress will someday match its military prowess."[15]

You may argue abortion is not the same because a fetus didn't experience life, but that doesn't hold true either. Would you dare accuse a woman grieving her miscarriage of being irrational? No, you would probably offer her condolences. Even if you view a fetus as a potential life rather than a life with potential, you still sympathize with that loss. When my cousin lost her newborn, it wasn't less sad because her daughter never got to live her life. It was more tragic because she barely lived. When a parent loses a young child, it haunts them. The younger you are—even if you're a young adult—the guests at the funeral will say, "They were gone too soon." When someone has lived a full and long life, we still mourn but we're at greater peace. My grandmother on my mother's side passed away at 102, completely content. I miss hearing her voice and seeing her smile, but I'm not sad a God-loving woman passed on.

When a father and soldier is killed in the line of duty, we think of how he'll never be able to walk his daughter down the aisle. When a mother passes, we lament about how she won't be able to send her children off to the prom or see them graduate. We talk about dreams they didn't get to fulfill and journeys they didn't make. We don't simply grieve the dead; we grieve for lost opportunities. Funerals are often a time families and friends are stirred to go make the most out of life, or at the very least, reach out to loved ones they've neglected. We make adjustments because we don't want to leave this world without feeling like we made the most of what we've been given.

Abortion is not immoral simply because that individual has intrinsic value. Abortion is immoral because *life itself is intrinsically valuable.*

Consciousness is valued by pro-choice activists because they presuppose it is wrong to rob someone of future conscious experience. They understand there is something good about being able to experience life itself. If that is the case, it's worth protecting the future conscious experience of the preborn, who possess the capacity to achieve consciousness and are on a self-determined path to actualize it. Even if you abort a fetus before achieving consciousness, it is possible to deprive someone of something, even if they are unaware of it. If I stole an inheritance from you, it would still be a deprivation, despite never knowing of the fortune you were rightfully entitled to. A harm would also be committed against a woman if she were raped in a coma, even if she never found out. It would be a violation of her bodily integrity, and so would tearing a child apart. Murder is wrong because it unjustly deprives a human of future conscious experience. Pulling the plug on a braindead patient doesn't deprive a human of future consciousness but an abortion certainly does.

Pro-choice activists will justify abortion in the interest of sparing a child from potential suffering and trauma. "Why would you want a child to grow up in a family that doesn't want them?" and so on. But I can never quite get an estimate on how much suffering is appropriate before it is justifiable to kill someone. Who made that scale and where is it located? No one is advocating we solve the massive homeless problem in California via mass execution or that we put foster care kids out of their misery. Even if someone chooses to take their own life, they will end up in a hospital on suicide watch if they survive. We value life so much; we don't grant blanket autonomy to end it. If someone even encourages suicide, they'll be kicked from major social media platforms. Perhaps we will one day become like *Futurama* with suicide booths, but we're not that far gone yet. If guaranteed suffering isn't a good enough reason to kill another human being, why is hypothetical or potential suffering adequate justification to end the life of a child in the womb?

If you're an atheist, you can take the approach that we're all primordial soup and nothing truly matters, or you can believe everything matters because this life is all we have.

The quality of our lives and how much we appreciate it may vary, but there is value in life itself. If we didn't believe that, would we bother spending our lives in a grand pursuit of meaning? You may find meaning, you may lose it, regain it, or never quite receive the answer you're looking for. There's still value in the search: the relationships we forge, the struggles that make us, the defeats we learn from, and the triumphs we savor. Life is worth living if we have the courage to explore its terror and its beauty.

The Societal Harm of Abortion

I'm often asked, *"What do you care if a woman has an abortion? It's between a woman and her doctor. It's none of your business, and it doesn't affect you."*

Many pro-life activists will reply by asking, "Would you stand up against child abuse, or would you mind your business? Can you speak out against rape if it's not affecting you?" And they'd go on with other examples. Evil is still evil, whether you're the victim or not.

No one would tell us to mind our own business if we were discussing school shootings like Sandy Hook, Parkland, or Uvalde. These were horrific tragedies. I didn't know a single victim personally, but I still empathized, prayed for the families, debated solutions, etc. The premise that someone can't or shouldn't care unless they suffer directly is dishonest.

Even so, I go a different route. I absolutely reject the notion that someone else's abortion does not affect me. Now, I could talk about my taxpayer dollars. I could talk about how abortion chains like Planned Parenthood receive funding, to my great disdain. I could talk about the government purchasing fresh, never frozen fetal remains for humanized mice experiments.[16] I could talk about the push to repeal the Hyde Amendment, which stops most federal dollars from funding abortions. I could talk about the Biden administration transporting illegal immigrants for abortions.[17] And the list could go on. "My money, my business," is a catchphrase I like to say, but it goes beyond that.

John R. Lott, Jr of Yale University and John Whitley of the University of Adelaide looked at the association between abortion and crime. "Abortion may prevent the birth of 'unwanted' children, who would have relatively small investments in human capital and a higher probability of crime. On the other hand, some research suggests that legalizing abortion increases out-of-wedlock births and single-parent families, which implies the opposite impact on investments in human capital and thus crime. The question is: what is the net impact? We find evidence that legalizing abortion increased murder rates by around about 0.5 to 7 percent."[18]

But it goes further beyond that.

Abortion causes great societal harm. Consider for a moment how we've been psychologically conditioned to accept abortion—not as a necessary evil—as an act of "self-care" and an "act of love." Women are taught to believe they cannot be equal or achieve their dreams if they do not have the freedom to sacrifice their children for it. To rationalize the sacrifice, we've been conditioned to dehumanize our children. To rationalize the dehumanization, we throw out the idea of natural laws, that we are created equal, and rights—such as the right to life—are transcendent. With so little regard for human life, is it any wonder how scientists are willing to play God with gain-of-function research and other experiments? After all, abortion has a deep history in eugenics. Eugenics is still used as a justification for abortion: minorities, the poor, and the disabled.

Women are also taught to believe they are inherently unequal to men. Jennifer Lawrence, who has a mega-successful career as a young actress thanks to franchises like *X-Men* and *The Hunger Games*, lamented to *Vogue* about the future of women after *Roe v. Wade* was overturned. "How could you raise a daughter from birth and believe that she doesn't deserve equality? *How?*"[19] If the natural ability to bear children makes women unequal to men, then it's fair to assume mothers are always inferior. Men and women are both unique—not unequal. Women carry civilizations in their wombs. They are so incredibly special, and women don't require the power to deliberately kill their children to be equal to their partners.

Feminists used to fight against being discriminated against in the workplace if they became pregnant. Now, they've concluded the natural and healthy process of their bodies is a liability. If pregnancy cannot be "treated" via abortion, pro-choice activists feel as though they are being violently aggressed upon. They claim you are "forcing" them to give birth and denying them health care. After *Roe v. Wade* was overturned, companies claimed they would pay or reimburse women who travel to have an abortion. It's certainly cheaper than paying for maternity care. It also has the makings of a dystopian novel.

The truth is abortion has only been able to flourish through the manipulation of women, whether it was groups like NARAL fudging the death of women during illegal abortions, or fearmongering the maternal mortality rate, prosecution of miscarriages, and ectopic pregnancies. Even now, social media companies like YouTube place links (to the National Library of Medicine) and disclaimers on abortion videos: "An abortion is a procedure to end a pregnancy. It uses medicine or surgery to remove the embryo or fetus and placenta from the uterus. The procedure is done by a licensed healthcare professional." What an abnormally politically correct way of saying an abortion deliberately and brutally kills your child. Based on their definition, a C-section would qualify as an abortion.

It's no wonder that Jessa Duggar Seewald, a Christian reality TV personality, was heavily criticized online for not calling her miscarriage an abortion. Abigail Disney, the heir to the magical world of Disney, scolded the grieving mother for not calling her D&C an abortion. "Contemptible cowardice." *Parade Magazine* claimed she had a "life-saving abortion," though they changed their article after facing backlash.[20] The reality is Seewald's baby died a natural death in her womb. Removing the baby's dead body was necessary to save Seewald's life. Though the procedure can still be heartbreaking for mothers, the ethics and details are obviously not the same as an induced abortion. The abortion activists who rushed to Twitter and TikTok to attack Seewald and capitalize off her pain proved they are not pro-woman. They aren't even pro-choice. They are pro-abortion. Nothing is off limits in the world of protecting abortion, not even the heart of a grieving mother, who had no say in whether her child lived or died.

While many uncompassionate opportunists took their swipes at Seewald, many attacks were also born from ignorance. Many young women genuinely believe a D&C is an abortion. Disney claimed Seewald advocates for making them illegal in many states, but that isn't true. Seewald wants the deliberate killing of the unborn outlawed, not miscarriage management. As Secular Pro-Life explained on Twitter, the difference is like having a cremation for the dead vs. setting an alive person on fire.

There are plenty of women who know better, but the conflation of miscarriages and induced abortions is used as a scare tactic to expand their base.

Women also do not benefit from a society that teaches men abortion is taking responsibility, and foregoing the responsibility of fatherhood and building families. A woman's body should be more than a thing to be enjoyed. She should be cherished and honored, instead of someone easily detachable by young and selfish men.

Abortion advocates say women choose to get an abortion, but how are abortion clinics not similar to predatory lenders? Abortion clinics are normally located in urban neighborhoods. Activists argue poor women of color need abortions, and even

President Joe Biden laments when they have limited access.[21] When Planned Parenthood makes ads for Mother's Day, they use black and Hispanic women. Should I not be concerned about the eugenics association with abortion, the disproportionate number of abortions from minority communities, and the stagnation of the U.S. black population? Activists who argue against racial disparities claim black people have no institutional power. Would that be different if 28 percent of black pregnancies didn't end in abortion?[22] According to the CDC, "in 2019, compared with non-Hispanic White women, abortion rates and ratios were 3.6 and 3.3 times higher among non-Hispanic Black women and 1.8 and 1.5 times higher among Hispanic women."[23] And the CDC does not require all states to report abortion data. Prominent abortion states like California, for example, often do not voluntarily report.

In my home state of Michigan, 53 percent of abortions were from black bodies in 2020. In this very same year, "non-essential" surgeries were not allowed because of the COVID-19 pandemic, yet women could have abortions. According to the Michigan Department of Health and Human Services, there were 29,669 sons and daughters deliberately terminated through induced abortions.[24] That would be the equivalent of half the population of my hometown of Pontiac being wiped out. Also, in the same year, Governor Gretchen Whitmer (D) declared racism a public health crisis because of the disproportionate impact on minority communities from COVID-19.[25] We have yet to see Whitmer address a desire for fewer black babies to be aborted.

When Whitmer vetoed millions of dollars of funding toward saving the lives of babies from the 2023 budget, her spokesperson, Bobby Leddy, spoke out against pregnancy crisis centers. Leddy said those centers "often use deceptive advertising that target young women and women with low incomes who are seeking abortion care." Why is it a bad thing for pregnancy crisis centers to target women who are desperate and let them know keeping their baby is an option they should consider? Why does Governor Whitmer's administration believe it would be better for these women to end up in Planned Parenthood where the workers have a financial incentive for pregnancy termination? Why shouldn't mothers be told if they need help, people are willing to do so? Pregnancy crisis centers can help pay for diapers, cribs, toys, strollers, parenting classes, help with babysitting, and so on. It all depends on how well-funded they are. Even though Gretchen Whitmer claimed she was "committed" to making Michigan a "model for equality, understanding, and fairness," she's presiding over a state where half the abortion business comes from black bodies.

Perhaps the saddest injustice is the aborted child and mother are both victims. Regret from abortion is real, and not enough women are elevated as a warning. Some are even scolded for possibly discouraging women who "need" an abortion. Even women who claim to have no regrets are often in denial. They will not admit to terminating a life. If you call it a "baby," they respond with "fetus" as if that erases their humanity. A human fetus is simply an "unborn human baby."

It's a stage of development, and that development begins the moment the baby is conceived. The abortion industry thrives on ignorance, and if women remain ignorant, they do not have informed consent. If we do not value and protect informed consent, the US could easily revisit the days of the Tuskegee experiments. And considering the ferocity with which the government recently mandated the COVID-19 vaccine, even though White House COVID-19 response coordinator Dr. Deborah Brix admitted recently that they knew it wouldn't stop the spread of infection,[26] is it hard to believe they'd make us do worse? In the earlier days of the COVID-19 pandemic, women sounded the alarm about how their periods were affected. Women on social media were silenced. It was not admitted until about a year later that vaccines affected menstruation.

If a stranger aborts their child, it does and will affect me because I live in a society that makes such an act thinkable and sustainable. And if society could inflict such evil upon an innocent and defenseless baby, I shudder at what it's willing to do to me. Americans despise the past and are ashamed of the sins committed by our forefathers, but if they could see the butchery rationalized by false rights today, they would see us as monsters and weep.

Chapter Nine
Healing of Women

Redemption Over Condemnation

It's a remarkable thing to be remembered because of death, but that is precisely what Stephen is remembered for. Before his stoning, the word mentions in Acts 6 that Stephen "was a man full of faith and of the Holy Spirit." But since Stephen was filled with the Holy Spirit, the men he debated couldn't keep up with him. So, they falsely accused Stephen of blasphemy and even produced false witnesses to lie. Before Stephen was stoned to death, he witnessed something remarkable; he saw a vision of Jesus standing at the right hand of the Father.

Normally, the word talks about Jesus "sitting" on the right hand the Father, so Christians question what was so special about this incident. Some pastors have said Jesus stood to receive Stephen because he was honoring him as a martyr. Some have said Jesus was standing to issue a judgment. I'll never forget a sermon from theologian Chris Palmer because he pointed out that God's view of judgment and justice is so dramatically different than ours.

> And Saul approved of his execution.
>
> And there arose on that day a great persecution against the church in Jerusalem, and they were all scattered throughout the regions of Judea and Samaria, except the apostles. [2] Devout men buried Stephen and made great lamentation over him. [3] But Saul was ravaging the church, and entering house after house, he dragged off men and women and committed them to prison. (Acts 8:1-3, ESV)

In Chapter 9, Saul is still persecuting Christians and "breathing threats and murders against the disciples," but then, he has a confrontation with Jesus. If you've ever heard the phrase "road to Damascus moment," it's a reference to Saul. While he was traveling, a light came upon him and asked, "Saul, why are you persecuting me?" Saul asked who, and the voice answered, "I am Jesus, whom you are persecuting. But rise and enter the city, and you will be told what you are to do."

The men traveling with Saul were stunned and speechless because they heard the voice but saw no one. Saul also saw no one because he was blinded by the light. The men led him to Damascus where the disciple Ananias happened to be.

The Lord spoke to Ananias and told him to find Saul, because he has been given a vision of Ananias laying his hands on him, and his vision returning. But Ananias questioned God because he had heard of all the evil Saul had committed against the saints. But the Lord had plans for Saul.

> [15] But the Lord said to him, "Go, for he is a chosen instrument of mine to carry my name before the Gentiles and kings and the children of Israel. [16] For I will show him how much he must suffer for the sake of my name." (Acts 9:15-16, ESV)

So, Ananias did as the Lord said. He found Saul, laid his hands on him, and "something like scales fell from his eyes." Saul was filled with the Holy Spirit and preached so mightily in Damascus; the Jews conspired to kill him. He had to escape from the city in a basket.

When Saul attempted to join the disciples in Jerusalem, they were terrified and skeptical of him. But Barnabas stood up for Saul and the change within him. Saul became the Apostle Paul, and of course, had a tremendous ministry.

Jesus didn't choose to take vengeance upon this man who had persecuted his saints enough to have them quivering in fear from his name alone. Jesus sought to redeem Saul and used him for his glory.

Abortion is indeed a terrible sin, but we were all sinners who fell short. We need God's grace and mercy. It doesn't matter if you're a liar, a fornicator, or a murderer. Jesus still died on the cross for you. Your debts were not merely forgiven; the wages of sin equal death and Christ was willing to die for you. Just believe in him and allow Christ to mend what you have broken inside of you.

I have spoken to so many women who carry the scars of their abortions, even women who are believers. They still believe they deserve to be punished and will have to answer to their maker. It is not God's will for us to carry the weight of our sins. He voluntarily bore the burden. His shoulders are big enough for the load; we were not created for it. God desires to alleviate your pain.

Perhaps we feel like carrying our shame is a necessary act of penance. We deserve the torture. We convince ourselves that living in a perpetual state of pain is an act of humility, but it is pride. We are not saved by our own works. We are saved by his grace. Holding onto our pain instead of allowing ourselves to be the evidence of God's redemption is a tragedy. How is God glorified through your chosen state of torment? What sort of testimony is that?

Do you truly think that Jesus Christ, who was severely whipped, beaten, disrespected, and outstretched on a cross and prayed, "Father, forgive them for they know not what they do," can't forgive you of your sins?

Toni McFadden is a pro-life author and speaker, who shares her abortion story. As a young woman, she had an abortion because she was headed off to college, she was afraid to tell her parents, and her boyfriend didn't want her to have the baby. She took an abortion pill in the clinic, but the second pill didn't cause a reaction until two months later while she was in class, severely hemorrhaging. Her boyfriend also broke up with her the day after the abortion.

McFadden was angry for a long time and tried to justify her abortion. When she began taking ownership of her actions, she began her path to healing. "Jesus helped me to see that he covers everything. It's not just one little part that he covers. Like, the gospel is enough. His blood was enough to cover my sins, so me condemning myself over and over again would be saying, 'your death wasn't enough for me.'" Once McFadden came to this revelation, she was able to turn her pain into a teachable moment. She spends her days breaking through the lies of the abortion industry and letting women know they don't have to suffer in silence. As for her ex-boyfriend, he also found forgiveness in Christ. The two reunited and honored their child on their wedding day. They've grown their family since then.

But perhaps you knew better. Some believers have abortions, knowing—deep down—they have taken a life. To that I say, Jesus walked with Peter knowing full well he would deny him three times. Even still, Jesus prayed that his faith would fail him not. And after Jesus rose from the dead, he sent a special word for Peter. Jesus asked Peter three times if he loved him, giving Peter the opportunity to reaffirm his love and commitment to Christ.

God is aware of the fact we are imperfect beings who will fail. There's a reason why one of the fruits of the spirit is longsuffering, or in other words, patience. If God is willing to be patient, kind, and forgiving to us, why can't we do the same for ourselves?

We value the unborn because they are made in the image of God and because God has a purpose for them before they are even born. The same is true for the mother. Before whatever tragic circumstances of life led her to the decision of that abortion, God knew her. We may make mistakes and allow outside forces to get between who we are and who God called us to be. But instead of deciding who we are now based on our scaled eyelids, why not go back to the source, and ask God ourselves?

Ask God to see yourself the way God sees you. Ask God to guide you on the path that he's predestined for you. And when God asks you if you love him, and you affirm your affections, don't be surprised when he commissions you to feed his lambs, feed his sheep, and take care of them.

My brother is the pastor of my church, and nearly two decades ago, he was involved in a terrible car accident. His femur was split into the shape of a "T," the ball of his pelvis snapped off; he had pins in his leg, nerve damage, and a host of other things wrong. The doctors were afraid he'd never walk again; only one hospital in the metro Detroit area would even take him, due to fear of lawsuits. But God had the right specialists there at the right time and worked miracles along the way, including supernatural healings after the doctors had done all they could. But it was a hard thing for my brother to go through, especially alone in the hospital while his family lived nearly an hour north. He often talks about how he listened to an Alvin Slaughter song, "Suddenly," because the Spirit of the Lord came into his room and assured my brother that he was not alone.

But my brother told the church that this moment and his accident are not what defines him. He thanked God for the testimony and God's goodness through it all, but he said, "Your pain should never define you. What you got delivered from should not define you."

When he thinks of a moment that defined him, he goes back to when he was a little boy, traveling with my father and two of our sisters on a Native American reservation in Canada. The Holy Spirit came upon him, and he sobbed at the altar for over an hour. Even though our father was also a pastor, and he hoped his children would follow in his footsteps of ministry, he did not know what God was capable of doing in his son.

Only God knows.

So, when you have your road to Damascus moment and God wants to reveal himself to you, open your eyes and see. And when God wants to use you for his glory, be brave enough to walk in the new path before you and speak of his goodness. It doesn't matter if you believe you're deserving of condemnation. God's view of justice is not ours. *It's his grace, not our grace.* Allow

God to use your life as an example of his love and redemption. Do not let your past or current pain be what defines you. Your purpose is in Christ. Your identity is in Christ. You don't have to be the woman with the issue. You're his daughter.

They Know Not What They Do

One day after church, my younger sister told me about a conversation she had online about abortion. A former classmate said on social media that she would rather die than have a child. Instead of engaging back and forth with the usual talking points, my sister privately messaged this young woman. My sister let her know that she didn't want to argue or start any drama. She just wanted some insight and to make sure she was alright.

Through their conversation, my sister was open and honest about some of the anxieties she had during her last pregnancy that other women didn't seem to relate to. Eventually, she opened up to a nurse, who assured my sister that her anxiety was from a place of trauma when she had an emergency C-section. She wasn't crazy; it was a legitimately frightening experience.

The young woman appreciated that bit of dialogue because too many people glamourize pregnancy and gloss over how difficult it can be. Eventually, she began to open up about her own traumas and explained because of what she had gone through, she never wanted to be a mother herself.

As I listened to my sister, I was very proud of her for taking the time to reach out to a woman in need. I was also a bit convicted. My sister knows more about pregnancy due to her firsthand experience, but I know far more about the topic of abortion. When I go on a rant about the issue, sometimes, the only commentary I'll get out of her is, "Yeah, it's sick."

But she, intuitively, knows what too many often forget: many of these women are hurting.

"No woman wants an abortion." I'm certain you've heard that before. Of course, that isn't true. Women march in the street for it, vote for this issue specifically, make appointments, and go to the clinics. Maybe it's not something they gleefully desire, but women cling to their need for it.

The question is *why*.

Pro-life activists can attend march after march, make signs and billboards, and argue until they're blue in the face, but they'll never truly end abortion unless we can get to the *why*.

Why do women *feel* like they *need* an abortion?

Nearly all abortions are elective. Women report they want abortions because they don't want to raise a child as a single woman or because of financial reasons.[1] Of course, women who are impregnated through consensual means have full control over whether or not they get pregnant. But we are human. Men and women can fall into temptation or even dive in. Sometimes, women don't take birth control. Birth control can fail, but it rarely does. Condoms are very reliable, but I've met a young woman who was a virgin and ended up with a baby when the condom, somehow, got stuck. A female comedian by the name of Chelsea Hart dragged a huge chunk of TikTok into her emotional drama with Lance "Modern Warrior" Tsosie. According to Hart's account, they had unprotected sex after mistakenly believing they were exclusive. Hart is hardly the first woman to make this mistake.

If such a huge chunk of abortion is not the result of rape, incest, the mother's life being in mortal danger, or even fetal anomalies, why do women feel entitled to abortion access?

Just because women are in an elective situation doesn't mean they feel the reality that it is a choice. If a woman has an abusive partner and doesn't know how to protect herself, how can she have the confidence to know she can protect someone else? If she goes to the police, will she be believed? What if she can't prove her abuse and is forced to share custody with a man who will privately abuse her child? What if she loses custody?

Situations like this are heartbreaking, and we should be sympathetic. Anecdotal stories like these are compelling. Not all women who have abortions are monsters out to kill children like some kind of goblin. Some believe they are deciding out of compassion for themselves and compassion for the child. However, we should not permit abortion simply because women are under extreme duress. We can empathize with her plight while acknowledging it's unethical. If the child was fifteen weeks outside of the womb rather than fifteen weeks in it, we'd be deeply disturbed.

We need to address the suffering instead of creating more victims. Instead of the abortion lobby figuring out how to gain access to this desperate customer, they could utilize their time to create more safe spaces for women, advocate for more safeguards and protections for women seeking custody, and also provide them with top-notch lawyers.

How can we help women, so they don't feel the need to have an abortion? That's the question too many abortion activists don't want to ask.

"My body, my choice" isn't the whole story. According to a study on women who suffer emotionally from abortion, the choice is not always about liberation; it comes from pressure. 58.3 percent of women had abortions to make others happy, 73.8 percent disagreed they were "entirely free" from pressure, 28.4 percent aborted in fear of losing their partner, only 49.2 percent believed the fetus was a human being when they had the abortion, 66 percent knew they were genuinely making a mistake at the time of the abortion, 67.5 percent said it was one of the hardest decisions of their lives, and 33.2 percent reported they already felt a connection with their baby at the time of the abortion.[2]

Think of men like Joss Whedon, the mastermind behind the *Buffy* universe and director of the first two *Avengers*, who paraded around as a male feminist. He's so pro-choice, Buffy had an abortion after a drunken hookup in the comics. But when Charisma Carpenter, who played Cordelia Chase on *Buffy: The Vampire Slayer* and spin-off series *Angel*, was pregnant, Whedon allegedly called her into his office and asked if she was going to "keep it."[3] According to Carpenter, Whedon attacked her character, mocked her faith, accused her of sabotaging the show, then fired her the following season after giving birth. Charisma kept her baby, though Joss "sucked" the joy out of motherhood with his verbal abuse and physically demanding work schedules. I wonder how many other women decided to terminate their pregnancies in Hollywood closed-door meetings or never got that far out of fear. The entertainment industry is fickle and cares little for women. They'll pack glittering celebrities into award shows and virtue signal for hours about the juiciest political topics while treating women in the most heinous manner. But this sort of pressure isn't unique to Hollywood and music.

No woman grows up wanting to feel the *need* for abortion. It took time to instill within the hearts of women and to become socially acceptable. It's a societal illness that developed over time. The public was manipulated into believing abortion was what society wanted and that it was necessary to protect women. The truth is multiple studies have concluded abortion has negative effects on the mental health of women.

David Fergusson, former director of the Christchurch Health and Development Study, is a pro-choice atheist. He was hoping to disprove abortion mental health researchers. Instead, "he found that even after controlling for numerous factors, abortion was indeed independently associated with a two-to threefold increased risk of depression, anxiety, suicidal behaviors, and substance abuse disorders."[4] When Fergusson submitted his findings for publication, the New Zealand government's Abortion Supervisory Committee asked him to withhold the results.[5]

When South Dakota created a statute requiring abortion providers to inform women of the research surrounding possible psychological risks of abortion, Planned Parenthood filed a lawsuit. The Eighth Circuit United States Federal Court of Appeals rejected their argument. Planned Parenthood argued there wasn't enough data to prove there was a "direct cause," while the courts ruled its standard practice to "recognize a strongly correlated adverse outcome as a 'risk,' even while further studies are being conducted to investigate which factors play casual roles."[6]

Before *Roe v. Wade*, NARAL deceived the public on abortion data to push for the elimination of restrictions. When co-founder Bernard Nathanson reflected on the lies told by his group, he believed the narrative was more important than the truth.

I confess that I knew that the figures were totally false and I suppose that others did too if they stopped to think of it. But in the "morality" of our revolution, it was a useful figure, widely accepted, so why go out of our way to correct it with honest statistics? The overriding concern was to get the laws eliminated, and anything within reason that had to be done was permissible.[7]

After *Roe v. Wade* was decided in 1979, organizations like Planned Parenthood wanted to know how they could increase their abortion numbers. Talking points emerged that belittled the humanity of the child. Even if a fetus was a life, so are bacteria and plants. Then, abortion became an act of empowerment, the only way a woman could be free and equal in a man's world. Then bodily autonomy became the most important argument, superseding any sort of parental or personal responsibility. It became about the worship of self.

Betty Friedan was an American feminist writer who was once fired from her job for being pregnant. She co-founded the National Organization for Women, and abortion activist Larry Ladder, who was also Margaret Sanger's biographer, desperately wanted Friedan to push abortion forward. His former partner, Bernard Nathanson, recorded some of Ladder's words in *Aborting America*. "If we're going to move abortion out of the books and into the streets, we're going to have to recruit the feminists. Friedan has got to put her troops into this thing — while she still has control of them." Ladder also believed they had to keep the women out front and wanted to get black women involved as well.

Friedan came around to their side, and abortion was adopted into the platform of NOW. But Friedan was never as radical as modern abortion activists today, who clearly fight to protect abortion over women. Friedan was a mother herself and believed feminists should focus on childcare and a better work environment for women. "Ideologically, I was never for abortion.

Motherhood is a value to me, and even today abortion is not." For Friedan, "the matter of choice has never been primarily the choice of abortion, but that you can choose to be a mother. That is as important as any right written into the Constitution."[8]

Of course, women have that right and that capability without abortion. Celibacy is an option available. But because of the over-sexualization of our society and the sexual revolution, any mention of abstinence practically spawns a demonic manifestation (figuratively). Women have told me it's "literally impossible." Well, women were sold a bill of goods. Instead of encouraging men to be chivalrous and holding them to a higher standard, women decided they needed to become more like men. Women resented being called "sluts," so they sought out to be "players." But as Louise Perry stated in her book, *The Case Against the Sexual Revolution*, "...women can all too easily fail to recognize that being desired is not the same thing as being held in high esteem."

Bridget Phetasy, a former writer for Playboy, was inspired to finally finish a phenomenal article, "I Regret Being A Slut," after reading Perry's book.[9] She defined herself as a case study for Perry's thesis, that the "dark side" of the sexual revolution—separating sex from consequences—has primarily benefited men. Though Phetasy would have denied drunken encounters left her "empty and demoralized" at the time, she came to realize she was using sex like a drug. Her "maneater" persona warped her mind to the point of being suspicious of decent and chivalrous men, and she thought of motherhood as a "trap."

Even more profoundly, Phatsey notes it's no wonder why so many young women look around at the consequences of the sexual revolution, outlined in Perry's book, "rough sex, hook-up culture, and ubiquitous porn" and decide they'd rather be a man. But truly, *they'd rather not be a woman.*

Inez Stepman is a senior policy analyst at Independent Women's Forum and a self-proclaimed "anti-feminist." She believes "transgenderism is not an aberration away from the fundamental assumptions of feminism, but their logical conclusion."[10] Feminists Simone de Beauvoir said, "Being a woman is not a natural fact. It's the result of a certain history. There is no biological or psychological destiny that defines a woman as such."[11]

Stepman says, "the central tenet of all waves of feminism has been that the differences between the sexes are not biological but socially constructed. That your sex should not matter." But this has always been a lie. Stepman points out that biology plays a huge role in the decisions we make and how society interacts with us.

Detransitioners like Sophia Galvin, founder of Rainbow Redemption Project, spoke of how the over-sexualization of women made her feel vulnerable and unsafe. On Allie Beth Stuckey's podcast, Galvin revealed transitioning didn't ultimately protect her anyway.[12] Social media platforms like YouTube, TikTok, and Reddit forums showcase women who fell victim to internalized misogyny.

But women are not men. They are not built like men. There's an appropriate saying: "God didn't make women to do what men can do. He made women to do what men *can't* do." Yet we've come to a place in society where women are discouraged from being women, and men pretending to be women are protected and uplifted above real women. The treatment of Lia Thomas, a transwoman swimmer at the University of Pennsylvania, compared to his teammates is a perfect example. In *The Daily Wire*'s documentary, *What is a Woman*, an anonymous female UPenn swimmer said Lia's swimming was non-negotiable. If any of the female swimmers needed help dealing with their new reality, the school could provide "counseling."

Traditional gender roles have become a thing to scorn, and biology is even met with more hatred. *Forbes* magazine reposted (then deleted) an article attacking de-transitioner Chloe Cole because she used phrases like "biological male," "biological female," and "biological sex."[13] The contributor calls these words "nonsense" and "transphobic." At the heart of it all, it's a rebellion against God's purposeful and beautiful design. Men and women are different, and they're meant to be.

Women are told if they do not have access to kill their sons and daughters in the womb, they are oppressed. When your default nature is privilege, not being catered to seems like oppression. That doesn't make it true. Who is oppressing them? God? Nature? Evolution? Women insist the medical advancements of the pill or abortion procedures have empowered them. Yet, women today are completely infantilized.

I once saw a viral TikTok video of a young woman dancing with a pregnant belly. The caption read, "When you've been with the same guy for 4 years and love kids, so you get pregnant at 19." Another caption said, "unexpected, but extremely blessed." She has over 2200 comments. She did receive congratulations and encouragement from other young mothers, but she also received many naysayers. They questioned how she would pay for the baby, and who would truly support the baby, and she was criticized for wasting the best years of her life. The mother was told she was too young to *have* the baby, though I noticed she wasn't condemned for being too young to *make* the baby.

Once the baby was made, what other options were there? Was she supposed to abort the child of the man she loves and go on with college like a life was never created, then killed? The two got engaged, and they have a supportive family. Even still, women were "sad" because she was "too young" in their minds.

Even more bizarre, *The Washington Post* did a story about a young woman who could not have an abortion due to the passing of the Texas heartbeat bill. [14] The headline reads: "This Texas teen wanted an abortion. She now has twins." The paper tried to cover the story as if it were a tragedy, but pro-life commentators elevated the beauty of life. If Brooke hadn't gotten pregnant, she'd be rushing from waitressing to real estate classes in community college, with the hopes of one day swimming with dolphins in Hawaii. Instead, she has two babies that she loves. Her boyfriend, Billy, would miss the freedom to "just chill," spending afternoons in skateparks and building burritos, but he now has a career path in the military and proposed to Brooke.

Reading reactions from this story was interesting. From the left, Twitter users remarked how the pregnancy crisis centers didn't do enough (they operated off a credit system if you took the parenting classes, and Brooke opted to not go and plan with Billy instead). Some said their "heart aches" because they've seen families with little resources before. Political commentator Erin Gloria Ryan tweeted under the author's thread, "Hard to pick the most craven, gross person in this story but I've gotta go with the local republican party cheerleading Brooke's forced motherhood without doing anything to help her financially." The attitude of Ryan's tweet reads like this: "Pay up or the babies get it!" Never mind that Brooke was about to get on the WIC program and raised 76K on GoFundMe.

Interestingly enough, Ryan didn't choose the pro-choice so-called "devout Christian" who kicked her daughter out of her house, after promising to take care of her and her grandchildren.

Left-leaning users, including journalists, commented on the reality of financial lack for women who procreate and cannot end the lives of their children. The "VoteChoice" account tweeted, "Our hearts are broken for women like Brooke."

But other users celebrated that two lives were not ended, and Brooke loves her children. Many were saddened when the twins would be old enough to read a national story about how their mother considered killing them, and all of the people who believed it was a better option. Allie Beth Stuckey said, "Sound like it's [the law] working then. Praise God." Jim Tretcher asked, "Why doesn't she just kill her own children? That would solve everything." Of course, Tretcher doesn't mean Brooke should literally do that. For some reason, society thinks it would be fine to save Brooke from motherhood by killing two fetuses that have begun to form their major organs, yet killing two newborns is monstrous.

A major commentary surrounding this story from pro-life activists was how the two teens came together and created a life plan. It's also important to note how the pro-life side of the aisle believed their family existing was a good thing and something they'd be able to handle, while the pro-choice community spoke doom and gloom into their lives. To them, being responsible for another human being is a detriment. Mothers internalize this type of judgment, and based on the article, Brooke has as well. Praise God, she's determined to prove the doubters wrong.

Responsibility can feel like a burden, but it is also a blessing. Just because your children are unplanned doesn't mean they'll be unloved, or they won't add value to your life. Maybe you can't take impromptu solo trips to Hawaii; that doesn't mean family vacations to Disney World with the kids won't be more meaningful. My parents have often expressed that Christmases are much more exciting when you have children. My mother will literally shop the entire year.

The responsibility of parenthood will dramatically change your life, but it's a necessary responsibility. If you engage in procreation and it results in a child, you are not being responsible by having an abortion like some pro-choice activists claim. Abortion is an escape hatch, and the entry fee is someone else's blood.

I'm always surprised by the reaction of pro-choice activists when I ask: "How did the baby get there?" It's a very simple question, but the amount of dodging is incredible. Barely anyone wants to answer because it makes the responsible party obvious, and they'd rather lay blame elsewhere. Even when I continue to press, women point the finger at men. Yes, they helped to make the baby, but men don't have abortions. As long as you allow blame to be such a central part of your life— whether the finger is pointed at other people or circumstances— you'll never be in control. You are not an NPC reacting to the commands of the user. You're the one driving the story.

Yes, being a parent will eat up your adolescence because it requires a certain level of maturity and responsibility. It's not a bad thing to be responsible for someone else. And though Brooke and Billy are teenagers, they are also adults. Billy is old enough to join the military, they're old enough to vote, drive, and sign contracts for student loans. No one thinks they're too young to procreate, yet pro-choice commentators are sad these "babies" had babies instead of being killers.

We have grandparents and great-grandparents alive today who were raised through the Great Depression, yet young adults in a first-world nation have to sacrifice their children to get by? It doesn't make any sense. Abortion isn't a new idea or invention, but if parents could survive in harsher societies of the past, it begs the question of why abortion is pushed in modern America as the answer.

I doubt more sex education would lead to less abortion. In 2020, only two percent of abortions in Michigan took place under the age of 18.[15] 66.9 percent of Michigan women with induced abortions had a previous term pregnancy, and 40.7 percent of those women had two or more. This isn't a sex education problem. They know how babies are made.

If sex education classes had extensive embryology, a devotion to acknowledging the human life of fetuses, and instilled within the population that abortion is a bad thing, sex education would be a different story. When I took health class in high school, abortion was a completely forbidden topic. We couldn't even discourage it. But a dear friend of mine who had an abortion was first introduced to the idea that she could have one, without parental consent, while in an inner-city sex education class from other students.

We have an abortion problem because we've been conditioned to devalue human beings, and we justify that devaluation by enforcing the idea that parental responsibility is solely a burden and not a duty, therefore, it is immoral.

That is why during the *Dobbs v. Jackson* case when Justice Amy Coney Barrett mentioned adoption as an option to transfer parental responsibilities, the mainstream media wrote hit pieces on adoption. Many pro-life adoptees fight for the right to life for the unborn, but it is not uncommon now to see pro-choice adoptees rail on social media against adoption. They'll use their right to life advocating against that same right for others.

Adoptees can face trauma, even if they grow up to be the next Steve Jobs (who was adopted and glad to not be aborted). They still deserve to be protected from violence. If mothers are concerned about the longing of their child and vice versa, the woman always has the option to raise a child herself. But convincing a young and desperate mother to keep her child is also attacked.

The Whitmer administration in Michigan accuses pregnancy crisis centers of deception. ArborWoman, a pregnancy crisis center in Ann Arbor, plainly says on its website that they do not perform or refer abortions, and they have OBGYNs on staff. But more importantly, they've had tearful and desperate women come into their clinics. Why does Whitmer's administration have an issue with any organization talking to these women and encouraging them to weigh their options and lean toward life? If you're genuinely pro-choice, why not uplift all of the options? Why does Whitmer fight so hard to protect the ones that result in tens of thousands of deaths?

Minnesota Attorney General Keith Ellison (D), who was also the former co-chair of the National Democratic Committee, issued a consumer alert for Minnesotans seeking abortions on August 22, 2022. "The Minnesota Constitution guarantees the right to safe and legal abortion. Many crisis pregnancy centers claim to offer comprehensive health care, but their purpose is to prevent pregnant people from accessing that right — which sometimes they accomplish by misleading, misinforming, or deceiving people."[16] Ellison is using terms like "pregnant people" to avoid the controversy of simply acknowledging only women can get pregnant, yet he is concerned about "misinformation?" I doubt it.

In modern America, discouragement of abortion is looked at as a heinous act. Abortion is a terrible thing, and most people can acknowledge that. Elected officials should be happy pregnancy crisis centers outnumber abortion clinics, but Ellison and Senator Elizabeth Warren look at it as if their team is losing. They don't want women to walk into these clinics, have a sonogram, and hear their child's beating heart at 180 bpm by week eight. By week ten, their brain, lungs, ears, and fine details like nails have begun to form.

If you had credible information that a mother was going to go home and murder her toddler, would you not do everything within your power to stop her? Wouldn't you at least try to convince her not to or alert the police? At the very least, women should be encouraged to not have abortions.

But abortion is described as an "act of love" by "experts" selected by the Democrats to speak before Congress in favor of abortion. In July of 2022, a law professor at Berkeley University in California was asked by Senator John Cornyn (R-Texas), "Do you think a baby that is not yet born has value?"[17]

Professor Khiara Bridges replied, "I believe that a person with a capacity for pregnancy has value, they have intelligence, they have agency, they have dignity." When she was pressed for not answering the question, she said, "I'm answering a more interesting question to me."

Senator Cornyn asked, "You think that a baby that is not yet born—let's say the day before his mother delivers—do you think that baby has value?"

Bridges tried to dodge again by stating, "I think the person with the capacity for pregnancy has value and they should have the ability to control what happens to their lives." But Bridges didn't dodge the question. She certainly demonstrated that even at nine months, she will not grant the unborn moral consideration. That is how radical the professors at universities are, and these people train up more generations of women.

Bridges' testimony was extreme, yet headlines from *Yahoo*, *The Huffington Post*, *The Washington Post*, and so on focused on Bridges calling Senator Josh Hawley (R-MO) "transphobic" because he took issue with her phrase "capacity for pregnancy" as opposed to "women." She even accused Senator Hawley's words of being violent toward transpeople because merely believing only women can be pregnant is "denying" their existence. She was very aggressive and emotional with Senator Hawley, but Bridges was lavished with praise by the political Left.

We've driven far off the path from Friedan not wanting to be fired by sexists for being pregnant. Now, pregnancy is being reshaped to include "men" (or rather women who reject their womanhood).

Lila Rose from Live Action noted, "To say that abortion was the solution to her pregnancy is, in essence, to agree with her boss. It is to say that her pregnant self is the problem, that her natural ability as a woman is the problem, that her child is the problem. Abortion has done nothing to correct the oppression and inequality that women in these situations face; it perpetuates it. Abortion is an excuse for men, businesses, and communities to neglect, exploit, and discriminate against women. Rather than support the mother and her child, they forcibly divide the two, pressuring the mother to have her child killed." [18]

Women need to be told they are capable of succeeding in motherhood, and men need responsibility to make them whole. But we've raised a generation of men and women who believe it's noble to sacrifice others rather than be accountable. They deserve to embrace selfishness and self-idolatry, and they believe the lie that gratification can be granted through pleasures of flesh rather than righteous pursuits. We are told the "future is female" yet compassion and parental responsibility are treated like kryptonite.

A biblical Proverbs 31 woman is a "girl boss" but she is also a mother and a pillar to the community. It is God's design that women are strong, capable, honorable, and feminine. The world desires to deconstruct that design through sexual exploitation, gender identity, and abortion.

Undoing much of the societal harm of abortion will take time, with an enormous effort and commitment to education. The media, academia, legal activists, lobbyists, entertainers, and politicians didn't warp minds overnight. It will take patience, compassion, and dedication to untwist depraved minds. The only way to speed up the process is with a supernatural intervention and a divine revelation that we are made in the image of God.

And those women who had an abortion should not be met with scorn. They should be met with compassion and understanding. It's okay to acknowledge abortion ended a life because there is a path forward, toward redemption. Too many women are made to feel like they'll be perpetual villains if they let the reality of their decision sink in, so they harden their hearts and belittle the lives of the unborn. I've heard many pro-life activists admit to being avid pro-choice proponents in the past, after having their abortions. Some even planned to have careers in Planned Parenthood, but the reality of abortion eventually opened their eyes to the truth.

Chelsea Hart opened her body up to Lance Tsosie in such a vulnerable way because she was first emotionally open with him. She shared the trauma of "losing" her "child." On TikTok, she said the contraction pain was so excruciating that she threw up and passed out in a puddle of sweat. Hart watched her child leave her body "in tiny pieces." Hart isn't describing a miscarriage. She's describing an abortion. In a video addressing Tsosie, Hart said she has an "ache that lives deep in her womb, Lance. And, sometimes, I just cry from my soul about it." Hart claims to still have anxiety and panic attacks that result in vomiting.

Some people gave Hart a difficult time after discovering her traumatic experience was about abortion, including "pro-choice" activists. Some people were afraid her experiences would be used for political talking points against abortion, and some believed she had no right to mourn and speak on the experience since it was initiated through deliberate actions. Also, Hart has openly mocked 900,000 deaths of babies murdered every year. She even wrote a little song to the tune of "Seasons of Love" from *Rent*. But Hart is still pro-choice and has done videos warning about the possible complications from abortion pills that health professionals rarely talk about.

Some of the biggest pushback was from women who also had elective abortions but also experienced miscarriages. They said the grief for each experience was totally different. I don't doubt that. There is a difference between playing God—deciding who lives and dies—versus coming face-to-face with the powerlessness of humanity and the pain of its mortality. But whether a child meets their end via spontaneous or induced abortion, they were still alive and very much the mother's child. Perception is a powerful tool. It can't change objective truth, but it can warp the world of an individual and those around them.

Pro-choice women empathize so strongly with a "woman's choice" because they realize how difficult of a decision it is to make. They can relate to the dread of being tied to a terrible father, perhaps even a dangerous one. They can relate to the anxieties and insecurities of not feeling up to the task of taking care of another human being, especially when it's so difficult to take care of themselves. Women can relate to having a dream within arm's reach, and the grief of having to give that up for someone else. Women are not generally pro-choice because they are uncaring monsters. They are pro-choice *because* they do care and have a warped sense of compassion, with tunnel vision focused on one party. The abortion lobby has perfected the weaponization of their skewed compassion. Even women who are gung-ho about abortion have likely gone through a hardening process, like Pharaoh. They've hardened their hearts to deepen their resolve, to protect their emotions, their friends, and their family.

The pro-life message has to be that we can love them both. We need to love women and encourage them. We empathize with their pain and their fear, but we don't always make the best decisions in such emotionally heightened states. We need time to process the gravity of the situation, weigh options, and discover a speck of hope.

Abortion advocates will often cite the Turnaway Study as evidence that 95 percent of women do not regret their abortions five years later. Though the mainstream media has fawned over the study with praise, its methodology has been criticized as flawed, the results as misleading, and the bias of the researchers (who seek to get rid of abortion restrictions) as obvious. Dr. Priscilla Coleman, professor of human development and family studies at Bowling Green State University, said, "In any other field, you wouldn't be able to publish this stuff."[19] For example, only 37.5 percent of women invited to participate agreed to it. Across the study, 42 percent dropped out, so the final result was based on 22 percent of eligible women. Coleman also notes not every woman will regret her abortion, but women still need to be made aware of risks, particularly to their mental health. There are hundreds of studies the media chooses to ignore, and women are not being properly informed.

Monica Snyder from Secular Prolife notes even if we grant the methodology of the Turnaway Study, something that has not been highlighted in the media coverage is that women who are denied abortions overwhelmingly do not regret birthing their children. Only 65 percent of participants still reported wanting an abortion after the first week of being denied. After birth, only 12 percent wished they could have aborted. By the child's first birthday, it was down to 7 percent. By the end of the five years, only 4 percent wished they had an abortion.[20]

Isn't it worth noting that 96 percent of women who are denied abortions, ultimately, do not regret that their children weren't violently killed in the womb?

At the revelation that a third of women don't have regret within the first week of being denied, Snyder was surprised at the ambivalence. "The pro-choice side frequently discusses how abortion restrictions pressure women to carry pregnancies they may not want, but it's also worth discussing how unrestricted abortion access can pressure women to get abortions they may not want."[21]

It's also important to note, that five years is a short time. I know pro-life activists who came to regret their abortions, but it took a few years to realize they made a mistake or took a life. Deborah Tilden is the co-creator of Life Victory, and she uses the pain, knowledge, and healing from her own abortion 40 years ago to help other women. [22] One thing that disturbs Tilden is the same misinformation told to her is still given to women today. She wasn't told how her abortion would affect her mental, emotional, and psychological health. It affected her marriage in ways she had to unpack years later. It led to overeating, obsessive exercising, alcohol, and drug abuse. Even her ability to bond with her children was hindered. Abortion peddlers claim life will go back to normal, but Tilden says life was never normal again. Tilden went through years of not knowing why she was depressed in October (when she had the abortion), around the would-be delivery date of her child, and on Mother's Day. After going through a healing recovery group, she realized other women who had abortions shared similar grief. Like Tilden, they were suffering in silence and were robbed of true informed consent.

Tilden said the first step in recovery was acknowledging the character of God. "God loves me unconditionally—no matter what I did, what I've done in the past. He wants me to get back on the path of wholeness, but that's through him. He wants us whole."

Women deserve better than abortion. Women should be *better* than abortion. Women don't only have to share each other's pain. We can share our burdens, and we can help to lift each other's loads. We don't have to buckle under the pressure. And if we feel our knees begin to wobble and shake, know that we will find the strength to endure and thrive. And if you're questioning how that's possible, I'll confess, "With man this is impossible, but with God all things are possible," (Matthew 19:26).

Chapter Ten
The Role of Christians

Roe v. Wade has been overturned, but the battle for life is not over. If anything, it will be more tumultuous, depending on what state you're in. And even if abortion was outlawed in the United States, the killing of the unborn is still unethical globally. Truthfully, the US had laws that were much more extreme than much of the developed world before *Dobbs v. Jackson*, and states like Colorado or the District of Columbia, which allow abortions up to nine months, are as extreme as they come.

So, what is the role of Christians? It's obvious Christians should not be in support of abortion, but how can we end it, and how aggressive should we be?

Offense Not Defense

If you intend on living your Christian walk while minding your own business, let me ask you this important question: does evil operate in a perpetual truce or does it advance if given the opportunity?

I've already spoken about Hobby Lobby and the Little Sisters of the Poor. They were minding their own business when the government came knocking at their door, requiring them to operate in a way that would violate their faith. But there are more examples.

In 2019, Foothill Church, Calvary Chapel Chino Hills, and The Shepherd of the Hills Church filed a lawsuit because the California Department of Managed Healthcare (DMHC) forced religious groups to pay for abortions. At first, DMHC wasn't enforcing churches because religious groups had exemptions. Internal documents obtained from 2014, revealed Planned Parenthood affiliates pressured lawmakers to force Christian groups to fund elective abortions. Brianna Pittman wanted to "fix" the issue of the exemptions. Pittman wrote to the health agency:

> Going forward, DMHC will not approve any further plans that exclude coverage for abortion or other reproductive health care service. This includes a clarification that there is no such thing as an elective or voluntary abortion exclusion. Simply saying that plans

need to cover "medically necessary" abortions has been the source of the issue and does not solve the problem.[1]

In August 2014, DMHC made a declaration that abortion was "basic health care" under Obamacare. They were clearly influenced by the abortion lobby.

President Joe Biden once believed in exemptions like the Hyde Amendment, but he let it be known on the 2020 campaign trail that he no longer does. He now holds the position that abortions should be funded by the taxpayers. After *Roe v. Wade* fell, his administration began to strategize how they could protect abortion statewide. Secretary of Health and Human Services Xavier Becerra immediately began looking into how women could be transported from state to state. He told *Meet the Press* on July 3, 2022, "We are exploring the opportunity to work with others to make sure that if a woman is trying to access that care that she needs, that will be supportive of that. There are a lot of partners, public and private, who are looking into this. We're one of those partners."[2]

Congresswoman Alexandria Ocasio Cortez and Senator Elizabeth Warren suggested putting abortion clinics on federal lands.

Regardless of how passive you wish to be about abortion, you're involved. Apathy won't spare you; it will simply leave you to be taken advantage of.

There truly is no common ground on the issue. The abortion extremists are not fringe. It goes all the way up to the

White House. If Christians do not stand up and at least allow their voices to be heard through their votes, we may not be able to turn back.

Politicians don't even want women to be encouraged to not have abortions. Some plan to target pregnancy crisis centers and the Biden DOJ had an underwhelming response when catholic churches and crisis centers were threatened and vandalized. After the *Dobbs v. Jackson* draft opinion was leaked to the press, activists illegally protested in front of the homes of Supreme Court Justices. A man traveled from California to assassinate Justice Brett Kavanaugh. It is still unknown who leaked the opinion, even though the pool of suspects should be small.

Some Christians debate whether or not they should be politically active at all. Abortion should not be a right or left, red or blue issue. It's an issue of right and wrong and, unfortunately, there is a big political divide on the issue. There are a few issues worthy enough to become single-voting issues. Abortion is one of them. We're talking about whether a child can live or die.

Some Christians believe they should absolve themselves from politics; some will cite Romans 13 to uplift the authority of the government. In the United States, our government operates on the consent of the governed. We have a say in our laws and who is elected to office. If Christians surrender their vote, they'll surrender their rightful power as citizens and allow secularists to have all the say. We're not *of* the world, but we're still *in* it.

It's all the rage in 2022 to shriek at the prospect of "Christian nationalists," which politicians are accused of being if they have typical conservative values and happen to be Christians. The media has a particular gripe with white evangelicals even though black churches are very political. The reason is black churches, uniformly, vote Democrat. When and if black churches start voting on the issues rather than the party, attitudes toward them will change as well. When people yell, "separation of church and state" and "tax the churches," it has nothing to do with protecting the integrity of our nation. They want to punish churches because they are seen as the political opposition. "Oh, you speak up against the thing we don't like? Well, we don't think you should be able to do that. Let's make you bleed." The church should not have loyalty to one party or the other, but it should—indisputably—be against abortion.

When William Wilberforce became a Christian, he considered whether he should continue his life in politics or retire to a private life where he could focus more on spiritual matters. Pastor John Newton, a former slave ship captain who wrote the famous hymn "Amazing Grace," encouraged Wilberforce to stay in politics as a Christian influence.

> Some of his people may be emphatically said, Not to live to themselves. May it not be said of you? Would you not be glad to have more command of your time, and more choice of your company, than your situation will admit? You meet with many things which weary and disgust you,

which you would avoid in a more private life. But then they are inseparably connected with your path of duty. And though you cannot do all the good you wish for, some good is done, and some evil is probably prevented, by your influence and that of a few gentlemen in the House of Commons, like-minded with yourself. It costs you something, many hours, which you could employ more to your own personal satisfaction, and exposes you to many impertinencies from which you would gladly be exempted; but if upon the whole you are thereby instrumental in promoting the cause of God and the public good, you will have no reason to regret, that you had not so much leisure for more retired exercises than some of us are favoured with. Nor is it possible at present to calculate all the advantages that may result from your having a seat in the house, at such a time as this. The example, and even the presence of a consistent character may have a powerful, though unobserved, effect upon others. You are not only a Representative for Yorkshire. You have the far greater honour of being a Representative for the Lord, in a place where many know him not, and an opportunity of showing them what are the genuine fruits of that religion which you are known to profess. [3]

Newton is referencing Queen Esther. When Haman is offended by her cousin Mordecai, Haman plots to have all Jews in Persia killed. Mordecai asked Esther to plead for her people, but she was hesitant. If she were to go inside the king's inner court without being summoned, she could be killed.

> [13] Then Mordecai told them to reply to Esther, "Do not think to yourself that in the king's palace you will escape any more than all the other Jews. [14] For if you keep silent at this time, relief and deliverance will rise for the Jews from another place, but you and your father's house will perish. And who knows whether you have not come to the kingdom for such a time as this?" (Esther 4:13-14, ESV)

William Wilberforce became one of the most renowned abolitionists in history and lived to see the dismantling of the slave trade in Britain shortly before he passed away. Wilberforce wrote in his diary at the age of 28, *"God Almighty has set before me two great objects, the suppression of the slave trade and the reformation of manners [morals]."*

Christianity influenced other great abolitionists, such as Pastor John Rankin in the United States. Frederick Douglass was also a strong Christian. When he gave his famous "What, to the Slave, is the Fourth of July" speech, he openly rebuked Christians for passively standing by while the brutality of slavery waged on. He thought the Fugitive Slave Act should have been seen as an assault on religious liberty.

Christians are not called to conform to evil simply because it is permitted or ordered by the government. When

Shadrach, Meshach, and Abednego would not bow before Nebuchadnezzar, they were rebelling against the government. Daniel was thrown into the Lion's den for breaking a decree to not pray. We may have to face persecution for standing for our religious convictions. We have to be ready to face the consequences, just as Jesus repeatedly warned in the New Testament. But the three Hebrew boys and Daniel have something in common: they stood for their God, and God's glory was revealed.

Christians are supposed to be living sacrifices, holy, and acceptable unto God. It's our reasonable service (Romans 12:1). It's the least we can do to worship a good, loving, all-powerful, and merciful God. We live our human lives, for as long as our God permits, with unbelievers. True. We live in the world, but we are not of the world.

If you are a Bible-believing Christian, you should never support legislation that allows for elective abortions. Even if you claim you're merely supporting "choice," you are signing your name on that child's death warrant. It's not like supporting the right to bear arms but not being culpable if someone misuses it to infringe against someone's rights. The purpose of abortion is to infringe against the child's right to life. If you support the legalization of child murder, you will share that collective sin, and that blood will also be on your hands.

Every voting believer needs to ask politicians where they stand on the issue of life. If you live in a heavily Democrat area, you may still find a politician who supports protecting the unborn. Not all Democrats believe in abortion without limitations. Vote for the best option, while evangelizing in between election seasons. If citizens are only engaged between August to November, they'll receive the representation they deserve. If they are working to change hearts and minds throughout the year, educating their communities, mobilizing, and recruiting good candidates, they'll make a difference.

Go to your local pregnancy crisis center. Get educated. Volunteer.

Go to your church and strike up conversations with members and leadership. Break down the biblical arguments against abortion and the real-world effects. Compel them to get engaged with the issue and build a network of people who will do the work.

You may go to a political event, even filled with Republicans, and come to find they are not nearly as passionate about the issue as you. The truth is many are afraid of the backlash. After the *Dobbs v. Jackson* decision was issued, many Republicans voiced concern about how abortion would play in the 2022 mid-terms. Pro-life activists have been fighting against this ruling for fifty years, and now people are too afraid to know what to do with it.

Go make your case to the voter.

You can't be too afraid to do good works because you've got a messaging problem. If you fail in 2022, that doesn't mean you'll fail in 2024. Life is worth fighting for. Republican consultants and politicians aren't going to fight against abortion as vigorously as possible—especially in local politics—unless the numbers look good. Sadly, that's how it works. But there will be standout candidates and PACs willing to boldly proclaim the message. Knock on doors, drop literature, and make phone calls. Complaining on the internet isn't going to change the nation, and if you're too persuasive, tech giants might conspire to have you banned. Besides, nothing is better than face-to-face interaction.

Groups like the Equal Rights Institute train pro-life activists to make more persuasive arguments. Live Action has been a thorn in the side of the abortion lobby for a long while. Kristen Hawkins is raising a pro-life generation with Students for Life, and she inspires others to be bold. Abolitionist Rising has also risen in popularity from their street evangelism and uncompromising convictions.

Look up the actual abortion numbers and statistics. Misinformation, euphemisms, and secrecy is the abortion lobby's greatest weapon. After all, they convinced the world murdering babies is about a "right to privacy." Learn how many babies are killed in your state per year. Compare that to a local city. Put the numbers in perspective and remind your neighbors nearly all abortions are elective.

Show the humanity of the children. Learn embryology. Ask people *when* they believe it's acceptable to kill an unborn child and if they know how developed they are in the womb.

You won't be able to persuade everyone, but apathy and ignorance have been the sword and shield of the abortion industry. Disarm them.

And when it's all said and done, fight for a ban. Will a ban put a stop to abortion? Laws against murder don't stop all murders, but human beings should not be granted free reign to kill each other. We should want an abortion ban because the unborn are entitled to a right to life.

Pro-choice activists will claim more lives will be killed if abortion is banned. There is no data to suggest more than 800,000 to 1,000,000 lives will be lost if we ban abortion. Abortion clinics are already shutting down. Children are being born who would have otherwise been aborted. Studies show that women who are denied abortions ultimately come to be glad they didn't receive one.

It will take time for the United States to completely get rid of abortion—if it can even happen at all. But I pray our children and their children will, onc day, look back on our nation and abhor the atrocities of abortion just as we abhor the atrocities of slavery.

Rejoice, But Don't Get Cocky

After the *Dobbs v. Jackson* opinion was issued, many Christian influencers were calling for empathy for those who were hurting. In Emmanuel Acho's *Uncomfortable Conversations*, he asked Pastor Chelsea Smith of Churchome why the church was "silent."

Smith referenced the verse, "Rejoice with those who rejoice, weep with those who weep," (Romans 12:15). Smith said she was "embarrassed" by the rejoicing at the cost of other people's pain. Pastor Smith never once, in the 27-minute video, expressed joy for the lives that would be saved or mourned the millions of lives lost.

If Pastors like Smith were back in the US during the 1800s, would they sour the mood of abolitionists as they rejoiced at the end of slavery? It would be appropriate to have compassion for those who lost loved ones and were in ruin after the Civil War. The country dedicated itself to reconstruction rather than grudges. Christians should commit to redemption over condemnation. But we wouldn't weep because slavery ended, and we shouldn't weep because abortion is no longer federally protected by terrible legal rulings.

Acho even asked Smith what the church should do to help women who are now "not empowered to make the decision." Abortion isn't empowering. If you need abortion to feel liberated, you're bound. There was a cry, throughout the world, when the Supreme Court issued its opinion on *Dobbs v. Jackson*. It wasn't the cry of women losing their freedom. It was a cry of addicts aching from the pain of no longer having a fix. There is no liberation in sin. Where the spirit of the Lord is, there is liberty.

Pastor Smith answered with the story of Jesus saving an adulterous woman from being stoned. She was quick to point out Jesus said, "He without sin cast the first stone," but she failed to mention Jesus also told the woman to "go and sin no more." Christians should have empathy and compassion for women who have an abortion, but it is not compassionate to encourage or pacify sin. No one on Acho's panel condemned abortion or discouraged women from having one.

Pastor Smith says, "Saving a life is a very valid cause, but that's not the only life that we're called to save. If you're pro-life, there's a lot of life." Upholding the institution of abortion will not save a woman's life, especially not her eternal life. "For whosoever will save his life shall lose it: and whosoever will lose his life for my sake shall find it," (Matthew 16:25, KJV).

James Forsyth, the senior pastor at Cedary Springs Presbyterian Church, wrote in *The Gospel Coalition*, "Now isn't the time for the church to beat its chest in celebration of a victory in the culture war. This is a moment for us to step up in love."[4]

Proverbs 21:15 says, "When justice is done, it brings joy to the righteous but terror to evildoers."

Though Forsyth offered good advice such as calling for Christians to be compassionate, actively helping women in distress, organizing within the community, and so on, some Christians took offense to the "finger-wagging."

"You have no idea what we have been doing for women," Allie Beth Stuckey said on her podcast. "And if you still have no idea at this point, that is a choice you have made. Because there are thousands of pro-life pregnancy centers that exist that have been doing all of the things that you're saying that Christians need to do before they can celebrate the overturning of *Roe v. Wade.* So, if you're worried about the deficit of compassion in Christians towards these vulnerable women, then you need to get up off your couch."[5]

Stuckey is correct. Pregnancy crisis centers exist throughout the country. Groups, like Save the Storks, are even mobile! Churches and charities are willing to help women in need. Christians also adopt. There is no such thing as an unwanted child. There is a pair of open arms waiting somewhere in the world; we just have to present the opportunity for those hearts to connect. There are presently more children waiting to be adopted than newborns available for adoption.

Some systems need improvement. For one, adoption is extraordinarily expensive. Many parents are willing to adopt who cannot simply afford to do it. But if parents choose to go through foster care, the Adoption Network notes those expenses are "generally covered by the taxes paid to a community and state." There are over 400,000 children in U.S. foster care, and 114,556 are waiting to be adopted.

There is also presently persecution of religious adoption agencies. The government would rather risk putting

Christian adoption agencies, like St. Vincent in Michigan, out of business than allow them to operate based on their religious convictions regarding marriage. The Michigan Department of Health and Human Services sued the Lansing-based charity in 2019 but announced a settlement in 2022 after a U.S. Supreme Court decision in favor of the Philadelphia Catholic foster care agency.[6]

Pro-life activists are normally rebuked by pro-choice activists when they will not sign onto Democrat wish lists like government-funded college, paid maternity leave (via government regulation), paid pre-K, and so on. But there are dangers to government-funded programs. Government money comes with government strings attached.

For example, the Biden Administration adjusted Title IX to include gender identity protections. If schools do not allow boys who identify as girls to go to locker rooms, bathrooms, and play on sports teams of their choosing, schools are in danger of losing their "free" lunch programs for underprivileged children. Grant Park Christian Academy in Tampa, Florida already found itself in battle with the Biden administration. Alliance Defending Freedom reported on August 15, 2022, the USDA issued the academy an assurance of exemption after pushback, but the mandate is still in place. Other school lunch programs are still in danger.[7]

Another example is when the Biden administration issued COVID-19 mandates, the Supreme Court shot down his edicts for businesses through OSHA. However, the

Supreme Court did uphold the mandates for healthcare workers because they receive Medicare and Medicaid.

Royal Meeker was a Princeton scholar and labor commissioner to President Woodrow Wilson. He was also a eugenicist. He believed the minimum wage would lead to job loss, but he thought that was a good thing. It would lead to welfare, and welfare would lead to control. "It is much better to enact a minimum-wage law even if it deprives these unfortunates of work. Better that the state should support the inefficient wholly and prevent the multiplication of the breed than subsidize incompetence and unthrift, enabling them to bring forth more of their kind."[8]

There is more than enough charity in this world. Black Lives Matter raised $90 million in 2020. People gave nearly $100 million to an organization that seeks to "disrupt the nuclear family" because of their emotional reaction to perceived injustice.[9]

The Minnesota Freedom Fund raised $40 million in 2020 because Kamala Harris (who was running for Vice-President), actor Steve Carell, singer Harry Styles, and other celebrities elevated this group to bail out rioters arrested during BLM protests. But MFF doesn't believe in cash bail. They'll bail out anyone, even accused murderers. They've freed criminals who went on to be charged with murder.[10]

Think of how much money we spend on elections. Beto O'Rourke (D) raised $80 million to challenge Ted Cruz (R) in 2018 and lost. Kimberly Klacik (R) raised $8 million in 2020, and her seat was virtually unwinnable. Biden (D) raised over a billion dollars to win in 2020.

Comic book movie adaptations and fantasy films generate billions at the box office domestically, according to Box Office Mojo. *Avengers: Endgame* grossed $853,373,000, and *Spider-Man: No Way Home* grossed $814,866,759. *Black Panther* grossed $700,059,566. *Star Wars: Episode VII: The Force Awakens* grossed $936,662,225. *The Last Jedi* grossed $620,181,382. Disney holds these properties and announced they would reimburse women for their travel to seek abortions in different states.[11]

Depravity also generates a lot of money. *Variety* reports "OnlyFans' net revenue grew 160 percent, to $932 million, and the company had pre-tax profits of $433 million (up from $61 million in 2020), its biggest yearly growth in profits."[12] PornHub makes $97 billion a year.[13]

We are not lacking in funds to take care of women and children in need. We are lacking in compassionate hearts. Abortion is an easy way for society to sweep "undesirables" under the rug and continue living life without giving thought or care to these people. Society doesn't fight for abortion because it's compassionate for women. Society fights for abortion because it's convenient for society. They are looking for absolution of responsibility.

Well, Christians are called to help those in need, and many Christians do. That doesn't mean we cannot do more. But Christians should not allow the world to psych them out of pushing for abortion bans because women will fall through the cracks. Christians should prove them wrong, but we should also challenge our secular society to be charitable as well.

It is perfectly fine for Christians and pro-life activists to celebrate a hard-fought victory. This particular battle is fifty years long. To ask Christians to weep for those who weep but expect them not to rejoice is insincere. But the celebration cannot lead to arrogance and laziness. The state-to-state fight will be just as if not more difficult, especially in radically pro-abortion states.

While anti-abortion activists should be glad that *Roe v. Wade* will no longer prevent states from protecting the unborn (if the states decide), abolitionists argue that *Dobbs* was wrong to send abortion back to the states at all. Under the 14th Amendment, abortion shouldn't be permitted in any state. There is nothing in the 14th Amendment that excludes the preborn from equal protection.

All persons born or naturalized in the United States, and subject to the jurisdiction thereof, are citizens of the United States and of the state wherein they reside. No state shall make or enforce any law which shall abridge the privileges or immunities of citizens of the United states; nor shall any state deprive any person of life, liberty, or property, without due process of law; nor deny to any person within its jurisdiction the equal protection of the laws. (US Constitution, XIV, Sec 1)

Some argue that you must be "born" to have equal protection, but the "born or naturalized" requirement deals with citizenship, not whether you should be entitled to unalienable rights. We wouldn't say a migrant who illegally crossed the border could be killed without any sort of repercussions because they aren't a citizen. The right to life would still apply, and they can't be deprived of it without due process. Just as they are entitled to equal protection, so is the preborn.

An unfortunate side-effect of *Dobbs* is that many people who may dislike abortion are arguing it's a states' rights issue under the 10th Amendment and quickly becoming apathetic in the fight for life. Even if it were a 10th Amendment issue meant to be up to the states, it's worth fighting in each state to make them protect life. When gay marriage was banned in California back in 2008, the gay lobby did not shrug their shoulders and accept the will of the people. We need to have more conviction to save the lives of children than homosexuals had for marrying each other.

We could fight to amend the Constitution—if that were necessary. That was the goal of the Republican platform for years. But it shouldn't be necessary. We should insist the law and our elected officials protect life equally under the 14th and demand our courts make it abundantly clear.

Allowing abortion to continue because it's a "state's right," would be like arguing that the states have a right to slavery. Either human beings have equal human rights or they don't. You should not be allowed to disqualify certain humans from human rights based on descriptive characteristics.

So, this is absolutely not a time to pat ourselves on the back and pretend we did a job well done. The fight has just begun.

Preach the Word

Honestly? Christians should be embarrassed that abortion has been rampant in a nation founded on Judeo-Christian values. It's the job of the church to make abortion unthinkable, and we have not succeeded.

There were over 30,000 abortions in my home state of Michigan in 2021. 55.6 percent of those abortions were from black bodies. In inner cities, you can barely throw a stone without hitting a church, whether it be a beautiful cathedral or a storefront. Black Americans attend church regularly more than any other group, yet the abortion industry is thriving off robbing black children of their futures. Generations gone.

How is the church lacking in such effectiveness? Why is there such a high rate of children born out of wedlock, fatherless homes, and abortion? When I was a young teen traveling with my father, he'd take his children church to church and one of us would testify: "I'm saved, sanctified, and still a virgin." The church would roar in applause—as if it were such a miracle—but there were always girls in the crowds with their mouths hanging low from shock.

"Purity culture" is looked at today as toxic. Though church hurt is real and Christian leaders may not have always expressed the gospel in the most constructive ways, we mustn't overlook the sincerity of past teachings. We can, however, perfect our teaching styles.

Celibacy isn't a game to determine who is good and who is not. It is not a measurement of one's value and self-worth. God's commandments on sexuality are not issued because he is a control freak who wants to complicate your life. God's commandments are issued in love. If anyone believes the Bible is "outdated," read the book of Proverbs. "For a whore is a deep ditch; and a strange woman is a narrow pit," (Proverbs 23:27, KJV). Go ask a man who has his check cut up all kinds of ways from child support and dealing with "baby mama drama" if this verse is true. If fornication weren't such an abundant issue, we wouldn't have almost 90 percent of abortions that occur. Yet, Christians in the church have abortions, whether they've engaged in intercourse with a boyfriend or have committed adultery.

Choosing to be celibate is the wise and moral choice for single people. Anyone who claims abstinence doesn't work is blatantly dishonest. Whether you choose to practice abstinence or not, doesn't take away from the fact that it works. If you choose to have sex, you have failed—not abstinence.

And despite what critics say, there is data to support that some abstinence-only education is effective. Not every program or purity pledge will make a statistical difference, but studies show abstinence-focused programs reduce or delay sexual activity.[14] A 2010 study of 662 black students in grades 6 and 7 found, "Abstinence-only intervention reduced sexual initiation," and those students were less likely to have sex than the control group that focused on health. The study also didn't find the safe-sex group and comprehensive intervention (which mixed abstinence and safe-sex education) to have more significant effects on intercourse or initiation than the control group.[15] A Southeast Texas school, predominantly African American and Hispanic, found that students who received a curriculum on delaying sexual activity were less likely to have had sex in the next two years.[16]

However, David B. Muhlhausen, Ph.D., evaluated the effectiveness of replicating teen pregnancy prevention (TPP) "evidence-based" programs and concluded, "the federal government has a dismal record of replicating social programs thought to be effective." Due to the "overpowering evidence of TPP ineffectiveness," Muhlhausen believes funding for these grants should be terminated.[17]

Furthermore, economist Thomas Sowell has often spoken out against sex education in school because it hasn't achieved its intended goal of less pregnancy and venereal diseases. As the government pumped more money toward sex education and "family planning" clinics in the 1960s, the more teen pregnancy and diseases increased. Though syphilis and gonorrhea had been on a steady decline from 1950-1960, they felt as though they had a crisis to solve. By 1975, the gonorrhea rate tripled. The pregnancy rate between 1970-1984 rose 29 percent for 15-17-year-olds, despite a spike in abortions.

Sowell said, "The primary objective of Federal efforts in family life and sex education has been to reduce unwanted pregnancy rates among teenagers, while the primary goal of most sex educators appears to be the encouragement of healthy attitudes about sex and sexuality."[18] Sowell believes the goal is to "brainwash" children and "supplant the values they have been taught at home." Sowell points out sex education is now pushed to K-12. How long does it take you to learn about puberty and sex? Sex education is not about biology; it's an ideological matter.

The Guttmacher Institute lends credence to Sowell's theory since their criticisms of abstinence-only education include "stigmatizing sex, sexual health, and sexuality," and they don't like the shame associated with young premarital sex. They're also upset abstinence education will "perpetuate harmful gender stereotypes" and "emphasize heterosexual relationships as the expected societal norm and not only ignore, but often undermine, the sexual health and overall well-being of LGBTQ youth."[19]

The teen pregnancy rate has been dropping since the 90s. "In 2018, the birth rate among 15-19-year-old girls and women was less than half of what it had been in 2018."[20] Pew Research notes fewer teens and young adults are having sex, and contraceptives are better nowadays. However, the CDC reported an all-time high for chlamydia, gonorrhea, and syphilis in 2019.[21]

You can't depend on the world to teach your children morality. The church world, especially at home, has to do a better job preparing young people for the temptations of the world, give them the knowledge of the risks, and while explaining the sinful nature of out-of-wedlock intercourse, come from a place of love.

MJ Acosta-Ruiz claims: "You can love God, you can be a member of your church, you can choose to have an abortion, and you can still be a good person, all at the same time."

You can be a member of your church and not even be saved. Plenty of people go to church and run around doing little jigs on Sunday, then go on being the biggest devil in town until they sit in the pew once more. By what standard do we judge if someone is "good?" If we accept the objective morality of God and base morality on his standards, abortion is undoubtedly evil. And if you love God, you will keep his commandments. That's not my opinion; that's what Jesus said (John 14:15).

Can you be a Christian, make a mistake, commit a grave sin, then be redeemed? Absolutely. But you cannot love God and reject his word. It's who he is. His goodness is reflected in his commandments. If you encourage other women to have abortions, you're not being a witness to his goodness. You're being an adversary.

Christians must come to know the difference between practicing religion and developing a relationship with God. Every time my father gets up to preach, he quotes the same scripture. "Thy word have I hid in my heart that I might not sin against thee," (Psalm 119:11, KJV). The word has to be something Christians study. How can Christians truly know God without understanding him? Have you ever heard a woman wake up from a terrible relationship because her partner did something that made it so obvious that he knew nothing about her or cared so little about her feelings? Why do Christians do this?

Reading the Bible isn't what makes you saved. But when you love someone, you don't want to openly offend and drive them away. That's why you must hide the word in your heart; make it so a part of you, that sinning against him becomes unnatural. Our hearts alone are deceitful. We need the word of God, so we are not betrayed by our own emotions. If you want a relationship with God, spending time in prayer and reading the word is how you get to know him.

If Christians cannot grasp the goodness of God's word, how will they convey it to the world? If you want to end abortion, start by strengthening your own heart in Christ.

Treat others with the love of Christ. If we are all made in the image of God, we need to act like it. We need to bear the fruit of the Spirit, which is not running around the church and doing a little two-step after rounding the altar for the second time.

¹⁹ Now the works of the flesh are evident: sexual immorality, impurity, sensuality, ²⁰ idolatry, sorcery, enmity, strife, jealousy, fits of anger, rivalries, dissensions, divisions, ²¹ envy, drunkenness, orgies, and things like these. I warn you, as I warned you before, that those who do such things will not inherit the kingdom of God. ²² But the fruit of the Spirit is love, joy, peace, patience, kindness, goodness, faithfulness, ²³ gentleness, self-control; against such things there is no law. ²⁴ And those who belong to Christ Jesus have crucified the flesh with its passions and desires. (Galatians 5:19-24, ESV)

It needs to be evident that God has made you into a new creature (2 Corinthians 5:17) because people need to know God can remake them as well. People in the modern world, particularly the West, are in desperate search of an identity. Some find it in race and obsess over it; every daily struggle is surrounded by it. Some find it in their proclaimed gender. If they want to know who they are and who they're meant to be, they can go before their Creator, who knitted them so thoughtfully in the womb.

The more you come to know Christ, the more you come to know you can do all things through him, because he'll strengthen you. You'll know with God, all things are possible. You'll know all things work together for the good, for those who are called according to his purpose (Romans 8:28).

Whatever trials a woman faces that may leave her desperate and considering an abortion, know that God is great enough to help her overcome. If it's financial, medical, or any other desperate situation, God can grant provisions, mercy, healing, divine protection, or even supernatural peace to endure hardship. As believers, we have to know that, and we must testify to believers and nonbelievers as well.

Before I became political, it was obvious to me that abortion was wrong. It was antithetical to my biblical upbringing. Pastors shouldn't need to tell their congregation abortion is evil; it should be obvious while observing the nature of God. It certainly doesn't hurt to point it out and make a strong case, especially when political activists openly misrepresent God from the pulpit for their agenda.

Stacey Abrams received a round of applause from Allen Temple AME Church in Woodstock, GA, after claiming: "I was trained to read and understand the Bible, and I will tell you this, there is nothing about the decision to eliminate access to abortion care that is grounded in anything other than cruelty and meanness."[22]

You can only have this view if you do not see the unborn as a human being made in the image of God. Even when Abrams went on to criticize six-week abortion bans, she never addressed the humanity of the child. She talked as if the unborn was no better than cancer pressing against a woman's uterus. Abrams said, "Lives are in danger," without addressing the obvious elephant in the room. She said, "It is now lethal to be a woman in the state of Georgia," because they won't grant a license to kill. Abortion is a complex issue, but anyone who will not address the humanity of the child killed, should not be taken seriously.

Abrams told *CNN* she was anti-abortion until college, then a pro-choice Christian friend persuaded her to change her mind. Now, Abrams is so radically pro-abortion that she won't condemn it in the ninth month.

When Jesus told the parable of the sower, he explained not everyone who hears the gospel will be rooted in it (Matthew 13:1-23). Not everyone is good ground. You must make certain that you are, so when a deceiver comes to pull you away from the faith, you won't let them choke the word out of you. Bear good fruit.

Men Must Step Up

If a man has children out of wedlock and dodges child support payments, he is criticized by society heavily. He is called a "deadbeat." Even if they give a little money here and there but don't come around, he'll be criticized for being an absentee father. Men need to be called out for rejecting their parental obligations through abortion as well.

Pro-choice activists claim it's a terrible thing for women to give birth to "unwanted" children. But women who have abortions often want children at later points of time in their lives.

A high level of desire for future children suggests an aborted pregnancy was most likely problematic due to specific circumstances or lack of sufficient social support. Among a sample of women seeking counseling for post-abortion distress, 64 percent felt "forced by outside circumstance" to have an abortion and 83 percent indicated they would have carried to term if significant others in their lives had encouraged delivery.[23]

Men are often nagged about supporting a "woman's choice," but many women are waiting for men to care. They're waiting for men to stand up and protect their progeny. If a man is not father material, why would she want to be tied to him for at least 18 years? Even worse, allow her child to suffer through a poor father?

Abortion Mental Health advocates criticize "relief" as a factor in determining the success of abortion outcomes because it's such a broad term with so many variables. Relief might come from not having the baby, but it may come from the procedure being behind her, and that her friends and family won't ever know she was pregnant. Relief may also come directly from her partner. Perhaps he'll finally stop harassing her or she's happy to not be tied to him any longer. Mental health counselor Robin Atkins admitted she felt relief after her abortion due to her ex, but she would take it back in a heartbeat to have her child alive now.

Women often are very irritated that so much of the abortion debate and blame are laid at their feet, even if they want all the control in the matter. Women can and should be more responsible with who they choose to sleep with and when, but sex is at least a two-partner dance. The egg is fertilized by a male's sperm. The man is absolutely involved and bears responsibility.

God created women to work in concert with men. Men should not be a burden to their helpmeet, nor should they make a woman feel like their child is a burden. Children are a challenge, but they are not an obstacle or a roadblock to a path of happiness.

We have generations of men being raised without fathers, who have no idea how to be a good father or a good husband. They haven't experienced it; they only know what not to do, and many will make those same mistakes anyway.

Pastors, deacons, elders, etc., need to take more time out to disciple these men. They hurt just like women do, even if they can't express their pains as plainly or articulately. Mentorship is sorely lacking in the body of Christ. A summer event full of pizza and the hottest worship bands is not adequate.

Too many leaders fill men with the arrogance of patriarchal authority without instilling the duty to protect and cherish their partners. They create churches of misogynists full of ego but with no leadership skills to back it up.

When God made man, he saw it was not good for him to be alone. He didn't give Adam a male companion. He gave him a woman to fill the void. "This at last is bone of my bones and flesh of my flesh," (Genesis 2:23, ESV). A man cannot reproduce without a woman. He can have no lineage without her, and she sacrifices her body and time to give him a child. This should produce gratitude. He should want to love, protect, and honor her.

Ephesians 5, says a man should love his wife as he would his own body. And even more specifically, "He who loves his wife loves himself."

Many women in the world are not ready for relationships, and the same is true for men. If they don't love themselves, how can they truly love a woman? And not love in a vain or self-serving way. Men aren't patient with themselves. They're unforgiving and critical instead of constructive and optimistic. Men aren't kind to themselves. Men put themselves down because they compare their accomplishments to others and judge their lives off perceived lack rather than God's blessings. So, instead of being inspired to achieve they become greedy and covet. They look out for themselves instead of helping others. They're angry, bitter, and delight in wickedness. And of course, they do not protect, and they lack the valor to be loyal. It takes no courage to live your life in self.

Men *need* responsibility. It's like an anchor keeping them from going adrift and becoming lost at sea. There's meaning in raising a family with a partner you can love and trust. "He who finds a wife finds a good thing and obtains favor from the Lord," (Proverbs 18:22, ESV). Your children are a blessing and a reward (Psalm 127:3).

Chapter Eleven

Establishing Justice

An induced abortion is an unjustified premeditated killing of a preborn image bearer of God and our neighbor, who we are called to love as we love ourselves. It is, undoubtedly, a great evil in our land that needs to be eradicated. The question of how we go about it is crucial. There are debates between the pro-life community and abolitionists regarding the effectiveness and morality of enacting incremental laws to end abortion. That is a topic that will need to be addressed in greater detail at a later time. But it's worth touching on the arguments of who should receive punishment for taking the lives of the preborn.

No one should be retroactively punished for a crime committed when it was legal. If a nationwide ban is enacted today, abortionists wouldn't be prosecuted for abortions performed years ago. The Constitution forbids the making of ex post facto laws. If there was a nationwide ban today, there isn't much debate that abortion providers should face consequences for performing illegal abortions, and things like abortion pills should be outlawed. Pro-choice activists gasp at the prospect of arresting doctors, but if a doctor was purposely killing toddlers, they'd make no fuss about it. Just imagine if that same toddler was younger and in the womb. That same child still deserves protection, and they deserve justice.

Equal Justice

The great debate is if abortion is murder—similarly or just as much as purposely killing a newborn—should a woman be punished for committing an abortion? Some Republican politicians will claim, "No one wants to punish women." This isn't true. I understand why Republicans want it to be true politically, but it isn't, and the number of anti-abortion activists who share this sentiment is growing. I've also heard Republican politicians plead, "Can't we agree that women shouldn't be punished?" They speak as if the position is absurd without genuinely debating the issue.

Abortion abolitionists are sometimes accused of picking on women because they believe if a woman commits an abortion, she should be punished by law. But their position is anyone who commits an abortion should face justice. Sadly, women are the primary abortionists because the majority of abortions are performed with abortion pills. If a man forces her to take a pill, she and her child are both victims and he should be punished. But if a mother willingly and purposely takes actions to end the life of her child, she should also face justice, just as she would if that child were outside of the womb. To grant the mother a special exemption would be to show partiality, and there is no partiality with God (Romans 2:9-11). God is a righteous judge and doesn't give preference to the rich or poor (Leviticus 19:15). It is not good to show partiality to the wicked or to deprive the righteous of justice (Proverbs 18:5). Even if the mother has a surgical abortion, she is still hiring a hitman to kill her child.

Major pro-life organizations and influential activists have argued abortion is murder, but mothers seeking abortion do not meet the requirements to be mentally culpable for their actions. *Mens rea* is a concept in the law that considers your intention or knowledge of wrongdoing when it comes to committing a crime. Pro-life activists will argue that society has indoctrinated women so much that even if you did charge women, many of them would needlessly go through a trial and be found innocent because they don't have true culpability for their crimes. Charging them in the future, once we rewire the minds of the culture, might be the right way to go, but they do not advocate for immediate arrests.

I agree with the pro-life position that our society has been largely brainwashed, and that case has been made in this book. However, if the mothers who committed the abortion are brainwashed, how can the same not be said about the doctors who perform the abortions? They live in the same society. They are being raised and taught that abortion is health care. Abortionists, indeed, have enough medical information to know they are killing living humans, but they are taught not to value them unless the mother wants them. They are taught the bodily autonomy of the mother supersedes the life of the fetus because as Dr. Warren Hern would note, all abortions are a matter of the health of the mother because the fetus is in her body.

It is also difficult to swallow the idea that women are not culpable. Sometimes, I listen to abortion debates, and I'm horrified at how little women know. I listened to a young woman describe an abortion with the pill, and she didn't understand how she had suffocated and starved her child. She believed it was a "clump of cells" that came out during a heavy period. Many women have no grasp of embryology at all. Fair enough. But some women have had abortions, don't like them, believe it's killing a child, yet have gone on to do it again anyway. There are informed consent laws on the books with waiting periods that require the mother to go online and read about the abortion procedure and the child's development, yet they still choose death. Many women have abortions after carrying multiple children to full-term. Many women claim they don't care that the fetus is alive; they can do as they please. Perhaps they "know not what they do," but that is mostly because they suppress the truth (Romans 1:17) that has been written on their hearts. Practically every day, I hear abortion defenders claim no woman wants an abortion, and then they go on to defend their need for the most trivial reasons. They know it's not good, but they love their sin. Perhaps some women are not culpable, but why shouldn't that be determined on a case-by-case basis? If a woman is an abortion doctor and performs an illegal abortion, anti-abortionists would likely agree that she should go to jail. If that same woman ingested an abortion pill for herself, much of the pro-life community would say our laws should give her immunity for taking the life of her child.

Besides, the primary argumentation of the pro-choice movement is that even if it is a baby and alive, it doesn't matter. They believe women should be allowed to kill their children because it's in their bodies.

Sometimes, pro-life activists will bring up that our culture normalized abortion just as slavery was once normalized, and the culture needs to be adjusted so we hate abortion like we hate slavery. I agree, but that doesn't mean we shouldn't seek justice. What's the argument here? If people were still holding slaves after the 13th and 14th Amendments were passed, should slave masters have legal immunity and face no justice because their culture instructed them that it was perfectly normal? When Captain Collingwood threw the slaves of the Zong overboard and faced no punishment because they believed those black men had the same moral status as planks of wood, do you genuinely believe that was the moral call that would have been just in God's eyes?

The law has a purpose besides protecting our liberties. The law is also a tutor. Many times, abortion activists will appeal to legality. They'll say, "If abortion was bad, it would be illegal." I once heard a pro-choice lawyer baffled by the idea that pro-lifers believe so many politicians in New York could make such an immoral mistake as if we don't have a history and current examples of enacting unjust laws. By not outlawing abortion, we are teaching society that it must be moral or that we don't truly believe it to be murder. Even legislation like the Unborn Victims of Violence Act signed in 2004 by President George W. Bush, which charges people for a separate crime for causing the death or injury of a child in the womb, has a special carve out for abortion. We are misinforming the public about the value of life and when children should be protected. Even the overturning of *Roe v. Wade* by the *Dobbs* decision is misinforming the public because many Republicans, such as Donald Trump, are claiming the rights of a preborn child should range from state to state based on their laws. Slavery was once argued as a "states' rights" issue. Human rights should not end once you cross a state line. The Democrats, on the other hand, believe the right to kill a preborn child should not be limited by state borders. If only those who fight on the side of righteousness had as much conviction as those who fight on the side of ungodliness!

Even well-intended legislation such as the six-week "heartbeat" bills are misinforming the public on the value of life. We do not become human and alive when our heartbeats are detected. We should be protected at conception. The political reason these bills exist is to claim that a heartbeat bill is not a total ban. You can have an abortion, for any reason, until that heartbeat is detected. Once it is, the baby cannot be killed. The true strategy is to virtually outlaw abortion because most women won't know they are pregnant before the heart begins to develop. This has led to two side effects in the debate. The first is that people are denying the significance of the fetal heartbeat or claiming what we hear isn't actually a true heartbeat of a fully developed heart anyway. The second is to argue if women should have some time to decide whether they can abort, six weeks is completely unreasonable because most women do not discover they are pregnant until later. In reality, women should not have more time to decide to kill their children, and they should be told that plainly. Despite Florida's six-week ban having exceptions for rape, incest, life of the mother, trafficking, and fetal anomaly, people still want the bill to compromise more. We could argue a six-week ban is better than nothing, but there are consequences to misinforming the public about the value of human life, when it begins, and when it should be protected.

You might be asking, how do we uplift redemption over condemnation if mothers are charged and convicted? Being found guilty of a crime doesn't mean that you cannot find redemption and salvation, nor does it mean Jesus Christ didn't die on the cross for your sins. We all know women who have had an abortion, and we wouldn't want them placed behind bars for that crime, especially if they have repented and carried grief for their sin. But ask yourself this question: would they have likely committed the abortion if there was a severe punishment? Likely not. Justice doesn't deter all crime, but an allowance of injustice spreads more injustice. If retail theft, for example, is not properly prosecuted, mobs will repeatedly break into stores like in California.

Some women only require a strong deterrent, and they will choose a different path. If punishing the guilty would deter women from choosing death, keep their little ones from being slaughtered, and preserve the mother's innocence, how is justice not mercy? I've seen too many women express the horror of guilt after their abortion, whether it happens immediately after surgery, when they carry their next child to term, or years down the road. I've read their comments as they cope with fantastical ideas that the soul of the child they killed will return to them, and I've seen women comfort each other, claiming the baby understands because it was best for the mother. Women ache after abortions, and it should not be our intention to drive a knife further into their hearts. I've cringed at some of the language pro-life debaters online use when addressing these women. We should seek to reconcile her with Christ, but we should prevent this tragedy from occurring if we can.

Abortion abolitionists, such as groups like Abolitionist Rising, don't argue that they can end abortion. They argue that we should establish justice. The child who is killed deserves justice and whoever committed the injustice should face penalty. Micah 6:8 says God requires us to do justice, but it also requires us to love mercy. You wouldn't need mercy if there was no guilt or no law in place. And once justice is sought, perhaps mercy will be granted depending on the circumstances, such as coercion, for example. There are different degrees of murder based on the facts of the case, and those who commit homicide can be exonerated based on the circumstances. And if we establish justice, that will significantly decrease the number of abortions.

Pro-life organizations such as Live Action argue that we need to make abortion "unthinkable." Perhaps that is a possible goal. Men fought and died over slavery in the past, but owning a slave is mostly unthinkable in the US. There are still people who are trafficked and forced to do things against their will, but society as a whole shuns and is disgusted by the practice and our ugly history. If we keep informing the public about the true horrors of abortion, if we support women, and criminalize providers, we may get to a place where abortion is mostly "unthinkable."

As to which approach is correct is being debated. But the abolitionists do have a very compelling question to ask of the pro-life community. Let's say pro-life legislators had the numbers across every state and federally to ban it. If abortion is outlawed at the moment of conception, any person who provides an illegal abortion will be prosecuted, and anyone who traffics in the abortion pill will be punished. Mothers who receive an illegal abortion are legally immune when it comes to committing an abortion. What would happen if women across the country went to their local courthouse with an obvious baby bump, pulled out an abortion pill, and announced, "I am having an abortion right now?" If these women committed such an act, even in front of police officers, pro-life laws would protect them from prosecution. At most, she could be punished for buying or possessing the pills, but it would be odd to send a mother to jail over possessing the drugs to kill her child, yet not prosecuting her for the actual killing. Even if the pro-life community got everything they supposedly wanted, they would disarm the government from being able to enforce the laws against the majority of perpetrators by granting them immunity. Just as women have special murder rights today, they would exist under pro-life laws.

God let it be known that Israelites or foreigners living among them who committed child sacrifice needed to be punished. If the people did not seek justice, God would turn his face from them. We do not want the sin of child murder to be shared among our nation.

I have also heard pro-life Christians argue that we are living under a new covenant and a law of grace, therefore, women don't need to be punished for abortion. I've also heard the claim that women don't need to be held accountable for abortion in the way a man would be for coercing her because God has a special authority given to men, and women are underneath them. Though I'm sure this is meant to be chivalrous and protecting, this line of thinking is condescending and misogynistic. Pro-life Christians would not argue that no woman should be held accountable for any crime, especially murder. They would have to argue pregnancy and abortion are such unique and special circumstances that women deserve an exemption only for this particular human rights violation, but pro-choice activists would make a similar claim that pregnancy is such a unique circumstance that it justifies the special right to kill their child. If abortion is murder, treat it as such or concede that it isn't.

Incrementalism and Immediatism

Christian pro-life activists have argued incrementalism is Biblical because God regulated actions that he didn't necessarily endorse, but his people were not ready for large leaps of moral progress, such as laws dealing with slavery and divorce. Jesus said that divorce was never God's design, but Moses permitted men to put away their wives because of the hardness of their hearts (Matthew 19:8-9). The heart of the world is very hard on abortion, and there is no foreseeable path for a nationwide ban. Not only would it be difficult—if not impossible—to get enough anti-abortion votes in the House and Senate, but a majority of anti-abortion politicians would simply lack conviction. Pro-life activists like to take victories where they can get them and save as many babies as possible.

Abolitionists, however, would argue there is no incrementalism for child sacrifice. God clearly hated it, forbade his people from participating in it, and shunned them for not enacting justice. Abolitionists endorse immediatism because it's a matter of obedience to God and dealing with sin as Christ commanded. If your eye causes you to sin, pluck it out. If your hand causes you to sin, cut it off. Even though there were laws in place for divorce, Jesus still said divorcees who go on to have relations are committing adultery, unless the marriage ended due to sexual immorality (Matthew 5:29-32). Legality doesn't erase disobedience to God's design. Abolitionists believe we should obey God's word immediately and fully instead of passing iniquitous decrees (Isaiah 10:1). They do not want legislation passed that permits the regulation or allowance of premeditated preborn homicide.

Pro-life activists will argue the historical success of incrementalism when it comes to slavery in the UK and the US, but abolitionists would argue that incrementalists slowed the progress of defeating slavery by regulating it instead of supporting abolition. Pro-life activists would argue *Roe v. Wade* was defeated through incrementalism, and abolitionists would argue taking fifty years to defeat an unconstitutional legal ruling, that still allows the sin of abortion, is hardly a cause for celebration.

The Government's Duty

Many Christians believe abortion is wrong, yet the government has no place in this particular matter. Some may claim to be "personally pro-life" yet pro-choice for everyone else (which is just pro-choice). This is nonsense. Christians don't say, "I believe rape is wrong, but it's none of my business. If someone else wants to choose rape, it should be legal." We don't argue that murder should be permissible. We even want thieves to face penalties for their crimes. We recognize that laws are put in place to protect citizens from being unjustly aggressed upon. You wouldn't personally believe it's wrong if you didn't believe the child was being aggressed and deprived of their life and future conscious experiences. And despite how we personally feel about the preborn, they are image bearers of God.

Based on the Declaration of Independence, the government exists to secure our unalienable rights, the first being the right to life. According to Romans 13, the government is a legitimate authority instituted with the permission of God. It says, "for he is God's servant for your good. But if you do wrong, be afraid, for he does not bear the sword in vain. For he is the servant of God, an avenger who carries out God's wrath on the wrongdoer. Therefore one must be in subjection, not only to avoid God's wrath but also for the sake of conscience," (Romans 13:4-5).

Unfortunately, not all governments are good, but they are meant to be. Nothing is wrong with advocating for limited government and insisting it shouldn't be involved with certain aspects of our lives, but the government does serve a legitimate purpose: to protect our liberties. There is a legitimate right to life, but there is no special right to murder your children.

As Christians, we should urge our government to meet its obligation to defend life and seek justice for our defenseless neighbors. The intricacies of how justice should be enacted and the political ramifications will have to be debated amongst ourselves, but throwing up our hands and allowing the secularists to have their way is unacceptable.

Even if banning abortion will not end it totally, it should not be permitted. We should not make murder "safe" and more convenient for the aggressors, and there should be some form of protection for the unborn. And if the law fails to persuade the aggressor and the conspirators from their act of violence, the victim—at the very least—deserves justice.

Women will always have the "choice" to choose abortion, even if it were to become illegal. But the greater question is why are we choosing to permit unjust violence against an innocent victim? Whether we as a society establish justice is a choice but it is also our duty.

<u>Conclusion</u>

Ministers from Light Bearers Ministry had a
fascinating discussion about Satan's greatest weapon in his
arsenal: his ability to deceive. [1] "Genesis 3 is, in so many ways,
the story of the first deception and the first victimization, but
it's not a victimization of control. It's not of power or of
strength. It's of manipulation—psychological deception." The
serpent unleashes what they call a "tripod of deception,"
which leads to the fall of mankind.

**The serpent introduced the idea that Eve had
restricted freedom.** The serpent asks, "Did God actually say,
'You shall not eat of any tree in the garden'?" He made it
seem like she had a tiny bit of freedom when the opposite was
true. There was *only one* tree God commanded them not to
eat from.

**The serpent introduced the idea that God was
untrustworthy.** The serpent told Eve she would not die if she

partook of the fruit, planting the idea God was lying to her, trying to control and manipulate her.

The serpent introduced the reason God was being deceptive and alleged God was looking out for himself, rather than acting out in their best interest. The serpent told Eve God was withholding the fruit because if she partook of it, she would be like God. He makes God self-serving and threatened rather than protecting and loving.

It was not until these deceptions took root that Adam and Eve sinned against God and broke his commandments.

An abortion ban is not a restriction on a woman's "reproductive freedom." She has many other options: celibacy, birth control, fertility tracking, condoms, and sterilization. If she becomes pregnant, she has adoption, safe harbor laws, or the choice to mother her child. Denying abortion as an option is not a lack of freedom. **That is the perspective of the serpent.**

If you can terminate the life of an innocent child—made in the image of God—based on your insufficiencies as a human instead of trusting God as your source, **you have the perspective of the serpent**.

If you agree with Stacey Abrams and believe a restriction on abortion access is rooted in "cruelty and meanness," rather than compassion and love for all parties involved, you have **the perspective of the serpent**.

The Bible says the devil prowls around like a roaring lion, seeking someone to devour (1 Peter 5:8). When a woman is faced with hard pink lines—full of anxiety—the devil doesn't emerge from a puff of smoke and command you to give up your baby via ritual sacrifice. He's cunning, and at times, very subtle. *How are you going to pay for a baby? What will your parents think? What will the church members say? You're not ready for this! You can barely take care of yourself. He'll leave you if you keep this baby. How can you raise a child alone?*

Satan is the accuser, and he'll accuse you of being ill-equipped, ill-prepared, and even incapable of loving your child. He will tempt you to fall into sin, and then use that sin to call you unworthy of God's love and forgiveness.

The devil is a liar.

In a woman's limited wisdom, she may conclude abortion is the best decision, for her and her child, at the time. But that's the problem. *Our wisdom is limited.* You can't possibly know. You can make whatever justifications to convince yourself that you made the right call. After all, "The way of a fool is right in his own eyes," (Proverbs 12:15). But the foolishness of God is wiser than even the wisest human (1 Corinthians 1:25).

It's okay to not know what's going to happen today. It's okay to not know what's going to happen tomorrow. But one thing is certain; God is sovereign, he is just, and he is a loving God. Your heavenly father knows all that you have need of, and he can more than meet those needs. But it is important to first seek the kingdom of God and his righteousness. And after you do that, all these things shall be added unto you (Matthew 6:25-34).

When Jesus told the Pharisees they were of their father, the devil, he said, "He was a murderer from the beginning, and does not stand in the truth because there is no truth in him. When he lies, he speaks out of his own character, for he is a liar and the father of lies," (John 8:44).

Do you believe God is strong enough, great enough, wise enough, and loving enough to help you through your time of need? If you knew God, you would trust him. And if you understood the character of the deceiver, you would flee from temptation as fast as possible and reject every lie from his lips.

If you are a woman who had an abortion, know that Jesus died on the cross not only for the liars, drunkards, adulterers, fornicators, etc. He also died on the cross for the sin of your abortion. Women should not hold onto their guilt and shame forever. We are all sinners in need of a savior.

If you're a Bible-believing Christian, abortion is never the answer. *Jesus is the answer*, and he came to give us life and life more abundantly (John 10:10). So, I implore you to choose life.

If you are a pro-choice and self-identified "Christian," you make that choice knowing it is antithetical to God's holy word. You can't love God and openly reject who he is and his commandments. You'd be serving an idol of your own making; not worshiping the one true God. The only "choice" to make is to "choose you this day whom ye will serve...but as for me and my house, we will serve the Lord," (Joshua 24:15, KJV).

For it is abundantly clear, God is blatantly against abortion.

About the Author

Christina L. Barr was born to Keith and Isabelle Barr on June 10, 1989, in Pontiac, MI. She and her six siblings were always active in her father's church. By the age of nine, Barr was writing worship music, and as a teen, she was designing graphics and cutting commercials for TV spots.

Barr has had the honor of singing in front of thousands in the Philippines, for the President of the United States, and for congregations—large and small—across the US. She's an eloquent speaker and loves to minister and worship.

She's always been a determined and creative mind and achieved her writing goal of completing 30 books by her 30th birthday. In 2012, she published her first book, *Superkid*, and began her indie publishing company, Ninja Dust Publishing. Barr also runs *Black Tea News*, a political and cultural news and commentary website. *Of Course, God is Blatantly Against Abortion* is her 16th published book.

Christina L. Barr is also a political activist. In 2014, she ran to be a state representative and a congresswoman. The next year, she became the Creative Director for the Michigan Republican Party. She still consults with various campaigns today.

On February 9, 2020, Barr was ordained into ministry with her five sisters by her father. Her only brother was ordained a few years prior and is the pastor of their church in southeast Michigan.

Barr is also a talented graphic designer and videographer and has designed all of her book covers, except for, *Of Course, God Is Blatantly Against Abortion*. Her youngest sister, Tina, drew and then digitally painted the hand of God reaching out to the child.

Stay Connected

Thank you for taking the time to read *Of Course, God Is Blatantly Against Abortion*. I pray it was a blessing to you. If you did enjoy it, I ask you to take a moment to review it on Amazon, Goodreads, Barnes & Noble, Google, and wherever else readers dwell. And please, share it on social media.

If you would like to read my other works, you can visit **NinjaDustPublishing.com**. For my thoughts on news, politics, pop culture, and so on, you can visit **BlackTeaNews.com**. And if you enjoy my work, I hope you'll consider becoming a supporter.

Thank you, and God bless.

BLACK TEA NEWS

AUTHOR CHRISTINA L. BARR
NINJADUSTPUBLISHING.COM

To learn more about the artist who designed the book cover, visit:

Tina's

Text Portraits and Designs

TinasTextPortraits.com

Notes

Introduction

[1] Biden, S. J. (2006, March). (T. Monthly, Interviewer) Twitter. Retrieved from Twitter: https://twitter.com/RNCResearch/status/1540400912199458817

[2] Charlotte Lozier Institute. (2022, August 17). *Fact Sheet: Reasons for Abortion*. Retrieved from Charlotte Lozier Institue: https://lozierinstitute.org/fact-sheet-reasons-for-abortion/#_ednref9

[3] Guttmacher Institute. (2022, June 15). *Long-Term Decline in US Abortions Reverses, Showing Rising Need for Abortion as Supreme Court Is Poised to Overturn Roe v. Wade*. Retrieved from Guttmacher Institute: https://www.guttmacher.org/article/2022/06/long-term-decline-us-abortions-reverses-showing-rising-need-abortion-supreme-court

[4] Planned Parenthood. (2020). *Planned Parenthood 2019-20 Annual Report*. Retrieved from https://www.plannedparenthood.org/uploads/filer_public/67/3

0/67305ea1-8da2-4cee-9191-19228c1d6f70/210219-annual-report-2019-2020-web-final.pdf

[5] AP News. (2022, August 17). *Planned Parenthood to spend record $50M in midterm elections.* Retrieved from AP News: https://apnews.com/article/abortion-2022-midterm-elections-health-congress-71871318f3c725a7df0bbe183e6c84be

[6] Yu, Y. S. (2022, October 28). *Proposal 3 abortion measure generates $57M in Michigan campaign donations.* Retrieved from Bridge Michigan: https://www.bridgemi.com/michigan-government/proposal-3-abortion-measure-generates-57m-michigan-campaign-donations

[7] Harvard CAPS Harris Poll. (2022). *Approval and Mood of Country.* The Harris Poll CAPS (Center for American Pollitical Studies) Harvard University. Retrieved from https://harvardharrispoll.com/wp-content/uploads/2022/07/HHP_June2022_KeyResults.pdf

[8] Cawthorne, C. (2022, June 26). *Stacey Abrams refuses to say whether she supports restrictions on abortions up to 9 months.* Retrieved from Fox News: https://www.foxnews.com/politics/stacey-abrams-refuses-say-supports-restrictions-abortions

[9] Silva, C. D. (2019, March 19). *Beto O'Rourke on Third-trimester Abortion: 'That Should Be a Decision That the Woman Makes...I Trust Her'.* Retrieved from Newsweek: https://www.newsweek.com/beto-orourke-third-trimester-abortion-should-be-decision-woman-makesi-trust-1367376

[10] Brest, M. (2019, March 20). *Beto Refuses To Endorse Bill That Would Ban Infanticide.* Retrieved from Daily Caller: https://dailycaller.com/2019/03/20/beto-2020-infanticide-bill-ban-abortion/

[11] Cohen, L. (2020, January 6). *Michelle Williams advocates for abortion rights in Golden Globes acceptance speech.* Retrieved from CBS News: https://www.cbsnews.com/news/golden-globes-michelle-williams-advocates-for-womens-rights-in-golden-globes-speech/

[12] RNC Research. (2022, May 20). *Rep. Alexandria Ocasio-Cortez Rants About How Babies In Wombs Are Not A Life .* Retrieved from Twitter: https://twitter.com/realdailywire/status/1527728634244608005

[13] Shapiro, B. (2022, May 23). *AOC And Ilhan Omar Have LOST THE PLOT.* Retrieved from Youtube: https://youtu.be/lxbAiU1dhYI

[14] Biden, J. (2022, May 3). *Remarks by President Biden Before Air Force One Departure.* Retrieved from The White House: https://www.whitehouse.gov/briefing-room/speeches-remarks/2022/05/03/remarks-by-president-biden-before-air-force-one-departure-15/

[15] White, S. P. (2012, August 17). *Above My Pay Grade . . . Four Years Later.* Retrieved from National Review: https://www.nationalreview.com/corner/above-my-pay-grade-four-years-later-stephen-p-white/

[16] Harvard CAPS Harris Poll. (2022). *Approval and Mood of Country.* The Harris Poll CAPS (Center for American Pollitical Studies) Harvard University. Retrieved from https://harvardharrispoll.com/wp-content/uploads/2022/07/HHP_June2022_KeyResults.pdf

[17] Acho, E. (2022, July 10). *Pro-Life vs Pro-Choice: Overturning Roe v. Wade | Uncomfortable Conversations with Emmanuel Acho.* Retrieved from Youtube: https://www.youtube.com/watch?v=_1kM0LA9G7c

[18] Josephus, F. (2015). *Writings of Josephus, Book 2.* Lulu.

[19] Sanger, M. (1939, December 10). Letter to Dr. C. J. Gamble. Retrieved from https://libex.smith.edu/omeka/files/original/d6358bc3053c931 83295bf2df1c0c931.pdf

[20] Hawkins, K. (2020, July 23). *Remove statues of Margaret Sanger, Planned Parenthood founder tied to eugenics and racism.* Retrieved from USA Today: https://www.usatoday.com/story/opinion/2020/07/23/racism-eugenics-margaret-sanger-deserves-no-honors-column/5480192002/

[21] Johnson, A. M. (2021, April 17). *I'm the Head of Planned Parenthood. We're Done Making Excuses for Our Founder.* Retrieved from The New York Times: https://www.nytimes.com/2021/04/17/opinion/planned-parenthood-margaret-sanger.html

Chapter One

[1] Moore Ph.D., K. L. (2016). *The Developing Human: Clinically Oriented Embryology, 10th Edition*. Philadelphia, PA, USA: Saunders, 2016. p11

[2] Sadler Ph.D., T. (2015). *Langman's Medical Embryology 13th Edition*. Lippincott Williams & Wilkins.

[3] Jacobs, Ph. D., S. (2019). *Balancing Abortion Rights and Fetal Rights: A Mixed Methods Mediation of the U.S. Abortion Debate*. The University of Chicago. Retrieved from https://knowledge.uchicago.edu/record/1883?ln=en

[4] Hitchens, C. (1988, January). *A Left-Wing Atheist's Case Against Abortion*. Retrieved from Crisis Magazine: https://www.crisismagazine.com/2019/a-left-wing-atheists-case-against-abortion

[5] Zhang, S. (2015, Oct 2). *Why Science Can't Say When a Baby's Life Begins*. Retrieved from Wired: https://www.wired.com/2015/10/science-cant-say-babys-life-begins/

[6] Gargollo, M.D., P. C. (2022, May 5). *How long do sperm live after ejaculation?* Retrieved from Mayo Clinic: https://www.mayoclinic.org/healthy-lifestyle/getting-pregnant/expert-answers/pregnancy/faq-20058504#:~:text=Ejaculated%20sperm%20remain%20viable%20for,alive%20%E2%80%94%20up%20to%20five%20days.

[7] Sarkar, S. (2022, June 27). *Defining when human life begins is not a question science can answer – it's a question of politics and ethical*

values. Retrieved from The Conversation: https://theconversation.com/defining-when-human-life-begins-is-not-a-question-science-can-answer-its-a-question-of-politics-and-ethical-values-165514

[8] Warren, M. A. (1973). On the Moral and Legal Status of Abortion. *The Monist*. Retrieved from https://rintintin.colorado.edu/~vancecd/phil215/Warren.pdf

[9] Bigelow M.D., H. (1848). Ether and Chloroform: A Compedium of their History, Surgical Use, Dangers, and Discovery. p. 15.

[10] McRobbie, L. R. (2017, July 29). *When babies felt no pain*. Retrieved from Boston Globe: https://www.bostonglobe.com/ideas/2017/07/28/when-babies-felt-pain/Lhk2OKonfR4m3TaNjJWV7M/story.html#:~:text=But%20it%20wasn%27t%20until,harm%20or%20kill%20the%20child.

[11] Bingham, J. A. (1866, February 28). One country, one Constitution, and one people." Speech of Hon. John A. Bingham, of Ohio, in the House of Representatives. USA. Retrieved from https://archive.org/stream/onecountryonecon00bing/onecountryonecon00bing_djvu.txt

[12] Michigan Department of Health & Human Services. (2022, June). *Induced Abortion in Michigan 2021*. Retrieved from Michigan.gov:

https://vitalstats.michigan.gov/osr/annuals/Abortion%202021.
pdf

[13] Standford Students for Life. (n.d.). *The Violinist Argument.* Retrieved from Stanford Students for Life: https://prolife.stanford.edu/qanda/q2-2.html

[14] Boonin, D. (2003). *A Defense of Abortion.* Cambridge University Press.

[15] Foothill Email Exhibits. (2017, October 23). Foothill Email Exhibits. Retrieved from https://adfmedialegalfiles.blob.core.windows.net/files/Foothill EmailExhibits.pdf

[16] Black Tea News. (2022, November 2). *Michigan Democrats Tried to Repeal Parental Consent Twice, Prop 3 is the Third Attempt.* Retrieved from Black Tea News: https://www.blackteanews.com/columns/2022/11/2/mnvtnic0 da3wiz5575ib9dxp6vpbmi

[17] Selective Service. (2022, October 7). *Selective Service.* Retrieved from Twitter: https://twitter.com/SSS_gov/status/1578505754470154241

[18] United Nations, N. Y. (2021, April 14). *Bodily autonomy: Busting 7 myths that undermine individual rights and freedoms.* Retrieved from United Nations Population Fund: https://www.unfpa.org/news/bodily-autonomy-busting-7-myths-undermine-individual-rights-and-freedoms

[19] Harris, K. (2023, January 23). *Remarks by Vice President Harris on the 50th Anniversary of Roe v. Wade.* Retrieved from The White

House: https://www.whitehouse.gov/briefing-room/speeches-remarks/2023/01/22/remarks-by-vice-president-harris-on-the-50th-anniversary-of-roe-v-wade/

[20] The World Medical Association. (1949, October). International Cod of Medical Ethics. London, England. Retrieved from https://www.wma.net/wp-content/uploads/2018/07/Decl-of-Geneva-v1948-1.pdf

[21] United States Holocaust Memorial Museum. (n.d.). *Women During the Holocaust.* Retrieved from Holocaust Encyclopedia: https://encyclopedia.ushmm.org/content/en/article/women-during-the-holocaust

[22] Knowles, M. (2022, December 3). *Michael Knowles DEBATES Viral Pro-Choice Activist | Bronte Remsik.* Retrieved from Youtube: https://www.youtube.com/watch?v=yiNW84kJy_k

[23] Dr. Flowers, L. (n.d.). *The Age of Accountability.* Retrieved from Soteriology 101: https://soteriology101.com/2018/06/21/the-age-of-accountability/

[24] Black Tea News. (2023, January 14). *Pro-Choice "Christian" from Michigan Votes Against Medical Care for Abortion Survivors.* Retrieved from Black Tea News: https://www.blackteanews.com/columns/2023/1/14/pro-choice-christian-from-michigan-votes-against-medical-care-for-abortion-survivors

[25] Copan, D. P. (2011). *Is God a Moral Monster?* Grand Rapids: Baker Books.

Chapter Two

[1] Ark Encounter. (2022). *About the Ark.* Retrieved from Ark Encounter: https://arkencounter.com/about/

[2] Maller, A. S. (2014, April 4). *Why God spared almost all Egyptians.* Retrieved from The Times of Israel: https://blogs.timesofisrael.com/why-god-spared-almost-all-egyptians/

Chapter Three

[1] Merriam-Webster. (2022, September). *abortion.* Retrieved from Dictionary, Merriam-Webster: https://www.merriam-webster.com/dictionary/abortion

[2] LifeSite. (2013, January 29). *Planned Parenthood 1952: Abortion 'Kills the Life of a Baby,' Danger to Mother.* Retrieved from LifeSite: https://www.lifesitenews.com/news/planned-parenthood-1952-abortion-kills-the-life-of-a-baby-danger-to-mother/

[3] Mazziotta, J. (2019, May 22). *Keke Palmer Shared Her Abortion Story After Feeling 'Disheartened About the News in Alabama'.* Retrieved from People: https://people.com/health/keke-palmer-shared-abortion-story/

[4] Cho, D. J. (2022, July 15). *Celebrities Who Have Shared Their Abortion Stories to Help Women Feel Less Alone.* Retrieved from People: https://people.com/health/celebrity-abortion-stories-busy-philipps-jameela-jamil/

[5] CDC. (2022, November 25). *Centers for Disease Control and Prevention.* Retrieved from Abortion Surveillance — United States, 2020: https://www.cdc.gov/mmwr/volumes/71/ss/ss7110a1.htm?s_ci d=ss7110a1_w

Chapter Four

[1] Hansler, J. (2017, September 27). *Michelle Obama: 'Any woman who voted against Hillary Clinton voted against their own voice'.* Retrieved from CNN: https://www.cnn.com/2017/09/27/politics/michelle-obama-women-voters

[2] ChurchPop. (2016, January 16). *Atheist Penn Jillette Doesn't Respect Christians Who Don't Evangelize.* Retrieved from Church Pop: https://www.churchpop.com/2016/01/16/atheist-penn-jillette-christians-evangelize/

[3] Lewis, C. (2001). *The Weight of Glory.* HarperCollins.

[4] Spielberg, S. (Director). (1991). *Hook* [Motion Picture].

Chapter Five

[1] Guttmacher Institute. (2018, January 11). *About Half of U.S. Abortion Patients Report Using Contraception in the Month They Became Pregnant.* Retrieved from Guttmacher Institute:

https://www.guttmacher.org/news-release/2018/about-half-us-abortion-patients-report-using-contraception-month-they-became

[2] Peterson, J. B. (2017, March 29). *2017 Maps of Meaning 09: Patterns of Symbolic Representation*. Retrieved from Youtube: https://youtu.be/yXZSeiAl4PI

[3] RNC Research. (2022, June 27). *Harris Says Abortion Limitations Would Limite the "Choices" of Men*. Retrieved from Twitter: https://twitter.com/RNCResearch/status/1541520693535309 826?ref_src=twsrc%5Etfw

[4] Lowery, W. (2022, September 7). *AOC's Fight for the Future*. Retrieved from GQ: https://www.gq.com/story/alexandria-ocasio-cortez-october-cover-profile

[5] Black Tea News. (2021, March 10). *Christians were Duped by Black Lives Matter*. Retrieved from Black Tea News: https://www.blackteanews.com/columns/2021/3/10/christians-were-duped-by-black-lives-matter

[6] National Fatherhood Initiative. (2023). *2024. Father Facts: Ninth Edition*. Germantown: National Fatherhood Initiative.

[7] Bussemakers, C., Kraaykamp, G., & Tolsma, J. (2022, March). Variation in the educational consequences of parental death and divorce: The role of family and country characteristics. *Demographic Research*, 581. Retrieved from https://www.demographic-research.org/volumes/vol46/20/46-20.pdf

[8] Carlyle, R. (2016, February 19). *Family lawyer reveals divorce horror stories from 40 years of seeing the damage caused to children by their warring parents*. Retrieved from Daily Mail: https://www.dailymail.co.uk/femail/article-3447786/Family-lawyer-says-divorce-worse-death-children.html

[9] Marcuse, H. (1966). *Eros and Civilization: A Philosophical Inquiry into Freud 2nd Edition*. Beacon Press.

[10] Albert Mohler, J. (2004, November 16). *Kinsey as He Really Was-- What You Won't See in the Movie*. Retrieved from Christian Post: https://www.christianpost.com/news/kinsey-as-he-really-was-what-you-won-t-see-in-the-movie.html

[11] Freud, S. (1930). *Civilization and It's Discontents*.

[12] Katherine Kortsmit, P., Antoinette T. Nguyen, M., Mandel, M. G., Elizabeth Clark, M., Lisa M. Hollier, M., Jessica Rodenhizer, M., & Maura K. Whiteman, P. (2022, Novermber 25). *CDC, Centers for Disease Control and Prevention*. Retrieved from CDC: https://www.cdc.gov/mmwr/volumes/71/ss/ss7110a1.htm?s_cid=ss7110a1_w

[13] Wolfinger, N. H. (2016, June 6). *Counterintuitive Trends in the Link Between Premarital Sex and Marital Stability*. Retrieved from Institue for Family Studies: https://ifstudies.org/blog/counterintuitive-trends-in-the-link-between-premarital-sex-and-marital-stability/?utm_source=Media+List&utm_campaign=bd9aa76e b8-

sex_divorce_risk_2016_press&utm_medium=email&utm_ter
m=0_a2dbdbdf5e-bd9aa76eb8-109135973

[14] Haskins, R. (2013, March 13). *Three Simple Rules Poor Teens Should Follow to Join the Middle Class.* Retrieved from Brookings: https://www.brookings.edu/opinions/three-simple-rules-poor-teens-should-follow-to-join-the-middle-class/

[15] Frankl, V. (2006). *Man's Search for Meaning.* Beacon Press.

[16] Hamilton, Ph.D, B. E., Martin, M.P.H, J. A., & Osterman, M.H.S., M. J. (2021). *Vital Statistics Rapid Release.* CDC. Retrieved from https://www.cdc.gov/nchs/data/vsrr/vsrr012-508.pdf

[17] Acho, E. (2022, July 10). *Pro-Life vs Pro-Choice: Overturning Roe v. Wade | Uncomfortable Conversations with Emmanuel Acho.* Retrieved from Youtube: https://www.youtube.com/watch?v=_1kM0LA9G7c

[18] Scott, T. (2022, May 13). *Senator Tim Scott Questions Secretary Janet Yellen at Banking Committee Hearing.* Retrieved from Youtube: https://www.youtube.com/watch?v=H12yBkRxEK4

[19] Adoption Network. (2022). *US Adoption Statistics.* Retrieved from Adoption Network: https://adoptionnetwork.com/adoption-myths-facts/domestic-us-statistics/

[20] Planned Parenthood. (2021). *Annnual Report 2020-2021.* Retrieved from Planned Parenthood: https://www.plannedparenthood.org/uploads/filer_public/40/8f/408fc2ad-c8c2-48da-ad87-be5cc257d370/211214-ppfa-annualreport-20-21-c3-digital.pdf

21 Quinones, J., & Lajka, A. (2017, August 15). *"What kind of society do you want to live in?": Inside the country where Down syndrome is disappearing.* Retrieved from CBS News: https://www.cbsnews.com/news/down-syndrome-iceland/?linkId=40953194&utm_source=Yahoo&utm_medium=Beauty&utm_campaign=down-syndrome-iceland-abortion

22 Mancini, J. (2014, August 24). *People with Down syndrome are happy. Why are we trying to eliminate them?* Retrieved from The Washington Post: https://www.washingtonpost.com/news/posteverything/wp/2017/08/24/people-with-down-syndrome-are-happy-why-are-we-trying-to-eliminate-them/

23 Wulfsohn, J. A. (2022, June 24). *Roe v. Wade overturned: CNN pundit cites relatives with Down syndrome, autism to defend abortions.* Retrieved from Fox News: https://www.foxnews.com/media/roe-v-wade-overturned-cnn-pundit-abortions

24 The Bible Project. (2017, October 27). *Justice.* Retrieved from Youtube: https://www.youtube.com/watch?v=A14THPoc4-4&feature=share&si=ELPmzJkDCLju2KnD5oyZMQ

Chapter Six

1 Warnock, R. (2022, May 2). *Reverend Raphael Warnock.* Retrieved from Twitter:

https://twitter.com/ReverendWarnock/status/1521307205349
351424?s=20&t=noPi0_Y1RHxkkFHpKeMH2g

[2] Woodhouse, S. (2022, May 10). *Hochul Allots $35 Million to Protect N.Y. Abortion Providers.* Retrieved from Bloomberg: https://www.bloomberg.com/news/articles/2022-05-10/hochul-allocates-35-million-to-protect-n-y-abortion-providers#xj4y7vzkg

[3] Black Tea News. (2022, September 11). *Democrats VS Christianity: Tolerance vs Intolerance.* Retrieved from Youtube: https://www.youtube.com/watch?v=Oskm_fpTqFQ&feature=share&si=ELPmzJkDCLju2KnD5oyZMQ

[4] Black Tea News. (2022, August 3). *CA State Sen Who Lowered Criminal Penalties for HIV Transmission, Says Lecturing About Sex Won't Stop Monkepox.* Retrieved from Black Tea News: https://www.blackteanews.com/columns/2022/8/3/ca-state-sen-who-lowered-criminal-penalties-for-hiv-transmission-says-lecturing-about-sex-wont-stop-monkepox

[5] Democratic National Committee. (2020). *PARTY PLATFORM.* Retrieved from Democrats.org: https://democrats.org/where-we-stand/party-platform/

[6] Delgado, R., & Stefancic, J. (2001). *Critical Race Theory: An Introduction.* New York University Press.

[7] Danbury Baptists Association. (1801, October 7). Letter to Thomas Jefferson, Esq., President of the United States of America.

[8] Jefferson, T. (1802, January 1). Thomas Jefferson's Letter to the Danbury Baptist Association.

[9] Hochul, K. (2021, September 26). *Rush Transcript: Governor Hochul Attends Service at Christian Cultural Center.* Retrieved from Governor New York: https://www.governor.ny.gov/news/rush-transcript-governor-hochul-attends-service-christian-cultural-center

[10] Douglass, F. (1857, May). Speech on the Dred Scott Decision. Retrieved from https://www.utc.edu/sites/default/files/2021-01/fddredscottspeechexcerpt2018.pdf

Chapter Seven

[1] Sprinkle, P. (2023, February 9). *Does the Old Testament Dehumanize Women? Dr. Sandy Richter (Exiles 22 Talk + Q & A).* Retrieved from Youtube: https://youtube.com/watch?v=AjnMM36QUjA&feature=shares&t=942

[2] Jedediah Bila LIVE. (2022, October 26). *HOT DEBATE: Red Pill Movement, Andrew Tate, And Liberalism vs Conservatism w/ @Destiny.* Retrieved from Youtube: https://youtube.com/live/n_3wnUrOBAI?feature=shares&t=5884

[3] Live Action. (2020, February 4). *Raped at Age 11, My Mother Became Pregnant With Me.* Retrieved from Youtube: https://www.youtube.com/watch?v=ZkV0T-hTmXs

[4] Precious Life. (n.d.). *Conceived in rape, former Miss Pennsylvania shares why every human life is worthy of protection.* Retrieved

from Precious Life:

https://preciouslife.com/news/443/conceived-in-rape-former-miss-pennsylvania-shares-why-every-human-life-is-worthy-of-protection/

[5] Biden, J. (2022, July 8). *Remarks by President Biden on Protecting Access to Reproductive Health Care Services*. Retrieved from White House: https://www.whitehouse.gov/briefing-room/speeches-remarks/2022/07/08/remarks-by-president-biden-on-protecting-access-to-reproductive-health-care-services/

[6] Dr. Warren, H. (1984). *Abortion Practice*. Lippincott.

[7] Equal Rights Institute. (2022, July 26). *The Pregnant 10 Year-Old: Thinking Well About This Tragic Story (with Robin Atkins)*. Retrieved from Youtube: https://www.youtube.com/watch?v=YxOiMKnawM0&feature=share&si=ELPmzJkDCLju2KnD5oyZMQ

[8] Students for Life. (2019, May 28). *My Twins Conceived In Rape Just Graduated High School*. Retrieved from Youtube:

[9] Reardon, D. C., Makimaa, J., & Sobie, A. (2000). *Victims and Victors: Speaking Out About Their Pregnancies, Abortions, and Children Resulting From Sexual Assault*. Springfield, Illinois, USA: Aborn Books.

[10] The Ad Hoc Committee of Women Pregnant By Sexual Assault. (2004). *Hard Cases Petition*. Retrieved from AfterAbortion.Org: http://www.theunchoice.com/pdf/OnePageFactSheets/HardCasesPetition.pdf

[11] Mahkorn, M.D., S. K., & Dolan, M.D., W. V. (1981). Sexual Assault and Pregnancy. In D. H. Thomas Hilgers, *New Perspectives on Human Abortion* (p. 194). Frederick, MD: University Publications of America.

[12] Illinois State Senate. (2002, April 4). Senate Bill 1663 Floor Debate. Illinois, USA. Retrieved from https://www.ilga.gov/senate/transcripts/strans92/ST040402.pdf

[13] CNN. (2014). *Crossfire: Abortion exception for rape?* Retrieved from CNN: https://www.cnn.com/videos/bestoftv/2014/01/22/crossfire-abortion-exception-for-rape.cnn

[14] Hamill, M. (2022, July 2). *Mark Hamill.* Retrieved from Twitter: https://twitter.com/MarkHamill/status/1543317524908949504?ref_src=twsrc%5Etfw%7Ctwcamp%5Etweetembed%7Ctwterm%5E1543402944972095488%7Ctwgr%5E166889b637101e801d18a33aa6370ba76a8a9bfb%7Ctwcon%5Es2_&ref_url=https%3A%2F%2Fwww.theblaze.com%2Fnews%2Fmark-hamill-

[15] Vincent, I. (2016, September 11). *Luke Skywalker wants me to 'abort my baby,' says ex-porn star.* Retrieved from The New York Post: https://nypost.com/2016/09/11/hamills-pressured-me-to-have-an-abortion-nathan-hamills-ex/

[16] Spiers, E. (2021, December 3). *I Was Adopted. I Know the Trauma It Can Inflict.* Retrieved from The New York Times: https://www.nytimes.com/2021/12/03/opinion/adoption-supreme-court-amy-coney-barrett.html

[17] Hatzipanagos, R. (2021, December 13). *Adoption across races: 'I know my parents love me, but they don't love my people'.* Retrieved from The Washington Post: https://www.washingtonpost.com/nation/interactive/2021/transracial-adoption-racial-reckoning/

[18] Johnson, L. (2022, September 8). *Leonydus Johnson.* Retrieved from Twitter: https://twitter.com/LeonydusJohnson/status/1567943975335518213

[19] Life Site. (2022, July 27). *My unborn son may not live long, but he still deserves protection from those looking to end his life.* Retrieved from Life Site: https://www.lifesitenews.com/opinion/my-unborn-son-may-not-live-long-but-he-still-deserves-protection-from-those-looking-to-end-his-life/?fbclid=IwAR2JNIbWN1JLBUv3I9bGnRepNgjuli2_2-0GkkpS8_LDk7ZzN-8rIJjENpM

[20] Francis, D. C. (2021, March 6). *Your baby's prenatal diagnosis is not a death sentence. Just ask my giggling goddaughter.* Retrieved from USA Today: https://www.usatoday.com/story/opinion/voices/2021/03/06/pro-life-abortion-fetal-abnormlity-statistics-column/4579657001/

[21] Debost-Legrand, A., Laurichesse-Delmas, H., Francannel, C., Perthus, I., Lemery, D., Gallot, D., & Vendittelli, F. (2014, March 24). *False positive morphologic diagnoses at the anomaly scan: marginal or real problem, a population-based cohort study.*

Retrieved from National Library of Medicine:
https://www.ncbi.nlm.nih.gov/pmc/articles/PMC3994389/

[22] NBC News. (2014, December 14). *Prenatal Tests Have High Failure Rate, Triggering Abortions.* Retrieved from NBC News:
https://www.nbcnews.com/health/womens-health/prenatal-tests-have-high-failure-rate-triggering-abortions-n267301

[23] Resta, R. (2021, June 22). *Prenatal Testing – What Is It Good For? A Review and Critique.* Retrieved from Lidsen:
https://www.lidsen.com/journals/genetics/genetics-05-03-136

[24] Artukovic, K. (2022, May 23). *Why does prenatal testing exist? Perspectives from a parent of a child with Down syndrome.* Retrieved from Secular Pro-Life:
https://secularprolife.org/2022/03/why-does-prenatal-testing-exist/

[25] *Biotech firm: Screening to 'avoid' babies with Down syndrome is a 'cash cow'.* (2020, May 22). Retrieved from Live Action:
https://www.liveaction.org/news/screening-avoid-down-syndrome-cash/

[26] Campell, M., & Lyu, D. (2019, November 13). *China's Genetics Giant Wants to Tailor Medicine to Your DNA.* Retrieved from Bloomberg: https://www.bloomberg.com/news/features/2019-11-13/chinese-genetics-giant-bgi-wants-to-tailor-medicine-to-your-dna

[27] Savage, C. (2023, January 17). *chloeandolliex.* Retrieved from Tiktok:
https://www.tiktok.com/@chloeandolliex/video/7189720476279655686

[28] Baker, J. (2021, November 4). *Joe Baker*. Retrieved from Facebook: https://www.facebook.com/JoeBakersAdventures/posts/967058830892

[29] Baker, J. (2021, November 5). *Joe Baker*. Retrieved from Facebook: https://www.facebook.com/JoeBakersAdventures/posts/967121834632

[30] Live Action. (2019, July 30). *The Pro-Life Reply to: "Abortion Can Be Medically Necessary"*. Retrieved from Youtube: https://www.youtube.com/watch?v=5TmomK2RB2A&feature=share&si=ELPmzJkDCLju2KnD5oyZMQ

[31] Hamada, MD, MBA, O. L. (2019, January 23). *Omar Hamada*. Retrieved from Twitter: https://twitter.com/OmarHamada/status/1088136519146188800?ref_src=twsrc%5Etfw

[32] The American College of Obstetricians and Gynecologists. (n.d.). *Facts Are Important: Abortion is Healthcare*. Retrieved from The American College of Obstetricians and Gynecologists: https://www.acog.org/advocacy/facts-are-important/abortion-is-healthcare

[33] Mary E. Harned, J., & Ingrid Skop, M. (2023, March 7). *Pro-Life Laws Protect Mom and Baby: Pregnant Women's Lives are Protected in All States*. Retrieved from Charlotte Lozier Institute: https://lozierinstitute.org/pro-life-laws-protect-mom-and-baby-pregnant-womens-lives-are-protected-in-all-states/

[34] The Associated Press via Nexstar Media Wire. (2022, August 9). *Nebraska woman charged with helping daughter have abortion.* Retrieved from Fox 59: https://fox59.com/news/national-world/nebraska-woman-charged-with-helping-daughter-have-abortion/

[35] Salter, P. (2022, August 8). *Norfolk mother and daughter accused of illegal abortion, burning and burying body.* Retrieved from Lincoln Journal Star: https://journalstar.com/news/state-and-regional/nebraska/norfolk-mother-and-daughter-accused-of-illegal-abortion-burning-and-burying-body/article_ff99fd49-a710-5ec3-8d51-5aced3001c71.html

[36] Kimport, K. (2022, April 10). *Is third-trimester abortion exceptional? Two pathways to abortion after 24 weeks of pregnancy in the United States.* Retrieved from Wiley Online Library: https://onlinelibrary.wiley.com/doi/10.1363/psrh.12190

[37] Kliff, S. (2013, April 15). *The Gosnell case: Here's what you need to know.* Retrieved from The Washington Post: https://www.washingtonpost.com/news/wonk/wp/2013/04/15/the-gosnell-case-heres-what-you-need-to-know/

[38] CDC. (2021). *Maternal Mortality Rates in the United States, 2020.* Retrieved from CDC Centers for Disease Control and Prevention : https://www.cdc.gov/nchs/data/hestat/maternal-mortality/2020/maternal-mortality-rates-2020.htm#ref1

Chapter Eight

[1] Timcast IRL. (2022, June 15). *Timcast IRL - ANOTHER Poll Shows HALF Of U.S. Think Civil War is Coming w/Dennis Prager.* Retrieved from Youtube: https://www.youtube.com/watch?v=to8e0twePpo

[2] Nathanson, B. N. (1979). *Aborting America.* Life Cycle Books.

[3] Kessler, G. (2019, May 29). *Planned Parenthood's false stat: 'Thousands' of women died every year before Roe.* Retrieved from The Washington Post: https://www.washingtonpost.com/politics/2019/05/29/planned-parenthoods-false-stat-thousands-women-died-every-year-before-roe/

[4] Levine, P. B., & Staiger, D. (2004). Abortion Policy and Fertility Outcomes: The Eastern European Experience".

[5] Bilger, M. (2022, August 22). *Planned Parenthood Caught Changing Fetal Development Info, Calls Baby's Beating Heart "Cardiac Activity".* Retrieved from Life News: https://www.lifenews.com/2022/08/22/planned-parenthood-caught-changing-fetal-development-info-calls-babys-beating-heart-cardiac-activity/

[6] Nerozzi, T. H. (2022, September 22). *Stacey Abrams says 'no such thing' as 6-week fetal heartbeat: 'Manufactured sound'.* Retrieved from Fox News: https://www.foxnews.com/politics/stacey-abrams-says-no-such-thing-6-week-fetal-heartbeat-claims-manufactured-sound

[7] National Maritime Museum, London. (2023, March 23). *The Zong*. Retrieved from Understanding Slavery Initiative: https://understandingslavery.com/casestudy/the-zong/

[8] RNC Research. (2022, July 6). *Democrat Sen. Elizabeth Warren: "We Need To Put A Stop" To Crisis Pregnancy Centers "Right Now"*. Retrieved from Twitter: https://twitter.com/RNCResearch/status/1544707511906930690

[9] Wallace, D. (2022, July 25). *Whitmer vetoes $20M in pro-life adoption funding; rips crisis pregnancy centers as 'fake health clinics'*. Retrieved from Fox News: https://www.foxnews.com/politics/whitmer-vetoes-20m-prolife-adoption-funding-rips-crisis-pregnancy-centers-fake-health-clinics

[10] Taney, R. B., Van Evrie, J. H., & Cartwright, S. A. (1860). *The Dred Scott decision: opinion of Chief Justice Taney*. Retrieved from Library of Congress: https://www.loc.gov/item/17001543

[11] Mungin, L. (2013, September 10). *Man pleads guilty to tricking pregnant girlfriend into taking abortion pill*. Retrieved from CNN: https://www.cnn.com/2013/09/10/justice/girlfriend-abortion-case/index.html

[12] Mungin, L. (2013, September 10). *Man pleads guilty to tricking pregnant girlfriend into taking abortion pill*. Retrieved from CNN: https://www.cnn.com/2013/09/10/justice/girlfriend-abortion-case/index.html

[13] Cheng, M. (2022, August 11). *'Disturbing': Experts troubled by Canada's euthanasia laws*. Retrieved from The Associated Press: https://apnews.com/article/covid-science-health-toronto-7c631558a457188d2bd2b5cfd360a867

[14] Government of Canada. (2022). *Third annual report on Medical Assistance in Dying in Canada 2021*. Retrieved from Government of Canada: https://www.canada.ca/en/health-canada/services/medical-assistance-dying/annual-report-2021.html#table_3.1

[15] Farmer, J. (2022, April 24). *When will "Never Again" mean "Never Again?"*. Retrieved from The Jerusalem Post: https://www.jpost.com/diaspora/antisemitism/article-704953

[16] Judicial Watch. (2020, June 23). *Judicial Watch Obtains Records Showing FDA Paid for 'Fresh and Never Frozen' Human Fetal Parts for Use In 'Humanized Mice' Creation*. Retrieved from Judicial Watch: https://www.judicialwatch.org/fda-humanized-mice/

[17] Catenacci, T., & Shaw, A. (2022, July 15). *House Republicans demand Biden admin stop transporting illegal immigrants to get abortions*. Retrieved from Fox News: https://www.foxnews.com/politics/house-republicans-demand-biden-admin-stop-transporting-illegal-immigrants-abortions

[18] Lott, Jr., J. R., & Whitley, J. (2001). Abortion and Crime: Unwanted Children and Out-of-Wedlock Births. *John M. Olin Center for Studies in Law, Economics, and Public Policy*

Working Papers, 2. Retrieved from Abortion and Crime: Unwanted Children and Out-of-Wedlock Births

[19] Aguirre, A. (2022, September 6). *Jennifer Lawrence Talks Motherhood, Causeway, and the End of Roe v. Wade.* Retrieved from Vogue: https://www.vogue.com/article/jennifer-lawrence-october-cover-2022-interview

[20] Black Tea News. (2023, February 27). *Abigail Disney Calls Jessa Duggar a Coward for Not Calling Her Miscarriage an Abortion.* Retrieved from Black Tea News: https://www.blackteanews.com/columns/2023/2/27/abigail-disney-calls-jessa-duggar-a-coward-for-not-calling-her-miscarriage-an-abortion

[21] Biden, J. (2022, July 8). *FACT SHEET: President Biden to Sign Executive Order Protecting Access to Reproductive Health Care Services.* Retrieved from The White House: https://www.whitehouse.gov/briefing-room/statements-releases/2022/07/08/fact-sheet-president-biden-to-sign-executive-order-protecting-access-to-reproductive-health-care-services/

[22] Abort73.com. (2021). *U.S. Abortion Statistics.* Retrieved from Abort73: https://abort73.com/abortion_facts/us_abortion_statistics/

[23] CDC. (2021, November 26). *Morbidity and Mortality Weekly Report (MMWR).* Retrieved from CDC: https://www.cdc.gov/mmwr/volumes/70/ss/ss7009a1.htm

[24] Michigan Department of Health and Human Services. (2021, June). *Induced Abortions in Michigan: January 1 through December 31, 2020.* Retrieved from Michigan Department of Health and Human Services: https://www.mdch.state.mi.us/osr/annuals/Abortion%202020.pdf

[25] Michigan.gov. (2020, August 5). *Governor Whitmer Signs Executive Directive Recognizing and Addressing Racism as a Public Health Crisis, Creates the Black Leadership Advisory Council.* Retrieved from Michigan.gov: https://www.michigan.gov/whitmer/news/press-releases/2020/08/05/signs-executive-directive-recognizing-and

[26] Fox News. (2022, July 22). *Dr. Deborah Birx says she 'knew' COVID vaccines would not 'protect against infection'.* Retrieved from Fox News: https://www.foxnews.com/media/dr-deborah-birx-knew-covid-vaccines-not-protect-against-infection

Chapter Nine

[1] Institute, G. (2005, 13 4). *Guttmacher Institute.* Retrieved from Guttmacher Institute: https://www.guttmacher.org/journals/psrh/2005/reasons-us-

women-have-abortions-quantitative-and-qualitative-
perspectives

[2] Priscilla K. Coleman, P., Kaitlyn Boswell, B., Katrina Etzkorn, B., &
Rachel Turnwald, B. (2017). *Women Who Suffered Emotionally
from Abortion: A Qualitative Synthesis of Their Experiences.*
Retrieved from Journal of American Physicians and Surgeons:
https://www.jpands.org/vol22no4/coleman.pdf

[3] Carpenter, C. (2021, February 10). *Charisma Carpenter.* Retrieved
from Twitter:
https://twitter.com/allcharisma/status/1359537746843365381

[4] Reardon, D. C. (2018, October 29). *The abortion and mental health
controversy: A comprehensive literature review of common ground
agreements, disagreements, actionable recommendations, and
research opportunities.* Retrieved from National Library of
Medicine:
https://www.ncbi.nlm.nih.gov/pmc/articles/PMC6207970/

[5] Hill, R. (2006, Jan 4). *Abortion researcher confounded by study.*
Retrieved from New Zealand Herald:
https://www.nzherald.co.nz/nz/abortion-researcher-
confounded-by-
study/3FYSQTNVHDEWTOTS4HKSEYG6GA/?c_id=1&
objectid=10362476

[6] Planned Parenthood Minn, N.D., S.D. v. Rounds, 09-3362 (United
States Court of Appeals for the 8th Circuit September 2,
2011).

[7] Nathanson, B. N. (1979). *Aborting America.* Life Cycle Books.

[8] Friedan, B. (2006). *Life So Far: A Memoir*. Simon and Schuster.

[9] Phetasy, B. (2022, August 17). *I Regret Being A Slut*. Retrieved from Beyond Parody with Bridget Phetasy: https://bridgetphetasy.substack.com/p/slut-regret

[10] Stepman, I. (2022, July 12). *Inez Stepman*. Retrieved from Twitter: https://twitter.com/InezFeltscher/status/1546939481265168385

[11] Beauvoir, S. d. (1975). Simone de Beauvoir on Questionnaire. (J.-L. Servan-Schreiber, Interviewer)

[12] Stuckey, A. B. (2022, August 25). *After Hormones & Surgery, She Found Christ | Guest: Sophia Galvin | Ep 667*. Retrieved from Youtube: https://www.youtube.com/watch?v=m5LLuYxjQAg

[13] Ennis, D. (2022, September 11). *Ex-Trans Activist Chloe Cole In Her Own Words: 'I'm Autistic'*. Retrieved from Forbes: https://archive.ph/0UdCV

[14] Kitchener, C. (2022, June 20). *This Texan teen wanted an abortion. She now has twins*. Retrieved from The Washington Post: https://www.washingtonpost.com/politics/2022/06/20/texas-abortion-law-teen-mom/

[15] Michigan Department of Health and Human Services. (2021, June). *Induced Abortions in Michigan: January 1 through December 31, 2020*. Retrieved from Michigan Department of Health and Human Services: https://www.mdch.state.mi.us/osr/annuals/Abortion%202020.pdf

[16] Ellison, K. (2022, August 22). *Attorney General Ellison issues consumer alert about crisis pregnancy centers*. Retrieved from Attorney General Office of Minnesota: https://www.ag.state.mn.us/Office/Communications/2022/08/23_CrisisPregnancyCenters.asp

[17] C-Span. (2022, July 12). *Senate Judiciary Committee Hearing on Abortion Access and the Law*. Retrieved from C-SPAN: https://www.c-span.org/video/?521318-1/senate-judiciary-committee-hearing-abortion-access-law

[18] Live Action. (2019, January 15). *How the Sexual Revolution Hijacked Feminism*. Retrieved from Youtube: https://www.youtube.com/watch?v=T3KFXqOCE7c&feature=share&si=ELPmzJkDCLju2KnD5oyZMQ

[19] Rousselle, C. (2020, July 14). *Expert on abortion and mental health says Turnaway Study is 'flawed'*. Retrieved from Catholic News Agency: https://www.catholicnewsagency.com/news/45172/expert-on-abortion-and-mental-health-says-turnaway-study-is-flawed

[20] Diana Greene Foster, P. (2020). *The Turnaway Study: The Cost of Denying Women Access to Abortion*. Scribner.

[21] Snyder, M. (2021, March 10). *Five years later, 96% of women denied abortion no longer wish they could have had one. (Turnaway Study)*. Retrieved from Secular Prolife: https://secularprolife.org/2021/03/five-years-later-96-of-women-denied/

[22] Tilden, D. (2021). Learn to Heal After the Pain and Lies from Abortion. (L. Rowe, Interviewer) Retrieved from Support After Abortion: https://supportafterabortion.com/learn-to-heal-after-the-pain-and-lies-from-abortion/

Chapter Ten

[1] Foothill Email Exhibits. (2017, October 23). Foothill Email Exhibits. Retrieved from https://adfmedialegalfiles.blob.core.windows.net/files/Foothill EmailExhibits.pdf

[2] Aitken, P. (2022, July 3). *Becerra: Federal gov 'looking into' helping women cross state lines for abortions*. Retrieved from Fox News: https://www.foxnews.com/politics/becerra-federal-gov-looking-helping-women-cross-state-lines-abortions

[3] Newton, J. (1796, July 21). *Text of John Newton's letter to William Wilberforce, 21 July 1796*. Retrieved from The Christian Institute: https://www.christian.org.uk/news/on-this-day-newton-urged-wilberforce-to-keep-going/

[4] Forsyth, J. (2022, June 28). *After Roe, Choose Compassion over Culture War*. Retrieved from The Gospel Coalition: After Roe, Choose Compassion over Culture War

[5] Stuckey, A. B. (2022, June 28). *Evangelicals' Shameful Response to Roe v Wade | Ep 634*. Retrieved from Youtube: https://www.youtube.com/watch?v=kkodbYJamAI

[6] Thompson, C. (2022, January 25). *Michigan settles lawsuit with St. Vincent Catholic Charities over same-sex adoptions*. Retrieved from The Detroit News: https://www.detroitnews.com/story/news/local/michigan/2022/01/25/same-sex-couples-adoption-michigan-st-vincent-catholic-charities-lawsuit-settlement/9215191002/

[7] Alliance Defending Freedom. (2022, August 17). *Low-Income Kids at Risk of Losing School Lunches Thanks to Biden Admin Mandate*. Retrieved from Alliance Defending Freedom: https://adflegal.org/blog/low-income-kids-risk-losing-school-lunches-thanks-biden-admin-mandate

[8] Columbia University. (1910). *Political Science Quarterly*. Ginn and Company.

[9] Black Tea News. (2021, March 10). *Christians were Duped by Black Lives Matter*. Retrieved from Black Tea News: https://www.blackteanews.com/columns/2021/3/10/christians-were-duped-by-black-lives-matter

[10] Keene, H. (2022, August 30). *Minnesota bail fund promoted by Kamala Harris freed convict now charged with murder*. Retrieved from Fox News: https://www.foxnews.com/politics/minnesota-bail-fund-promoted-kamala-harris-freed-convict-now-charged-murder

[11] Keene, H. (2022, August 30). *Minnesota bail fund promoted by Kamala Harris freed convict now charged with murder*. Retrieved from Fox News:

https://www.foxnews.com/politics/minnesota-bail-fund-promoted-kamala-harris-freed-convict-now-charged-murder

[12] Spangler, T. (2022, September 1). *OnlyFans Creators Earned $3.9 Billion in 2021, Swelling 115% Year Over Year.* Retrieved from Variety: https://variety.com/2022/digital/news/onlyfans-financials-earnings-creators-1235357264/

[13] Spangler, T. (2022, September 1). *OnlyFans Creators Earned $3.9 Billion in 2021, Swelling 115% Year Over Year.* Retrieved from Variety: https://variety.com/2022/digital/news/onlyfans-financials-earnings-creators-1235357264/

[14] Kim, C., & Rector, R. (2010, February 19). *Evidence on the Effectiveness of Abstinence Education: An Update.* Retrieved from The Heritage Foundation: https://www.heritage.org/education/report/evidence-the-effectiveness-abstinence-education-update#_ftn4

[15] Jemott III, PhD, J. B., Jemmott, PhD, L. S., & Fong, PhD, G. T. (2010). Efficacy of a Theory-Based Abstinence-Only. *Archives of Pediatrics and Adolescent Medicine.*

[16] Tortolero, P. S., Markham, P. C., Fleschler Peskin, P. M., Shegog, PhD, R., Addy, MA, R. C., Escobar-Chaves, DrPH, L. S., & Baumler, PhD, E. R. (2009, August 18). *It's Your Game. Keep It Real: Delaying Sexual Behavior with an Effective Middle School Program.* Retrieved from National Library of Medicine: https://www.ncbi.nlm.nih.gov/pmc/articles/PMC2818029/

[17] Muhlhausen, D. (2017, July 31). *The Failure of the Teen Pregnancy Prevention Program: Advocates of Evidence-Based Policymaking*

Ignore the Evidence. Retrieved from The Heritage Foundation: https://www.heritage.org/public-health/report/the-failure-the-teen-pregnancy-prevention-program-advocates-evidence-based

[18] Sowell, T. (1995). *The Vision of the Anointed: Self-Congratulation as a Basis for Social Policy*. Basic Books.

[19] Boyer, J. (2018, February 28). *New Name, Same Harm: Rebranding of Federal Abstinence-Only Programs*. Retrieved from Guttmacher Institute: https://www.guttmacher.org/gpr/2018/02/new-name-same-harm-rebranding-federal-abstinence-only-programs

[20] Livingston, G., & Thomas, D. (2019, August 2). *Why is the teen birth rate falling?* Retrieved from Pew Research: https://www.pewresearch.org/fact-tank/2019/08/02/why-is-the-teen-birth-rate-falling/

[21] CDC. (2021, April 13). *Reported STDs Reach All-time High for 6th Consecutive Year*. Retrieved from CDC: https://www.cdc.gov/media/releases/2021/p0413-stds.html

[22] Abrams, S. (2022, August 22). *WokePreacherClipsTV*. Retrieved from Twitter: https://mobile.twitter.com/WokePreacherTV/status/1561868834813919233

[23] Reardon, D. C. (2018, October 29). *The abortion and mental health controversy: A comprehensive literature review of common ground agreements, disagreements, actionable recommendations, and research opportunities*. Retrieved from National Library of

Medicine:

https://www.ncbi.nlm.nih.gov/pmc/articles/PMC6207970/

Conclusion

[1] Light Bearers. (2019, October 8). *Cosmic War | Table Talk S01 E07*.
Retrieved from Youtube:

https://www.youtube.com/watch?v=7c3FCQT0BL4

www.ingramcontent.com/pod-product-compliance
Lightning Source LLC
Chambersburg PA
CBHW020817270326
41928CB00006B/380